Families, Work and Benefits

The Policy Studies Institute (PSI) is Britain's leading independent research organisation undertaking studies of economic, industrial and social policy, and the workings of political institutions.

PSI is a registered charity, run on a non-profit basis, and is not associated with any political party, pressure group or commercial interest.

PSI attaches great importance to covering a wide range of subject areas with its multi-disciplinary approach. The Institute's 50+ researchers are organised in teams which currently cover the following programmes:

Family Finances – Employment – Information Policy – Social Justice and Social Order – Health Studies and Social Care – Education – Industrial Policy and Futures – Arts and the Cultural Industries – Environment and Quality of Life

This publication arises from the Family Finances programme and is one of over 30 publications made available by the Institute each year.

Information about the work of PSI, and a catalogue of available books can be obtained from:

Marketing Department, PSI
100 Park Village East, London NW1 3SR

Families, Work and Benefits

Alan Marsh and Stephen McKay

Policy Studies Institute, London

The publishing imprint of the independent
POLICY STUDIES INSTITUTE
100 Park Village East, London NW1 3SR
Telephone: 071-387 2171 Fax: 071-388 0914

ISBN 0 85374 555 2

PSI Research Report 754

A CIP catalogue record of this book is available from the British Library.

1 2 3 4 5 6 7 8 9

PSI publications are available from
BEBC Distribution Ltd
P.O. Box 1496
Poole, Dorset BH12 3YD

Books are normally despatched within 24 hours of receipt of order. Cheques should be made payable to BEBC Distribution Ltd.

Credit card orders may be phoned to FREEPHONE 0800 26260

Faxed orders to FREEPHONE 0800 26266

Enquiries: 0202 715555 (BEBC Ltd)

PSI subscriptions are available from PSI's subscription agent
Carfax Publishing Ltd
P.O. Box 25, Abingdon, Oxford OX14 3UE

Laserset by AL Art, London
Printed in Great Britain by BPCC Wheatons Ltd, Exeter

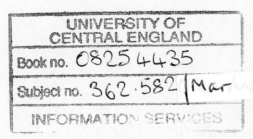
Acknowledgements

The authors bear full responsibility for everything in this volume. That there is anything to take responsibility for is due to the enormous amount of help they received from other people.

At PSI, Richard Berthoud helped to design the study, read it and improved it. At the Social Policy Research Unit at the University of York, Anne Corden gave us valuable advice.

The Department of Social Security paid for the study, also helped to design it, and carried out part of it. Kailash Mehta and his staff carried out a postal survey of 14,500 child benefit recipients with efficiency and great success. All this was organised by Tony Martin who was friend and mentor to the project throughout.

Drawing the sample involved the work of three computer centres. The DSS centres in Washington (Tyne and Wear) and North Fylde, and the Post Office national computing centre in Chesterfield. Without their help and ingenuity, the project could not have gone ahead in this form.

The fieldwork was carried out by National Opinion Polls (Social and Political). At NOP, Nick Moon and Marie Davison made important contributions to the questionnaire design and achieved an 82 per cent response rate from the sample.

Karen Mackinnon took on the task of setting up the data for analysis and often untangled puzzles in the analysis.

We are glad of this chance to thank everyone who helped us.

Alan Marsh and Stephen McKay
Family Finances Research Group
Policy Studies Institute

June 1993

Contents

Preface

This is the first report of the programme of research into Britain's low income families that is being carried out by the independent Policy Studies Institute for the Department of Social Security.

This study focused on incomes and social security benefits on the margins of work. It concerns the incentives and well-being of families with dependent children in and out of work. This report examines this issue of work and family well-being and the role played by family credit and allied in-work benefits.

The report is in two parts. The first part introduces the main arguments surrounding work, benefits and family credit and explains the research design. It compares low income families with the rest. It describes the circumstances of low income families and their use of benefits. It examines the special problems of take-up of 'means tested' or income-related benefits, particularly family credit, and includes a summary of the social and economic geography of low income families by introducing the four main 'actors' in the analysis that follows in the second half; these are:

- families receiving family credit;
- families who appear to qualify for family credit but do not claim it;
- families having no-one in full time work; and
- families who earn a little more than the amount that would qualify them for family credit.

These four analytical categories make up the 'within-range' population of actual and likely customers of family credit and provide the basis for the second part: an analysis of the effects of family credit. There are really 8 such 'target groups' in the study because the above four are almost always analysed separately among one parent and two parent families.

The second part of the study examines the effects of family credit on families' incentives to work in three ways:

- what are the constraints and opportunities facing low income parents in work, and what limits do they place on the incentives that benefits may provide?
- how do the current and potential customers see family credit and how it might affect their opportunities for work?

what are the actual incentives created and how do people apparently respond to them?

A fourth question is then asked: what difference does it make? What are the effects of claiming (and of not claiming) family credit on families' relative material well-being?

A final chapter summarises the whole report and discusses some of the wider implications of the findings in relation to policy for support for the incomes of families.

PART ONE

FAMILIES, WORK
AND SOCIAL SECURITY
BENEFITS

1   The study of in-work benefits

Introduction
This is a study of Britain's low income families, carried out in 1991 for the Department of Social Security. The main purpose was to study the effects of social security benefits on work and well-being among families with dependent children. There was strong interest in the effects of 'in-work' benefits, especially family credit. Nearly all parents of dependent children get child benefit and one in six get one parent benefit too. And anyone in low-paid work may claim income-related or 'means-tested' benefits such as housing benefit and help with their community charge. But only *working families* may claim family credit. Like housing benefit, family credit is means tested and only about six families in every hundred receive family credit nowadays. They get an average of about £42 a week.

Family credit is a cash benefit, with some associated welfare provisions, that may be claimed by parents who work more than 16 hours a week (though at the time of the survey, in 1991, the weekly qualifying hours were 24), whose children are of dependent age and whose net family income falls below a specified level. This threshold level is determined by the number and ages of the children in the family.

The amounts paid are linked to the amounts of income support and associated benefits that would be paid if the parents were not in full-time work. Although a relatively small part of the benefit system, costing in 1991 about £560 million a year from a total benefit expenditure of over £65 billion, family credit is aimed at families on the threshold between state dependence and employed self-sufficiency. For this reason, issues of welfare and issues of incentives coincide in ways that are important for the benefit system as a whole.

The main task, then, was to estimate and to explain the effects of family credit on its client population. This population is defined as the families who are within range of the qualifying provisions - including those who *might* claim the benefit if their circumstances changed, as well as those who actually received it. They may be either seeking or entering low-paid work, working and eligible to claim, claiming, or have incomes just beyond the scope of the benefit. Thus, the approach was one that sought to understand the relation of family credit to the whole low income population whose behaviour and whose needs it may affect. For this reason, the study is based on a survey of a representative sample of 2,300 of Britain's low income families.

The study had two main themes, the first focusing on the effectiveness of the benefit in reaching and then meeting the needs of its intended claimants, the second focusing on the incentives and constraints that affect the behaviour of potential and actual claimants. The main means of doing this was to compare family credit recipients with families out of work and on income support, with families who earned moderate incomes, just above the family credit limits, and with families who qualified for family credit but did not claim it.

There are a number of ideas in the above paragraphs that will need more detailed explanation: for example, the idea of a 'client population' who are 'within range' of family credit. These will be dealt with as the design of the study is described more fully in the later part of this introductory chapter. We will look now at some of the background to the study.

Background

PSI has been here before. In the early 1980s the Joseph Rowntree Memorial Trust supported PSI in a programme of research into family income support. Joan Brown's work in that programme (Brown 1983, 1987) focused heavily on the effects of the in-work benefit that family credit has now replaced, known from 1971 to 1988 as 'family income supplement' or FIS.

Brown reminds us that FIS was introduced in 1971 as a temporary measure, rapidly introduced in anticipation of Chancellor Barber's expected tax credit scheme. Tax credits did not come, though child benefit is an element that survived, and FIS remained for 17 years. It was introduced because something needed to be done about two problems:

- It was believed in the 1950s that hardship in work caused by very low wages was a thing of the past and would not return. Poverty, as Beveridge had predicted on the basis of earlier poverty studies, by Rowntree, Booth, Bowlby, and others, was thought to be limited to sections of the population who had no work or other income. Their needs would be met, he thought, by insured schemes like unemployment benefit and state retirement pensions. Later, uninsured social security, mostly national assistance and then supplementary benefit, became more important. But a succession of studies in the 1960s had shown that hardship in work had not, after all, been abolished. Its main victims were children and their parents. Single income families earning the lowest wages had not enough disposable income to maintain acceptable levels of well-being for themselves and their children, especially amid a population of others whose standards of living were rising more rapidly than at any time in the past.
- If the first problem was not sufficient cause for urgency, the second was. Families with dependent children and low wages could sometimes be better off out of work than in work. The amounts they would receive in what was then supplementary benefit could exceed their receipts from

work, especially if work related expenses like travel were considered. No-one was comfortable with the idea that benefits intended for the relief of need among those with no income were acting as a powerful disincentive for people to go to work and support their families through earnings.

Though these problems were clear enough, and were among the reasons offered in Parliament for legislation at that time, the social historians on the back benches enjoyed themselves debating what some called the 'awful warning' still echoing from Berkshire at the turn of the eighteenth century. There in 1795 the Justices of the parish of Speenhamland decided upon a modest intervention in the local labour market by supplementing the wages of poor labourers in line with recent increases in the price of bread. The awful warning they had in mind was said to be the events in France only six years earlier where want of bread among the masses, among other things, had led to the demise of most of the ruling class. But in Speenhamland it was wages that determined the amount given. As wages rose, supplementation was reduced. Thus Berkshire farm labourers became the first workers to experience something that waited another 176 years for a name: 'the poverty trap' (Piachaud, 1971).

The Speenhamland system was overthrown in 1834 by the Poor Law Report and an increased reliance on the deterrent effects of workhouses. The official view had moved against wage supplementation on the ground that it actually suppressed wages. This point has always remained controversial. Blaug, for example, claims to detect so much upper class prejudice in the 1834 report as to undermine its authority. There were anyway so many downward pressures on the wages of the recently dispossessed labouring masses in the early decades of the nineteenth century, that the effects of meagre levels of local wage supplementation must have been undetectable. But the prejudice against it remained and other forms of social security were always preferred to wage supplementation. Others have argued that the irony of this prejudice has been to keep down wages through a policy of withholding benefits from any among the unemployed who were heard to turn down work at even the lowest wages.

As Brown's account indicates, during the 1970s 'the ghost of Speenhamland' was laid and FIS was a qualified success, at least with most of the annual average of 205,000 families who received it. It made a substantial contribution to the incomes of many working families with larger numbers of children whose welfare had given proper cause for concern, and it was clearly helping the growing numbers of lone parents to manage to get into work and stay there. Brown's and others' accounts of the reaction of recipients was favourable. They particularly appreciated the business-like arrangements for paying FIS on a 'no further questions asked' basis for a whole year. It was not, they often said, like being on social security, and there was a strong preference for work over unemployment.

But some flaws were visible. Basically the levels of benefit were too low. This point had been made by a number of critics at its introduction. This still left

3

some families with total incomes (earnings plus FIS) below their level of entitlement to supplementary benefit - that they really would be 'better off on the dole'. The numbers affected in this way are open to controversy. But even using the most austere measures of short-term SB rates, the proportion of FIS recipients below that level was never less that ten per cent and similar numbers hovered only a pound or two above - amounts easily swallowed up by travel or similar in-work costs.

An even more serious problem was the creation of an intractable 'poverty trap' whereby most of the additional income earned by working longer hours or by getting better-paid work was lost because benefit was withdrawn at nearly the same rate. In the latter years of FIS, such adjustments were delayed by up to a year, but this too was a problem for those whose wages fell soon after being given an award.

Since FIS was based on gross earnings, and the rate of withdrawal was high, the poverty trap in the 1970s for FIS families had steep and slippery sides. For a few families on FIS it was unclimbable because for each extra pound they earned, up to £1.20 was withdrawn from their benefits if tax, national insurance, and rent and rate rebates were entered into their personal income equation. Nearly everyone on FIS had marginal rates of withdrawal between 70 per cent and 90 per cent. Thus, FIS caused marginal rates of withdrawal to be visited upon the lowest paid workers that exceeded even some of the most punitive rates of tax laid upon the best-paid workers by governments in the 1970s. This also raised concern for work incentives.

Concern was also raised about take-up levels. The initial target was 85 per cent of eligible families receiving FIS at any one time. This quickly proved an ambitious target and the earliest estimates, on what was admitted to be a shaky 'better than nothing' statistical basis, pointed to take-up rates as low as 35 per cent.

The highest estimates in the 1970s were about 65 per cent and the OPCS survey of family finances (Knight, 1981) suggested a figure of about 50 per cent. On the other hand, Knight was also able to confirm that the take-up by expenditure was likely to be higher - he suggested a figure of 65 per cent - since eligible non-claimants tended to be those with smaller than average entitlements. That is, the larger awards were more likely to be taken up, leaving 35 per cent of the money unclaimed.

Even so, a benefit that failed to deliver to its customers a third of the money voted for it by Parliament had an indifferent claim to effectiveness. Reasons given for this shortcoming have now become familiar ones. Low levels of consumer awareness remained resistant to government advertising. Claim forms were dauntingly complicated because an in-work means-tested benefit was never going to be anything but complicated to claim and assess. Fluctuations in working status caused by occasional part-time working by one or other member of a couple, and fluctuations in income caused by overtime, bonus and piece rates caused families to move swiftly in and out of entitlement. A fairly rapid turnover of claims suggested that take-up was being suppressed by movements of these kinds.

Low take-up and poor work incentives were held by critics to be part of the evidence that FIS, and other means-tested benefits that proliferated in the 1970s, was the wrong way to deliver social security to its claimants (see for example Deacon and Bradshaw, 1983, Parker, 1989). They also pointed to inefficiencies inherent in complex systems: high administration costs, and inequities beyond those caused by non take-up. For example, a means test is a household test and the benefit is added to household income. Income is not always fairly shared in households and its weaker members, especially children, can lose out. Means testing was held by critics to be an unacceptable procedure, involving unjustified invasions of personal privacy such as detailed disclosure of personal circumstances, endless checking and rechecking, and unpleasantness such as cohabitation investigations.

The system of social security set into place after the war was based on the Beveridge principle of universality, and it all but did away with means testing. The subsequent growth of selectivity undermined this principle to the extent that Deacon and Bradshaw were able to claim that the numbers receiving means-tested benefits rose from 2 million to 12 million between 1948 and 1982.

It is argued that this growth has re-created 'claimant' as a social role and it is one that is easy to stigmatise. Social security can become something for 'them' and not for 'us'. For example, a recent PSI study of elderly people selected its sample from pension records. The DSS wrote to 1800 elderly pensioners inviting their cooperation in the interview survey. Many of those who replied excused themselves on the ground that they would be unsuitable respondents because they had always provided for themselves and had '...never had anything to do with social security.'

Critics of means testing argue instead for the re-establishment of principles of universality. Some, Parker, for example, argue for a basic income paid to each individual on the sole ground of citizenship and in recognition of a principle that the first job of the state is to ensure a basic standard of living for everyone. Others look toward various negative income tax schemes. Indeed, FIS was introduced mainly to plug one of the wider gaps left by the non-implementation of the Barber/Joseph tax credit proposal. Supporters of universality also point out that degrees of targeting can be retained. Child benefit is everyone's favourite example of a universal but targeted benefit.

On the other hand, supporters of selectivity argue that it is indefensible to pay social security to people who do not need it. To do so would damage incentives to work in other ways. No opponent of selectivity has ever argued that the universal 'clean sweep' solutions would be cheaper, or would avoid higher taxation. They would also find it difficult to avoid the retention of some selectivity to meet exceptional need, such as disability, or large regional variations in housing costs.

The direction of social security policy in the 1980s was not towards universality, nor toward higher taxes, and selectivity increased. During this time,

FIS became rather a touchstone of the whole argument. It was probably the least effective among means-tested benefits. If it could be made to work better, then a case was made in favour of selectivity in general. Many of the particular deficiencies of FIS arose from the lack of a coherent policy toward income support for families, in and out of work. The reviews that led to the 1986 Social Security Act and its reforms that were introduced in April 1988, tackled a number of the most important problems with the introduction of family credit, which replaced FIS and introduced a number of reforms:

- Benefit levels were increased and hence more families were brought into entitlement.
- The 'poverty trap' was not abolished but it was made more shallow. This was achieved by basing entitlement on net rather than gross earnings and by arithmetically linking in-work and out-of-work benefits so that claimants ought no longer to lose more than a pound in benefits for every new pound earned; owner occupiers remain an exception. This made assessment even more complicated but it was designed to provide extra help for the lowest income families and, at the same time, improve work incentives.
- The number of qualifying hours for two-parent families (working 30 hours per week) was reduced to the levels applied since 1979 under FIS to one parent families only: 24 hours a week.
- Some passport benefits like free school meals and milk tokens were converted into cash equivalents, though others, like free prescriptions, eye tests and dental treatment remained.
- The period of award was brought back to the original FIS period of six months.
- New resolutions were made to improve take-up. These were enacted in a letter to 300,000 employers making them aware of the changes and asking them to tell their employees about it (8 per cent of DSS employees get family credit) and by spending over £8 million in advertising between launching the new benefit in April 1988 and January 1990.

Early measures of take-up of the new benefit showed no great improvement over the FIS figures. A hand count of returns in the last eight months of 1988 by the Family Expenditure Survey (based on less than 150 families) suggested that the proportions had remained stubbornly on 50 per cent by caseload and 65 per cent by volume. Though of course by widening the franchise of family credit, by larger entitlements and reduced hours, more people were drawn into benefit. The total monthly average of families in benefit rose and during 1991 an average of about 325,000 families received family credit at any one time. A high proportion were lone parent families. About a third of lone parents who work full-time claim family credit and 38 per cent of all recipients of family credit are lone parents.

A survey of family credit recipients carried out for the National Audit Office by NOP also suggested that improvements in the design of the benefit were having an impact on its customers. The 1990 NAO survey found that 38 per cent of recipients had come into family credit from income support or supplementary benefit. Half were new customers whose jobs had been taken up since April 1988. The NAO study concluded that a significant proportion of new claimants had been prompted into work by the introduction of family credit and that it was popular with a large and stable core of regularly renewing families. It was of considerable assistance to lone parents, though, realistically, their incentives were overlaid by greater issues that affected the opportunity to work and to claim. Majorities of lone parents said that unfavourable changes in their childcare arrangements, convenience of travel and hours of work and the chance to take time off when needed were the important factors in getting a job and being able to continue.

Echoing some of Anne Corden's conclusions (discussed below), the report said:

> '...there exists a sizeable group of family credit and income support recipients who are committed to finding or continuing work, almost irrespective of whether they perceive the level of their take home pay to be sufficient to meet their needs. And for a second group of benefit recipients, the availability of family credit influences their ability and willingness to take up or continue in work.'

> 'There is, however, a sizeable group of people receiving income support who believe they are better off on social security and that there is little likelihood of being able to get a job at a level of pay that meets their needs.'

For these and other reasons, the NAO recommended that more should be done to advise out of work families of the opportunities offered by family credit. The NAO also recommended an investigation of '...why families move into and out of entitlement to income support and family credit, in order to establish whether there is scope to improve the effectiveness of the work incentives provided by the schemes.' The commissioning of this study predated the NAO report but its design anticipated this need, among others, as an important research aim.

A more detailed evaluation of the working of family credit, and an invaluable starting point for the design of this study, was provided by Anne Corden's qualitative research with groups of eligible families, not all of them claimants, of recently rejected claimants and some out of work families who might claim in the future.

Corden also found that some of the reforms were visible as improvements on the ground. Paying family credit directly to women had given them highest awareness of family credit and its rules and they tended to direct how it was spent. Families successful in a claim said that 'the size of the award of family credit was often a pleasant surprise', but one that was promptly followed in some cases

7

by a nasty shock of the withdrawal of most or all of their housing benefit. It was particularly popular with lone parents, many of whom appeared to have '...built family credit into their plans...' for a return to work. The retention of health-related passported benefits was also '...highly valued.'

Corden's view of the incentive effects of family credit upon out of work families was also qualified. Women were better informed than men, but overall levels of awareness were low. Reading her accounts of exchanges with some of them gives an impression that family credit is seen at best through a haze of misapprehension which the least complication of circumstances thickens into a fog. Lone parents were aware that they had to solve their childcare problems simply and cheaply and reliably if a low-paid job on family credit was ever going to give them more than they got on income support. Even families who did see family credit as an incentive to work were often wary of the risks involved. As other work by the York University team at the Social Policy Research Unit has suggested, out of work families are often very anxious about how they will manage if they accept low-paid jobs, particularly if the job does not last long and they find themselves starting all over again on income support (McLaughlin, et al, 1988).

Corden's quest for eligible non-claimants to interview - 'the Holy Grail of research on income-related benefits' - proved vexingly difficult and leads her to sceptical conclusions about them. Those she found, she described as people who themselves find it hard to grasp the idea of eligibility; some among them were irretrievably bitter about a past rejection of a claim for family credit. She concludes:

> 'Research on take-up and incentives needs to get to grips with the structure of the eligible, potentially eligible and recipient populations. Research on incentives needs to look beyond the question of whether in-work benefits affect movements in and out of work, important though these are, and to look at the way benefits affect labour supply decisions while in work. Research on take-up needs to look beyond overall rates to look at how the various factors that constitute claiming decisions interact with each other and how they are distributed over the eligible population.'

This conclusion, similar in tone to the NAO study, was taken up in the design of this study. Having adopted a dynamic approach - an overused word but one that accurately describes the need to know what influences people to go from one state to another, from IS to FC, from FC to higher income, from FC back to IS and so on - it was obvious from the start that a claimant-only study would not do. Hence the adoption of an approach that was to embrace what was earlier introduced as the client population. The approach also introduced some very difficult methodological problems. The following section discusses the main issues of the research aims, content and sample design that resulted. These are a mixture of pragmatic aims to do with the functioning of family credit as a part of the benefit system and theoretically based aims about the relation of benefits to work.

The design of the survey

The sample design was not merely the usual technical matter of finding a representative sample of the population to be studied. It was an integral part of the methodology of the study. The target groups of families that were sought for interview represented the departures and destinations in and out of work that are affected by family credit, income support and other benefits. The paths between them are vectors defining direction and income values. Family credit, though, lies at the centre of this process. The main problem was to identify a population of families who were 'within range' of family credit. By this we meant:

1. PRESENT RECIPIENTS: families who were currently receiving or claiming family credit.

2. ELIGIBLE NON-CLAIMANTS: families who qualified for family credit but were not claiming it.

3. OUT OF WORK FAMILIES: families who, though without *full-time* work, might well be expected to claim family credit within the foreseeable future, as they entered full-time work.

4. MODERATE INCOME FAMILIES: families who earn a little more than the level that would entitle them to claim family credit but for whom a change of circumstances, a new child, or the loss of regular overtime payments, for example, would bring them within scope of eligibility.

There is a fifth group of interest that emerges naturally from each group except the present recipients: FORMER CLAIMANTS, successful and unsuccessful.

The definitions applied to select the fourth group, 'moderate income families' also defined what was meant by 'low income families'. It was:

> *families whose total income from all sources was between 1 per cent and 25 per cent more than the most they could earn before their entitlement to family credit expired.*

It is important to note that this definition of 'a low income family' depends on the numbers of children in the family and their ages. Thus a couple with one four year old child earning £162.50 a week net would not be selected. A couple with four children over 12 earning £180 a week net would be selected.

The focus of the content of the study also meant that we needed to talk to unequal numbers of these four groups. We needed a lot of family credit claimants, for example, but rather fewer higher income or out of work families. We needed just about all the eligible non-claimants it was practical to find, but again not as many as the numbers of claimants.

The real problem is that low income families, *in the population as a whole*, are not common. Families with dependent children are found in slightly fewer than four in ten households but only five or six in a *hundred* of these receive family credit. We started with a guess that another five in a hundred would be eligible non-claimants. So half the people we needed to find - all those entitled to family credit - are only 4 per cent of the population as a whole. Families living on IS or unemployment benefit are about another 10 per cent of families, or another 4 per cent of the population. Those hovering just above the family credit limit are probably another 5 per cent. Our total sample population is hidden away in only 12 per cent of all addresses. This is an unpromising prospect for a general population sift to find those wanted for interview. This is shown in Figure 1.1

It was decided to carry out a postal sift of families included on the child benefit record system in the DSS computer in Washington, Tyne & Wear. This sift would take the form of a postal self-completion questionnaire that would identify low income families among those who replied.

Hitherto, such a sample base has been helpful for postal rather than interview surveys because there is no way the system, which is designed to administer 6.67 million benefits and not provide researchers with samples, can cluster families into, in this case, 70 small postal areas that can be issued to interviewers in economical quotas. However, a method was discovered that involved using the Post Office's computer in Chesterfield to provide estimates of the numbers of child benefit encashments in each postal area. These estimates were then used as a basis for sampling 70 areas (in Great Britain, but none in Northern Ireland) proportionate to the numbers of families found in each, which is an indispensable step in such a sampling scheme. Complications were introduced by about 20 per cent of families who get their child benefit paid directly into their bank or building society account, and by a mixture of one-weekly and four-weekly order books that introduced variations into the local estimates of numbers of families.

The method was tested in seven areas and it was found to work. The numbers found by the sampling procedure in DSS Washington corresponded to the estimates made by PO Chesterfield. Variations introduced by account credit transfers (ACTs) and four-weekly order books produced variations in sample size of the predicted direction and magnitude. Consequently, the size of the main stage postal sift was calculated by grossing up the smallest group needed for interview: the eligible non-claimants, who were thought to be 5 per cent. We needed a minimum of 300 to interview and so would have to find 400 to approach. The resulting calculation determined a postal sift of 14,500 families.

To preserve confidentiality, the four page questionnaire was sent to each family directly by the DSS's research management division. But the replies were sent to PSI. Two reminders were sent to those who did not reply to the first mailing. Questionnaires were received from 70 per cent of those sampled (minus those 'gone away' etc) or 9,700 families, most of whom returned sufficient information to admit them to the selection procedure for the interview stage. Again, a higher-than-average response rate was obtained from target group members, especially those receiving income support and family credit. This may be because, receiving their form from DSS they thought they had to return it, even though the letter stressed the voluntary nature of response. Since so many

Figure 1.1 The location of the four 'target groups' in the relative income distribution among families

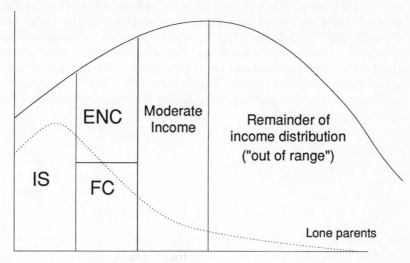

lone parents are receiving IS, the overall response rate for lone parents in the sift was nearly 80 per cent.

One difficulty remained. If we now had the basis for finding and interviewing 300 eligible non-claimants (plus all the out of work and moderate income families needed) the sample would yield a corresponding 300 families receiving family credit. This was not enough. We needed about 900.

The solution to this last problem was found in a third computer: the DSS family credit records in North Fylde. It was programmed to select in each of the same postal areas used for the child benefit sample, twice the number of family credit recipients discovered by the *sift*. Thus 300 would become 900 and retain the right proportions in each area.

Whereas the total sift results were below the originally hoped-for level of 75 per cent, the results from the interview stage, including the new North Fylde sample, exceeded expectations. The interviews were carried out by a team of NOP's more experienced interviewers, personally briefed by NOP and PSI researchers. Interviews were obtained from 82 per cent of those approached, though 7 per cent were interviews where only one partner in a couple had been personally interviewed and the partner data, where possible, completed by proxy.

The sift sample appeared accurate in the sense that its composition aligned very well with what is known about British families from other sources. The chief difference lies in a greater number of lone parents: 24 per cent among families replying to the sift compared with 18 per cent nationally. The majority of lone parents are already DSS customers and so they are rather used to filling in forms. The sub-sampling procedures used to select the interview sample corrected for this acquired bias.

Having quite a lot of information from the sift questionnaire allowed a second kind of comparison between families who were selected for interview and declined, and those who accepted and were interviewed. The 18 per cent of selected families who declined an interview, or who were not contacted, tended, on average, to have slightly fewer and slightly older children. Among couples, slightly fewer had male partners in work (61 per cent compared with 69 per cent) and among working lone parents, they earned a little more. There were no other significant differences and none that called for the introduction of special weighting procedures.

2 Who are Britain's low income families?

This chapter first places low income families into a wider context of families and work in Britain and the patterns of work associated with low income. This, essentially, is a comparison between those identified as low income families by the sift, and all those families who had higher incomes.

We then turn to the interview data to show in more detail what kinds of families have low incomes, relative to the numbers of their children. These are 'equivalent incomes' that place them in the lowest quarter of the national distribution among families with dependent children. We ask who, among these low income families, receive the very lowest incomes, including the families on income support? Who are among the lowest paid 5 per cent of working families who qualify for family credit? And who have 'moderate' incomes somewhat above this level? What, broadly, is the social construction of low incomes, work, and social security benefits?

First, though, how do families with children compare with other types of household? The concern is with *dependent* children: that is, children aged less than 16 years, or between 16 and 18 years of age but still in full-time education. Figures from the General Household Survey show that families with dependent children comprise 42 per cent of all family types. This compares with 26 per cent of families who are childless (cohabiting) couples, and 32 per cent who are one adult households, most of whom will be older people (see Figure 2.1).

Low income is not, of course, confined to families with children. People beyond retirement age, or single unemployed adults, frequently live on low incomes. But it is true to say that families with children make up nearly all of the *working* low income group. Low income among families containing children has been seen as one of the highest priorities for welfare policy and for the distribution of social security benefits. Conservative governments of the 1980s significantly raised the profile of low income families with children, and attempted to target resources in their favour (DHSS, 1985 - the Fowler Review). The emphasis on targeting was underscored by what was effectively a transfer of resources to the worst-paid working families from the rest.

Family credit was introduced and child benefit was frozen, though a small amount of uprating has now been restored for the first born. The debate over whether or not to maintain the value of child benefit against year on year inflation, however, indicates that the choice of ways of assisting families with children remains controversial. Although its value has been eroded, there is no doubt that child benefit, and one parent benefit where appropriate, remains an important

Figure 2.1 Composition of Households

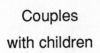

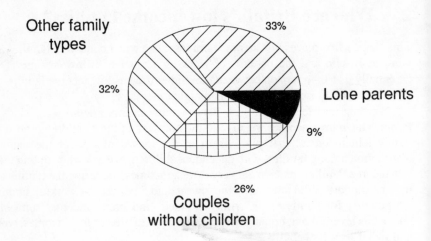

Other family
types

32%

33%

Lone parents

9%

26%
Couples
without children

source of income for those families we have called 'moderate income' families whose incomes keep them hovering just above the qualifying limit for family credit. Moreover, it is a source of income paid direct to the mother, in almost all cases.

Low income families
The analysis in most of this report seeks to look at the differences between the situations, constraints, and experiences of different low income families. These differences arise from differences in their relation to the labour market, on the one hand, and the social security system on the other. For example, are recipients of income support encouraged to enter the labour market by family credit? Or do they instead value the stability of remaining on out of work benefits (McLaughlin, Millar and Cooke; 1988)? Or are other factors, rather than benefits, determining whether or not they get paid jobs? This section considers the range of factors which distinguish low income from higher income families.

But there is one factor overriding all others: lone parenthood. Nine out of ten lone parents fall into our definition of low income families. Those who do not, tend to be lone fathers or divorced and widowed lone mothers. There is hardly a single or separated lone parent in the land who is not captured upon the uniform plain of low income. As Bradshaw and Millar showed in their 1989 survey, the majority of lone parents have more or less the same equivalent income. Among all lone parents, only a quarter have full-time jobs, 7 out of 10 get income support. Though only 1 in 6 of all families, lone parents are nearly half of all low income families and they make up nearly three quarters of all families on income support.

Lone parents compared to couples stand in a quite different relation to the forces that can tug people with children back and forth between work and life on benefits. Some of them face formidable barriers to work. A lack of affordable childcare is just one. Although their part-time earnings are more generously treated under IS rules than are couples', they still lose benefit pound-for-pound against earnings of more than £15 a week. Lone parents are therefore discouraged from the more usual route taken nowadays by mothers returning to work. They are much less likely to ease themselves into work part-time and gradually increase their hours as their youngest child passes first into nursery, then primary, then secondary school. In fact, only one in ten of all lone parents work part-time. They tend to have to jump straight into full-time work, or continue at home.

This, on the other hand, is where family credit comes into the picture. First, since most of them are women and, as Bradshaw and Millar show, they are less well educated, trained or qualified compared to other women, they tend to be offered low wages. This rather directs them towards family credit. Second, as we show in detail in a later chapter, lone parents stand to gain relatively more from family credit than do couples. The adult element in the amounts paid are the same for lone parents as for couples. Whilst lone parents have more than half the expenses of couples, and they are more likely to have to pay for childcare, family credit is more attractive to them than to couples, all other things equal.

Broadly speaking, the things that encourage or discourage lone parents from becoming low income one-earner families in work are the same things that encourage or discourage couples from becoming higher income two-earner families. This means that *as families* their relative positions with respect to benefits and work are different. For this reason they are treated separately in almost all that follows.

We start by comparing low income families with higher income families. Among couples we compare those selected as low income couples and those found by the sift. Among lone parents we have a special opportunity because we interviewed all the higher income lone parents found by the sift. We interviewed them for a special report to the DSS on lone parents. The following comparison, though, is virtually their only appearance in this volume.

The characteristics of low income lone parent families

Nearly all lone parents are low income families. Only 8 per cent of the lone parents in the sift were above the cut-off point of more than 25 per cent above the family credit threshold, calculated on the basis of earnings plus maintenance. Table 2.1 provides a number of comparisons between those lone parents identified as lower income and those few lone parents (just over 100 were interviewed) who were better off than this. While this is a comparatively small number for analysis, the differences between them and the remainder of lone parents are so wide that some confidence may be placed in the reliability of the

Table 2.1   Demographic characteristics of low income and higher income lone parent families

column percentages

	Low income	Higher income (over 125% of FC limit)
Weighted number	1690	151
Unweighted number	856	103
Sex and Marital Status	%	%
Male	4	17
Female		
Single	23	12
Separated	37	23
Divorced	31	44
Widowed	4	3
Total	*100*	*100*
Age of youngest child	%	%
0-4	46	16
5-10	32	37
11-15	19	31
Older	3	17
Total	*100*	*100*
Ethnic group	%	%
White	91	94
Black	4	1
Asian	2	-
Other	2	1
Refused/NA	2	4
Total	*100*	*100*
Tenure	%	%
Owner	24	86
Social tenant	60	4
Private tenant	9	3
Other	8	7
Total	*100*	*100*
Median age	31 years	39 years

findings. Note that these will, in this brief appearance, be called the 'higher income' lone parents, to distinguish them from the 'moderate income' lone parents who feature in later analyses who are those with incomes between 1 per cent and 25 per cent above their FC threshold. It is worth bearing in mind that many 'higher income' lone parents, and couples too, have only average earnings (see below).

Income status for most lone parents is bound to be related to earning power and employment opportunities. The only way for most lone parents to move off means-tested benefits is through paid work, either for reasonable hourly rates of pay or for a large number of hours - leaving aside the possibility of finding a partner.

A lack of childcare arrangements is an important barrier to paid employment, so it is not surprising that the low income lone parents were more likely to have younger children than the higher income group. Forty-six per cent of the lower income group had children less than five years old. This compares with only 16 per cent of the higher income group. For 34 per cent of higher income lone parents, their youngest child was 11 years of age or older. Older children place fewer demands on available childcare, since they spend lengthy amounts of time at school, and are in least need of adult supervision.

Not surprisingly, the lone parents in the higher income group were rather older. Their median age was 39 years, compared with 31 years for the lower income group.

The higher income lone parents were four times more likely to be lone fathers than the lower income group. Lone fathers comprised only 4 per cent of the lower income group, but 17 per cent of those lone parents with higher incomes. They were also more likely to be divorced lone mothers (44 per cent rather than 31 per cent), and less likely to be either single (never married nor cohabited) or separated.

The tenure profile of the higher income lone parents was striking - almost 9 out of 10 (86 per cent) were home owners - well above the national average. This may reflect their high earnings, or could have resulted from capital settlements on divorce. 60 per cent of the lower income group were living in social rented properties, compared with only 4 per cent of the higher income group.

The characteristics of lower income couples with children

Unlike the lone parents, none of the couples whose income, based on the sift, was more than the level of the family credit threshold plus 25 per cent were interviewed in the main stage project. Thus, we have to rely solely on information from the sift, or elsewhere, in order to make further comparisons between higher (again as opposed to the 'moderate income' group identified among the *interviewed* couples) and lower income couples. Table 2.2 compares the lower and higher income couples across a number of dimensions.

It was in the number of full-time earners (working 24 hours and more) that the main reason for the income difference became clear. One in three of the

Table 2.2   Characteristics of low income and higher income couples with children

column percentages

	Two parent families: Low income (up to 125% of FC limit)	Higher income (over 125% of FC limit)
Numbers (not weighted)	1935	4283
Age of youngest child	%	%
0-4	51	45
5-10	27	29
11-15	18	21
16+	4	5
Total	*100*	*100*
Number of children	%	%
1	29	39
2	41	47
3+	30	14
Total	*100*	*100*
Number of full-time earners	%	%
0	41	2
1	56	65
2	3	33
Total	*100*	*100*

higher income families had two earners, compared with about one in thirty of the low income families. Over 40 per cent of the low income couples had no full-time earner, compared with only a handful of the higher income couples.

We found that, among lone parents, those with the youngest children tended to have the lowest incomes, and were the least likely to be in paid employment. Among couples, we found no association between age of youngest child and income. However, it was much more common for families with three or more children to be on lower incomes. This is partly a result of the threshold adopted in this study. For a given wage, a family with many children is more likely to satisfy the threshold than a smaller family. Three (or more) child families represented 30 per cent of lower income couples, but only 14 per cent of those on higher incomes. The higher income couples are much more likely to have just one dependent child: 39 per cent of higher income couples had only one dependent child, compared with 29 per cent of the lower income couples.

Work and earnings

Families' work, and how much they earn, are central to this analysis. So it is worth looking in detail at the patterns of work and earnings that distinguish low income families from the rest. Social security benefits apart, what is low income? What do low paid families earn?

Table 2.3   Patterns of work and median net weekly earnings among low income and higher income families with dependent children.

	%	Low income Median earnings (£s p.w.)	%	Higher income Median earnings (£s p.w.)
Lone parents (n=2007)				
Working 24 hrs+ a week:	19	£105	95	£207
Working less than 24 hrs		}31%		}97%
a week	12	£28	2	-
Not working	69	-	3	-
Total	100		100	
Married women (n=6218)				
Working FT	9	£82	37	£134
		}26%		}71%
Working PT	17	£39	34	£67
Not Working	74	-	29	-
Total	100		100	
Married Men (n=6218)				
Working FT	54	£150	97	£293
		}55%		}98%
Working PT	1	(£56)	*	(£247)
Not Working	44	-	2	-
Total	100		100	
Couples with children (n=6218)				
Both work, 24hrs	4	£171	36	£340
He works, she works PT	11	£169	34	£278
He works, she does not	40	£140	29	£260
She works FT, he does not	5	£97	1	£224
She works PT, he does not	5	£40	*	-
Neither work	33	-	*	-
All	100	£139	100	£292

Table 2.3 shows, separately for low income and higher income families, the proportions of men and women working full-time or part-time (adopting the FC rules of 24 hours a week or more) and their median earnings. Table 2.4 shows earnings in greater detail.

Being a low income family is largely a matter of having no job or low pay, often low female pay. Being a higher income family is largely a matter of being a two-earner family or having high male wages, or both.

Among lone parents, almost all the higher income group work full-time, and a quarter of them are men. Among the low income group, only 19 per cent work full-time and 11 per cent part-time.

Among couples, the pattern is naturally more complicated. Nearly all the higher income men have full-time jobs, of course, and the majority of these have working wives too: only 3 in 10 higher income couples rely solely on male earnings, almost none on sole female earnings. In contrast, only 15 per cent of low income couples have two jobs, 40 per cent have sole male earnings, and, again unlike higher income couples, 10 per cent have sole female earnings, though half only part- time. A third of low income families have no work at all.

Table 2.4   The earnings of low income and higher income families

	Low Income			Higher Income		
	Lone Parents	Married Women	Married Men	Lone parents	Married women	Married men
Take home pay in £s per week	%	%	%	%	%	%
1-50	34	53	3	0	24	0
50-100	32	35	12	3	35	0
100-150	28	10	38	8	20	0
150-200	5	1	42	36	0	10
200-250	1	*	4	30	7	22
250-300	0	0	*	15	3	22
Over 300	0	0	0	8	3	46
Total	*100*					
Average earnings (£'s per week)	79	57	144	228	114	378
Median earnings	77	49	150	206	88	293
Average pay, (£s per hour)	3.10	2.9	3.2	6.1	4.5	7.0
Median pay, (£s per hour)	3.00	2.9	3.3	5.4	3.6	5.4

Among main wage earners - lone parents and husbands - the earnings distributions comparing low income with higher income families scarcely overlap. Among low income families, take home pay is typically less than £200 a week; among higher income families, £200 is almost universally a minimum take home wage. Higher income families do not merely earn more than low income families, they earn twice as much. For example, among lone parents working full-time the median take home earnings of low income families are £105 a week, among higher income families, £207 a week. Among full-time working husbands, the gap is widest: £150 a week among low income husbands, £293 a week among higher income husbands.

It is worth bearing in mind that lone parents are not a homogeneous group, except that most are women. There are important differences among them according to their marital history. Only among lone fathers and, marginally, among divorced lone mothers were the majority economically active. Activity rates among single lone parents and widows were lowest with less than a quarter in paid work of any kind; a fifth of the out of work singles and 28 per cent of the widows had never had a paid job. Those separated from cohabitation tended to have lower activity rates compared with those separated, but not (yet) divorced from a marriage.

Lone parents without paid work had typically been absent from the labour market for over five years, lone fathers less than three years, widows for more than nine, though lone fathers and widows had accumulated the greatest amount of earlier work experience (if they ever worked at all). Lone fathers and widows were, of course, noticeably older than other lone parents. The single mothers and those separated from cohabitation had the least work experience, averaging less than five years, while a further one fifth of the single mothers had had less than a year in paid work. So four out of ten single mothers had little or no work experience to offer a new employer.

The composition of low income families

We now turn solely to the interview data gathered from our 2,300 low income families and provide a first description of how they divide into the different target groups that distinguish the design of this study. But we start with a surprising finding: the numbers of self-employed families among them.

Self-employed families

Self-employment is not readily associated with claiming social security benefits, nor even with low income. But self-employed people are found in considerable numbers among those with the lowest incomes as well as among the more familiar professional and entrepreneurial groups. They are typically small traders and shopkeepers, often just starting in business, some with an enterprise allowance. Or they are manual workers, usually in the building industry, who work almost on a day-to-day basis, often through labour-only subcontractors. If such people have dependent children, they are often eligible for family credit. Official

Table 2.5   Self-employed workers by marital status

Weighted Numbers

	Percentage currently working as self-employed	Total
Lone parents	7.9%	492
Couple mothers	14.3%	467
Couple fathers	22.3%	819
All families	16.3%	

statistics show that 17 per cent of families receiving family credit base their claim on self-employed earnings. The assessment of earnings of self-employed claimants is typically more complex. It can take twice as long to process their claims as it does for employee claimants.

Among those in this survey of low income families who were in work, one in every six families defined themselves as self-employed, see Table 2.5. Fewer (8 per cent) of the lone parents were self-employed. While this was above the average for all women, given that there are only 23 cases (unweighted), further analysis cannot be reliable. Among married and cohabiting women, self-employment was much more common (14 per cent). However, within this sample it is usual for the women not to be in work, so the numbers of self-employed workers remain small.

It was amongst the working married men that we found the largest numbers of the self-employed: 22 per cent. They tend to work on their own account and three quarters of them do not employ other workers. They are heavily concentrated into construction work, other manual jobs and transport. Self-employed low income women are found, by contrast, in the retail and personal service sectors, or in cleaning and distribution work.

Having determined that the self-employed are a significant presence among low income families, how do they differ from other low income families? Among lone parents, the small number of self-employed workers were older than those who were employees, and less likely to be either single (never lived with a partner) or separated. Among couples, there were few differences in marital status or age. There were some differences in the housing tenure patterns of employees and the self-employed. Almost 80 per cent of two parent families with a self-employed chief wage earner were owner occupiers - much higher than for employees (58 per cent) and indeed above the national average.

The number and ages of children have been found to have an important influence on working patterns. There appeared to be little association with employment or self-employment among low income couples, however. Among lone parents, the self-employed were less likely than employees to have just one child. They were also older on average.

Table 2.6   Employment status

column percentages

| | Chief wage earner by marital status | | | |
| | Lone parents | | couples | |
	Employee	Self-employed	Employee	Self-employed
Base	492	39	1082	198
Unweighted number	373	23	647	122
Marital status	%	%	%	%
Married			91	94
Cohabiting			9	6
Single	16	-		
Separated	39	22		
Divorced	41	65		
Widowed	3	12		
Total	*100*			
Median age				
Respondent	34 yrs	42 yrs	33 yrs	34 yrs
Partner			35 yrs	37 yrs
Housing tenure	%	%	%	%
Owner occupier	40	48	58	78
Social tenant	41	52	35	17
Private tenant	9	-	3	3
Other	9	-	4	2
Total	*100*			
Age of youngest child	%	%	%	%
0-4	22	21	51	48
5-10	46	35	24	28
11-15	26	35	16	19
Total	*100*			
Number of children	%	%	%	%
1	50	24	19	19
2	36	55	47	46
3+	15	21	34	35
Total	*100*			

The 'target groups'

Having identified our sample of low income families, the next step was to divide them into the four target groups that formed the basic design, or rather the eight groups since we would want to look at lone parents and couples separately. The research design also required greater numbers of some kinds of family, particularly claimants, than of others. These are actual numbers interviewed:

	Eligible non-clmnts	FC claimants	Moderate income	Out of FT work
Lone parents	57	322	72	432
Couples	157	496	416	239

Two cells look unexpectedly large: out of work lone parents and moderate income couples. The first were selected deliberately to form the basis for a postal follow-up survey and to compare with a second lone parent survey in 1993. The second, like Topsy, just grew, because many of them were originally selected as eligible non-claimants. Many of these, as we expected, turned out to be ineligible but of course we had no way of knowing in advance *which* ones would do so. Since the take-up rate turned out to be higher than the design assumption of 50 per cent, rather more families ended up in the moderate income group because moderate income is what makes them ineligible. A few more transferred to the moderate income group because they had substantial savings which disqualified them from family credit.

Chapter 4 deals with the problems of take-up in great detail. For the moment, we introduce the actors who will play their parts in later analyses of take-up, of work incentives and so on. When the numbers above are re-weighted to reflect their true position, relative to one another, this is how the eight groups appear in the population of *low income families*.

	ENC	FC recipient	Moderate income	Not in FT work	
Lone parents	2%	5%	3%	38%	= 100%
Couples	6%	8%	20%	18%	

The pre-eminence of out of work lone parents as a presence among low income families is very striking: nearly 4 out of 10 of them. Family credit claimants total 12 per cent of low income families, eligible non-claimants 8 per cent and the moderate income group 23 per cent, nearly all of whom are couples.

Table 2.7 compares these eight types of low income family across all the principal social and economic characteristics that tend to be important in shaping peoples' economic activity.

One in ten of the couples had yet to marry. Most of the lone parents were formerly married, though more of the out of work lone parents were single. Lone parents had fewer children than couples and the point made earlier about working lone parents having older children is seen very clearly. Black people, of all kinds, are about 4 per cent of the British population but are 10 per cent of low income families. This figure of 10 per cent may also be low because the postal sift was addressed to women and it may have screened out some Asian women. Among couples in low income families, it is usually the male partner who has a paid job, if either of them have a job, though about one in seven of the working couples have two earners and one in ten of the out of work couples have some part-time work.

If the Standard Occupational Classification (SOC) is use to code the jobs reported by low income families, most of them end up in just a few categories of often unskilled work. This is made worse by the large numbers of women to be coded. In fact, the majority of jobs to be coded were women's jobs. Low-paid female workers are almost invisible to the SOC. Using the data, a new occupational scale was created for low-income jobs. It discriminates between 20 low paid occupations.

The women tend to be found in junior non-manual grades, selling and personal service jobs, or they are cooks and cleaners. In fact the majority of low-paid women do one of five jobs that all begin with 'C': cooks, cleaners, cashiers, childminders and clerks. The men are found more often in the less skilled manual grades in production, construction and food industries; others are drivers and warehousemen.

The 'benefit fault line'

The patterns shown in Table 2.7 point to a general conclusion that will shape much of what follows in this volume. There is a kind of geological 'fault line' that runs through the population of low income families that places the two 'benefit families' (those in work and claiming FC, or out of work and claiming IS) on one side and the non-benefit families (eligible non-claimants of FC and the moderate income families) on the other.

The benefit families, compared to the others, tend of course to be lone parents. This apart, they also tend, among couples, to marry less and cohabit more and, among lone parents, include fewer widows. They tend to be younger and to have more children. They are less well educated and have fewer qualifications. They are more often found in unskilled jobs. More than anything, though, they tend to be social tenants rather than owner occupiers, usually in council housing.

Readers may be surprised at this point to note that the social profile of eligible non-claimants is somehow more favourable than that of claimants, being typically home owners rather than social tenants. This is the first of a number of unexpected results that will be discussed below. Meanwhile, the next step will be to examine more closely the kinds of low income family who receive social security benefits, and those who do not.

Table 2.7   The composition of lower income families

column percentages

	Lone parents				Couples			
	Out of work %	Claim -ing FC %	Elig. non- clmts %	Mod- erate income %	Out of work %	Claim -ing FC %	Elig. non- clmts %	Mod- erate income %
Married					85	87	91	93
Cohabiting					15	13	9	7
Single	26	16	17	10				
Separated	41	34	26	26				
Divorced	28	47	47	53				
Widowed	5	2	8	10				
One child	44	39	53	49	22	13	20	21
Two children	13	42	31	42	42	38	40	49
Three	16	12	10	6	23	29	27	20
Four or more	6	6	6	1	13	19	13	10
Youngest child								
0-4 years	52	21	21	13	52	54	53	51
5-10 years	30	42	34	35	26	31	31	24
11-15 years	15	30	29	42	15	12	14	19
16-18 years	3	7	16	10	6	3	2	6
Median age of respondent:	30	34	38	39	33	32	33	32
Partner:					36	34	36	35
White	91	94	82	88	90	85	82	93
Black	4	4	10	7	*	1	3	*
Asian	2	*	4	-	6	11	10	4
Other	2	*	2	3	3	1	1	1
Refused/NA	2	1	2	1	1	2	5	2

Table 2.7   The composition of lower income families   *(continued)*

column percentages

	Lone parents				Couples			
	Out of work %	Claim -ing FC %	Elig. non- clmts %	Mod- erate income %	Out of work %	Claim -ing FC %	Elig. non- clmts %	Mod- erate income %
Tenure								
Owner- occupiers	17	33	53	67	30	40	64	67
Social tenants	65	52	27	18	61	52	29	27
Private tenants	9	6	10	7	4	5	3	3
Others	8	8	8	8	3	3	3	3
Economic Activity								
Women								
Work FT	-	92	100	94	-	19	17	14
Work PT	15	1	-	6	11	6	10	31
Seeking work	9	1	-	-	5	3	5	4
Sick, etc	6	1	-	-	6	2	1	4
At home	70	5	-	-	78	70	67	47
Men								
Work FT					-	77	90	89
Work PT					2	2	-	1
Seeking work					64	14	-	1
Sick, etc					29	5	7	8
At home					5	2	3	1
Income (£s per week)								
From:								
earnings	4	82	104	152	6	99	94	206
inc-related benefits	51	36	3	0	54	35	3	2
other DSS benefits	21	20	20	⸱ 25	48	23	24	27
Total income (including income from others sources)	82	148	138	203	111	162	126	259

27

Table 2.7   **The composition of lower income families**   *(continued)*

column percentages

| | Lone parents | | | | Couples | | | |
	Out of work %	Claim -ing FC %	Elig. non- clmts %	Mod- erate income %	Out of work %	Claim -ing FC %	Elig. non- clmts %	Mod- erate income %
Education								
Age left school (median age)								
Women	15.4	15.2	15.5	15.7	15.4	15.4	15.4	15.4
Men					15.0	15.3	15.2	15.3
Highest qualification								
Women								
None at all	46	47	29	11	56	52	39	42
CSE/RSA/C&G	27	27	32	31	20	22	27	26
O level	13	15	8	19	16	13	11	17
A level	4	2	9	6	1	2	5	3
Nursing	1	2	6	12	1	2	4	2
Higher quals	5	6	8	16	3	6	6	7
Others	3	5	8	4	3	3	7	4
Men								
None at all					58	51	45	37
CSE/RSA/C&G					24	25	26	27
O Level					6	8	9	14
A Level					1	1	1	3
Nursing					0	*	1	0
Higher quals					10	10	16	17
Others					2	5	3	2

Table 2.7   The composition of lower income families   *(continued)*

column percentages

	Lone parents				Couples			
	Out of work %	Claim -ing FC %	Elig. non- clmts %	Mod- erate income %	Out of work %	Claim -ing FC %	Elig. non- clmts %	Mod- erate income %
Present or last occupation								
Women								
Professional in health, education and welfare	2	2	7	13	2	2	7	3
Other professional	0	1	2	3	0	2	1	1
Intermediate non-manual	3	9	11	9	3	4	5	6
Junior non-manual	14	18	30	36	13	12	21	17
Junior retail & direct selling	18	14	11	5	2	16	11	20
Personal service workers	10	21	20	16	16	16	10	13
Child minders	0	*	0	0	0	0	1	1
Skilled and semi-skilled production	4	7	5	8	3	7	8	6
Skilled and semi-skilled construction	0	0	2	0	1	0	0	0
Other skilled and semi-skilled	1	0	0	1	0	*	0	0
Unskilled production workers	6	4	2	1	8	9	15	4
Unskilled in construction, etc	*	1	2	2	3	2	3	2
Agriculture & fishery	0	0	0	1	0	1	1	0
Catering staff	19	12	5	1	11	9	12	11
Cleaners	13	5	0	0	13	9	4	13
Transport workers	2	1	0	0	0	1	1	0
Distribution	6	3	2	1	3	8	0	3
NA/not classified	2	1	0	2	1	2	0	1

Table 2.7   The composition of lower income families   *(continued)*

column percentages

	Out of work %	Couples Claim -ing FC %	Elig. non- clmts %	Mod- erate income %
Present or last occupation				
Men				
Professionals in health education, and welfare	2	0	3	2
Other professionals	1	2	5	6
Intermediate non-manual	7	7	13	17
Junior non-manual	4	3	8	7
Junior retail & direct selling	3	7	7	3
Personal service workers	*	2	1	1
Child minders	0	1	0	0
Skilled and semi-skilled production	10	13	13	12
Skilled and semi-skilled construction	10	6	5	8
Other skilled and semi-skilled	3	3	1	7
Unskilled production workers	11	8	7	6
Unskilled in construction, etc...	17	13	10	9
Agriculture & fishery	0	4	2	1
Catering staff	3	5	2	2
Cleaners	0	2	1	1
Transport workers	16	13	10	11
Distribution	5	10	6	5
NA/not classified	7	3	6	4

3 Low income families and social security benefits

Many low income families rely heavily on social security benefits, even if they are in work. Other low income families who receive only child benefit will have had experience of claiming other social security benefits in the past and will have a higher than average probability of doing so in the future. Even those whom we have called 'moderate income' families will count child benefit alone a significant part of their net income.

There are two kinds of social security benefit claimed by low income families: 'income related', more often called 'means-tested' benefits like income support and family credit, and non-means-tested benefits like child benefit and unemployment benefit, though the latter is dependent on national insurance contributions. Among means-tested benefits, which of them they claim will depend on whether or not any adult in the family works full-time.

Income related or 'means-tested' benefits

There are four *primary* means-tested social security benefits potentially available to families with children. Two of these, housing benefit and community charge benefit, are available to families whether or not they are in work. The availability of the other two, income support and family credit, depends in the first instance on hours of work.

There are *secondary* benefits that are *indirectly* means-tested. These are often called *'passport benefits'* because they may be applied for only on production of proof of receipt of one of the primary means-tested benefits. Families receiving income support can apply for grants or loans under the social fund. They can also apply for benefits in kind, such as free school dinners and milk, cheaper spectacles and free dental treatment, free prescriptions, fares to hospital or prison visiting, and so on. Many of these are also available for families receiving family credit, except free school meals. They may not apply under the social fund for discretionary grants and loans, but certain payments through the regulated social fund (funeral expenses payment and maternity expenses payment, but not cold weather payments) are available to them.

Figure 3.1 illustrates these distinctions.

Figure 3.1   The availability of means-tested benefits

Families with at least one adult working 16 hours a week or more	Families with no adult working more than 16 hours a week
PRIMARY BENEFITS	
family credit	income support (including mortgage interest payments)
housing benefit	housing benefit
community charge benefit	community charge benefit
SECONDARY BENEFITS	
some passport benefits	all passport benefits
	social fund discretionary grants and loans
regulated social fund (not cold weather payments)	regulated social fund

Housing benefit (HB) provides help with paying rent, but not mortgages, for families on a sufficiently low income. Rates of housing benefit are set so that families receiving income support may claim 100 per cent of their (eligible) rental costs. For families with incomes greater than the amounts payable under income support, housing benefit may still be payable, but awards will be reduced by 65 pence for every £1 of income over their IS threshold. Community charge benefit (CCB) works in a similar way, but is designed to cover community charge bills. The maximum award is 80 per cent of the total bill that claimants have to pay (not 100 per cent as for rent), while the taper is much shallower (15 pence in every pound). Under the new Council Tax, the maximum will be 100 per cent of the bill.

Help with payments of mortgage interest is available for families receiving income support and is taken into account in calculating their entitlement. It is also worth bearing in mind that home buyers who have jobs also get help in the form of MIRAS rebates from their interest payments at the basic rate of income tax, even if they do not pay income tax, on up to £30,000 of their mortgage.

The two key means-tested benefits for families with children are income support (IS) and family credit (FC). There is a sharp distinction in the eligibility conditions for these two benefits, based upon the number of hours worked.

Income support is generally available to families where no adult works more than 16 hours a week or more (until April 1992, during the period of this study the relevant figure was 24 hours). During fieldwork for this study, the former rule was in operation and so this will be the dividing line between those called 'out of work families' and those in work. It is worth remembering, on the other hand, that there are some low income families who work part-time despite losing all of their earnings above £5 a week each for couples and £15 a week for lone parents. There are others who support themselves solely on part-time work and do not claim IS, even though some of them would be entitled to something. Typically they tend to be two-earner part-time working couples or lone parents who receive decent amounts of maintenance. Neither is common.

Family credit is available only where at least one adult works 16 (formerly 24) hours a week, or more. The amounts of either benefit payable depend on:

- the number and ages of children,
- the level of savings and investments,
- income from all earnings and elsewhere, except for some disability benefits which are ignored. Child benefit and one parent benefit are also ignored under family credit, but not under income support. For this reason the child credits under FC are smaller than those under IS to take account of the different treatment of ChB and OPB.

So 'family credit families' are those who were receiving family credit when they were interviewed, and the 'eligible non-claimants' are those meeting these conditions but not receiving FC.

The rates of family credit are calculated so that cash income for those families receiving it should exceed the income that would be available if out of work, on income support. This is a very important point. The two benefits, IS and FC are arithmetically geared together. The aim is to maximise the chances that a family in work and claiming family credit ends up with a higher total cash income than they would have if they were out of work and claiming income support. Thus the four means-tested benefits - IS, FC, housing and community charge benefit - are all bound together in a single system of support for the incomes of families, based on net income and capital.

On the other hand, as Figure 3.1 indicated, there is one potential flaw in this scheme. All these calculations take into account reductions in the amounts of housing benefit and community charge benefit that would be payable, but not awards of mortgage interest. Since mortgage interest is only paid to families if they receive income support, there is no *guarantee* that mortgage payers will be better off on family credit. Indeed, given the relatively small net gain from family credit over income support for tenants, the presumption is that many owner occupiers would be worse off. The group most likely to be worse off on family credit than on income support are those with higher mortgages, or repayment mortgages taken out recently. At the time of the study, mid-1991, there were a few of these around.

Income support, family credit and the 'unemployment trap'
The purpose of this wedge between amounts of family credit and amounts of IS is to provide an incentive to take paid work rather than stay on out of work

Additionally, it may encourage existing workers to remain in
it.

proportion of income that a family receives when not working compared
me they could receive in full-time work is known as the *replacement
ratio*. Thus, a replacement ratio of 50 per cent would imply that a family
receiving £200 in work, would be able to recoup £100 if they did not work. This
calculation also needs to take the value of passported benefits available to out of
work families, the treatment of in-work perks, and travelling expenses into
account. Dilnot and Morris (1983) provide a discussion of the calculation of
real-world replacement ratios. In strict cash terms, the higher the replacement
ratio, the lower the incentive to take (or remain in) paid work. Replacement ratios
of greater than 100 per cent, or close to this, constitute the unemployment trap.

Replacement ratios will be lower (and, hence, incentives to work greater) the
higher is earning capacity, the more generous is family credit (and other in-work
benefits), and the less generous is income support.

But maintaining incentives to work is just one objective of a social security
system. The main objective is that of maintaining decent standards of living for
all who need help to do so. This objective suggests that the value of income
support should, at least, be sustained. Hence, there will always be a tension
between ensuring the sufficiency of benefits, and promoting work incentives.

The product of these tensions is the difficulty in setting the value of benefits
at a point that meets need and maintains incentives to work. The extent to which
family credit achieves this balancing act successfully is the main preoccupation
of later chapters of this report.

In the final sections of this chapter, we take an overall look at the functioning
of income support, family credit and housing benefit. Who receives them? How
long do families stay on these benefits? Are they easy to claim and to gain
information about? And so on.

Income support

The social security systems of many countries have a safety net. There is usually
a benefit available to families who have insufficient income for basic living
expenses. In the UK, families with little or no income, and not engaged in
full-time work (now defined as employment for 16 hours or more each week),
may claim income support. It is the successor to supplementary benefit and,
before that, national assistance.

The amount of income support payable to each family depends on the type
of family, and the age and number of children. If they are home owners, and
increasing numbers are nowadays, they will have half their mortgage interest
paid during their first 16 weeks as claimants; all of it is paid in the 17th and
subsequent weeks.

In summer 1991, the date of the main stage interview, the amounts of money
payable to a lone parent (aged over 18) with one child aged 4 would have been
as follows:

Personal allowances:

for single parent	£39.65
for child aged under 11	£13.35

Premiums:

family	£ 7.95
lone parent	£ 4.45
Maximum income support	£65.40

(Plus mortgage interest)

These amounts are 'typical' in the sense that by far the majority of families with dependent children who receive income support *are* lone parents.

This is the amount of income that should be received by this type of family. If they have any income, the amount of income support payable is reduced pound for pound. So, if this lone parent was receiving child benefit of £8.25 and one parent benefit of £5.60 each week, the amount of income support that could be received would be £51.55. If maintenance was being paid then, in 1991, the amount of income support would be reduced by the value of the payments.

Total income will be equal to the maximum amount of income support: £65.40.

Maximum income support	£65.40
less child benefit	£ 8.25
less one parent benefit	£ 5.60
IS payable	£51.55

In order to promote continuing contact with the labour market, earnings (but not other income) below a certain level - the disregard - are ignored. Lone parents may earn £15 before losing any income support: couples may earn £5 each, increasing to £15 when they have been on IS for more than two years, or if they receive a disability premium.

The great majority of IS claimants are in rented accommodation. Those in council and housing association tenancies - most of them, in fact - have all their rent paid by housing benefit. Those in private tenancies have all or part of their rent paid, judged against an appropriate amount.

Various studies have suggested that families with children receiving income support face severe problems of low welfare. They have the lowest incomes among this low income subset of the population, and appear to face the greatest financial difficulties.

The receipt of income support

In 1990, there were more than four million recipients of income support: just over one million of these were also recipients of child benefit.[1] Among families with children, a large majority of the recipients of income support are lone parents rather than two-adult families. One parent families made up 72 per cent of the families with children receiving income support in 1990 (see Table 3.1).

Table 3.1   Numbers receiving income support 1990

Total receiving IS	4.18 million
of which numbers:	
Receiving child benefit	1.13 million
Lone parents	0.81 million

Source: DSS (1992)

Taking the PSI/DSS survey of low income families, 73 per cent of low income lone parents received income support.[2] This compares with only 24 per cent of the low income couples. To that extent, low income is associated with no work for lone parents: for couples being within scope of means-tested benefits is much more a matter of low earnings.

Table 3.2 compares certain of the characteristics of income support recipients with those of low income families as a whole. Lone parents formed a far larger proportion of income support recipients than of low income families overall. Widows were rather less likely to receive income support than other types of lone parents, but the number of widows in this sample was too small for very fine-grained analysis. Among low income couples with children, cohabiters were rather more likely than married couples to be on income support.

Housing tenure proved to be a significant difference between the different subgroups of low income families. Almost two out of every five low income families were home owners: half were social tenants. Among those on income support, over two thirds were social tenants, only 1 in 6 were home owners. The influence of social tenancy on economic participation, earnings and benefit incomes will be seen later as a key factor in shaping the social location of low income families.

The duration of income support receipt

Living on income support is difficult for all families and their difficulties are likely to increase the longer they remain on IS and without full-time work. There are two potential difficulties: budgeting may become more difficult and a return to work becomes less and less likely. These two problems may affect each other and life 'on IS' becomes self-perpetuating. As time spent on IS continues, so a family's 'accumulated human capital' will become depleted, just as their savings run down and their stock of household goods ages and goes unreplaced. The skills they might offer employers may become outdated. Positive motivation towards employment may fall. Some may become depressed, others ill (see Heady and Smyth, 1989). Getting back to work will to that extent become (even) more difficult. It is also possible that employers will prefer to recruit workers who are already in jobs rather than take on those who have been out of the job market for some time.

Table 3.2   The characteristics of income support recipients

column percentages

	Proportion of IS recipients		Proportion of ALL low income families	
Weighted base	1673		3562	
Unweighted base	578		2310	
	%	%	%	%
Lone parents of whom:	73		47	
Single		27		23
Separated		42		39
Divorced		29		32
Widowed		2		5
Couples of whom:	27		53	
Married		78		89
Cohabiting		21		10
Total	*100*		*100*	
	%		%	
Age of youngest child				
0-4	56		49	
5-10	29		29	
11-15	13		17	
Ethnic group				
White	91		90	
Black	3		2	
Asian	2		4	
Other	2		2	
NA/Refused	2		2	
Tenure				
Owner	17		38	
Social tenant	69		51	
Private tenant	7		6	
Other	6		5	

Table 3.3 shows the median duration on income support experienced by current IS claimants, by a number of characteristics. A cross section survey such as this will tend to find more among recipients of IS who have longer rather than shorter spells on IS. The proportion on IS only briefly, will be fewer in the sample than is the true proportion of brief spells among all spells on IS.

Table 3.3   The duration of income support receipt

	Median duration (in months) among current recipients
Base	1674
Unweighted base	578
All	25 months
Lone parents	29
Male	11
Female	
Single	39
Separated	18
Divorced	40
Widowed	24
Couples	14
Married	13
Cohabiting	17
Age of youngest child	
0-4	22
5-10	29
11-15	45
Ethnic group	
White	25
Black	35
Asian	12
Tenure	
Owner	15
Social tenant	29
Private tenant	24
Other	17

Half of the recipients had been receiving income support for two years or more. Among them were many single lone parents who had been on income support for rather longer than other families -typically for over three years - whereas lone fathers on IS had claimed for typically less than a year. This was even lower than that of couple claimants, who had been on income support for a median duration of one year and two months.

For lone parents, a comparison is possible with the figures published by DSS in their Annual Statistical Enquiry. They show a mean duration on income support of 31 months compared to our 29 months. The two distributions are very similar.

In the previous section we found that families with older children were less li ely to have a low income than those with younger children. This was counted for by the labour market constraints on lone parents. Table 3.3 shows that where a family was on income support, those with older children tended to ve the longest durations. This was partly due to an age effect -those with ildren just a year old are unlikely to have been on income support for longer an one year. It may also have indicated that some low income families with der children were likely to be trapped in benefit dependency. Many low income milies will leave low income when one or other partner goes out to work. This ecomes increasingly possible as children get older. But not all families can join his trend.

There is a strong relationship with housing tenure. The shortest durations /ere for home owners (15 months): the longest for social tenants (29 months). Private tenant claimants had been on income support for an intermediate period of two years.

Only those on income support may apply to the social fund. Most of those who apply for loans get them, 21 per cent in the case of our claimants in this sample, but fewer receive outright grants: 13 per cent in our sample which was just over half of those who had applied for a grant.

Family credit

Later in this volume we will be centrally concerned with the effects of family credit. In this section we look at the benefit itself, and differences between families receiving family credit and other low income families. We look at their use of passport benefits compared to similar use by income support claimants. We also use DSS data to examine broader details of the families who receive family credit.

Unlike income support, family credit does not attempt to ensure that each family of similar size (that is, numbers and ages of children and adults) receives the same income. Instead, families with higher earnings will typically be better off while receiving family credit than families with lower earnings -although not all that much better off. This is an important point to bear in mind while interpreting many of the findings in this report. It means that comparing *similar sized* families on FC, those who receive the largest awards of family credit have the lowest *total* incomes.

Under family credit, a family earning less than £62.25 is eligible for a maximum award for themselves and each child. A lone parent with a four year old child, earning £62.25 for a 24-hour week would receive in family credit:[3]

Adult credit	£38.30
Child credit	£ 9.70
Total	£48.00

A lone parent earning £62.25 per week (after national insurance) or less, and working for 24 hours a week or more, would receive this amount. For each pound by which net earnings exceed £62.25, family credit entitlement is lowered by 70 pence - not by a full pound above a disregard as for income support. So if this lone parent took home earnings of £72.25, the amount of family credit payable would be (£48 - £7 = £41). Family credit ceases to be payable at net earnings above £130. On the other hand, both child benefit and one parent benefit are disregarded under FC.

These amounts of family credit, plus earnings, are rather higher than the amounts of income support to which families are entitled (£65.40 for this family, with up to £15 of earnings disregarded on top). When housing benefit and community charge benefit are reduced as a result of this higher income, the calculation still favours family credit but with a less generous gap between the cash received in work and that payable out of work. Chapter 8 tackles these difficult problems of marginal incentives to work.

Who receives family credit?

In the sift, recipients of family credit formed 6 per cent of all respondents. This is consistent with administrative statistics which showed in 1991 that there were 6.7 million child benefit recipients, and 350,000 family credit recipients (ie 6 per cent). Within our low income sample - those on or below the level of family credit plus 25 per cent - recipients of family credit comprised 10 per cent of lone parents and 15 per cent of couples. This reflects the rather lower proportion of low income lone parents in paid employment.

Evidence from aggregate data

By the end of August 1991, at the time of the DSS/PSI survey, the number of family credit claims in payment had reached 355,000 (see Figure 3.2).

The Department of Social Security regularly examine their data base of family credit claimants. Statistics are based largely on a 5 per cent sample of cases, selected according to particular National Insurance code numbers. The most up to date information relates to April 1991, when there were 341,000 claims in payment. Lone parents represented 38.3 per cent of claimants: couples the remaining 61.7 per cent. It is worth bearing in mind that 16 per cent of family credit couples based their claim on family incomes where the woman's job is the main or the sole contribution. Some of these 'reverse-role' couples are self-employed, others have a single female employee claimant who has an

Figure 3.2 Family credit recipients

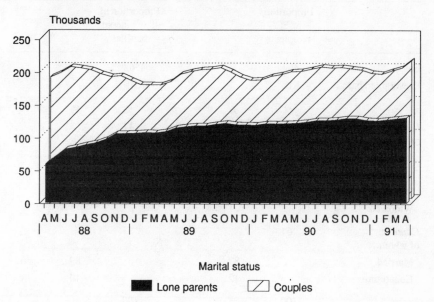

Marital status

■ Lone parents   ▨ Couples

Source: DSS analysis of 5% sample

unemployed partner, others a disabled partner. The latter two kinds of family attract special interest in Chapter 8.

The average award of family credit in April 1991 was £30.50. Even though they had fewer children than couples had (1.6 compared with 2.4), lone parents got higher awards: £31.50 compared with £29.80. This is because lone parents earn less than couples (see Table 2.7).

The overwhelming majority of family credit recipients are employees (84 per cent) rather than self-employed: 21 per cent of couples, but only 7 per cent of lone parents, are self-employed applicants.

The sample data

Within our study design, claimants of family credit occupied a middle station between those out of work, and those with incomes above eligibility for family credit. To that extent, we expected many of their characteristics to be similar to that of the low income group as a whole. In general terms, recipients of family credit were less likely to have children aged under five (41 per cent, compared with 49 per cent among low income families as a whole). This is consistent with young children presenting an important barrier to taking paid employment, at least among one parent families, and so being able to claim family credit.

Table 3.4   Receipt of family credit among low income families

column percentages

	Proportion of FC recipients		Proportion of all low income families	
Base	462		3562	
Unweighted base	818		2310	
	%	%	%	%
Lone parents	39		47	
of whom:				
Single		16		23
Separated		34		39
Divorced		47		32
Widowed		1		5
Couples	61		53	
of whom :				
Married		87		89
Cohabiting		12		10
Total	100		100	
Age of youngest child	%		%	
0-4	41		49	
5-10	35		29	
11-15	19		17	
Ethnic group	%		%	
White	89		90	
Black	2		2	
Asian	7		4	
Other	1		2	
NA/Refused	2		2	
Tenure	%		%	
Owner	37		38	
Social tenant	52		51	
Private tenant	5		6	
Other	5		5	

Among lone parents, receipt of family credit was rather higher among divorcees than chance would have suggested. Single lone parents and those who separated were under-represented compared to other types of low income one parent families.

The passport benefits

A family receiving income support becomes eligible to receive a range of benefits that are paid *in kind*. These include free prescriptions, free dental treatment, help with the costs of spectacles, and free school meals. All of these, except free welfare milk for the under fives and school dinners, are also available to recipients of family credit.

The existence of such benefits, rather than payment in the form of a higher rate of weekly benefit, may be justified either by an intention to meet certain needs directly rather than expect claimants to meet them out of their benefit, or by a recognition that meeting certain infrequent expenditures from income support (or family credit) is simply not practicable. It is also a way of dealing equitably with families with differing needs: a family with an ailing adult in need of multiple prescriptions will gain more than a family all in good health, though 'gain' may not be entirely the right word. For this reason, passport benefits can sharpen the unemployment trap for ailing families. It would be costly to have to meet prescription charges when in work, unless FC was also available.

We sought to find out how important these benefits were to low income families. Are they occasional benefits which meet need at a time of difficulty, or are they instead part of an accepted package involving widespread use of such benefits? Results for a range of passported benefits are presented in Table 3.5.

Table 3.5   Use of passport benefits among current claimants

row percentages

Benefit		Income support Used	Not used		Family credit Used	Not used	
Free school meals	%	57	43	= 100%	n/a	n/a	
Free eye tests	%	44	56		41	59	= 100%
Assistance with buying milk for under fives	%	43	57		11	89	
Legal aid	%	41	59		18	82	
(lone parents only)	%	(47)	(53)		(33)	(67)	
Fares to hospital	%	11	89		8	92	
Loft insulation	%	5	95		3	97	

Among claimants of income support, free school meals were received by 57 per cent of claimants. Chapter 5 indicates that this gives a take-up figure of around 80 per cent, once allowance is made for families with children below

43

school age. This indicates an amount of benefit support for children's welfare going unclaimed, though the preferences of the children themselves may well be a cause.

Among the other benefits, free eye tests were used by more than 40 per cent of both sets of claimants. Recourse to state assistance with fares to hospital, or to install loft insulation were rather rarer - typically fewer than 10 per cent of claimants used these benefits.

By and large, there were few differences between lone parents and couples in their use of passport benefits. The exception was in use of legal aid, which was more common among lone parents than among couples. This suggests that issues relating to separation, divorce or financial settlements form an important motive for seeking financial assistance with legal costs. However, even controlling for marital status, recipients of income support were more likely to have used legal aid than family credit claimants.

Housing benefit
Housing benefit is available to tenants whose income is below a certain level. This level is determined by the eligible rent, the size of the family, and the age of the dependent children. Families receiving income support will be eligible for the maximum 100 per cent rebate. Families receiving family credit are also eligible, although family credit counts against housing benefit entitlement. In fact, HB is supposed to be reduced by FC entitlement, even if the family has failed to claim FC. But it is not known how thoroughly local authorities implement this rule. In fact, most of those claiming housing benefit were on income support (82 per cent of cases) and only 8 per cent were on family credit. The steep housing benefit taper (65 per cent), and the treatment of family credit as income, means that eligibility does not extend far up the income distribution among families. For this reason, some have argued for a shallower taper (Kemp, 1992).

In this low income sample, 78 per cent of tenants were receiving rent rebates. Table 3.6 makes a number of comparisons between those families who were receiving rent rebates, and low income tenants as a whole. Overall, the differences were few. Recipients of housing benefit were more likely to be lone parents than couples. However, there were few differences in the types of lone parent who received or did not receive HB.

The number of full-time workers in the family unit was, unsurprisingly, closely linked to whether rent rebate was received. Almost no couples with two full-time earners received HB. Recipients, among both couples and lone parents, were most likely to have no full-time earner. While this was typical for all low income tenants, irrespective of receipt, there was more likely to be a single full-time earner for families not receiving HB - a combination of income being too high and, possibly, some non-take-up too.

Table 3.6   Receipt of housing benefit among low income tenants

column percentages

	Proportion of HB recipients		Proportion of all low income families	
	%	%	%	%
Lone parents	67		58	
of whom:				
Single		28		26
Separated		42		41
Divorced		27		29
Widowed		2		3
Couples	33		42	
of whom:				
Married		81		85
Cohabiting		19		15
Total	*100*		*100*	
Age of youngest child	%		%	
0-4	53		53	
5-10	30		30	
11-15	14		15	
Ethnic group				
White	92		92	
Black	3		3	
Asian	1		1	
Other	3		2	
NA/Refused	2		2	
Other benefits received				
Family credit	8		13	
Income support	82		64	
Number of full-time workers				
Lone parents				
None	95		88	
One	5		12	
Couples				
None	81		52	
One	17		44	
Two	1		5	
Weighted base	1567		2005	
Unweighted base	560		838	

Social security and the self-employed

DSS statistics show that 17 per cent of family credit recipients are self-employed. We found a similar or even higher proportion for *all* jobs of these low income families, which suggests that the number of family credit recipients who were self-employed is not disproportionate.

Table 3.7 gives the proportion of couples who received family credit, by combinations of employment status. Clearly, some of the permutations of respondent and partner work statuses were commoner than others. The most typical employment combination is a male employee with a non-working partner. The largest category for analysis of the self-employed is where the male is self-employed and his partner is not in work. These two groups represent the most reliable basis of comparison.

Self-employment was not closely related to receipt of family credit. Take-up of family credit is anyway thought to be lower for self-employed than employed families. Among low income families, those with a male employee are more likely to receive family credit than those with a self-employed male (where both have a non-working wife).

Where both partners in a couple worked, unusual among low income families, the presence of a self-employed adult did add to the proportion receiving family credit. However, it remained true that family credit is most likely where there is only one working partner. Looking at the chief wage earner, we found no difference in the proportion of recipients among self-employed and employed families.

Table 3.7   Couples receiving family credit, by employment status

Employment status combination of family		Bases		Receiving FC
Wife	Husband	Wtd	Unwtd	
No work	Employee	632	395	27%
No work	Self-employed	107	64	24%
Employee	Employee	250	142	8%
Employee	Self-employed	46	30	18%
Employee	No work	137	72	22%
Self-employed	Self-employed	28	18	9%
Self-employed	Employee	24	15	21%
Self-employed	No work	11	7	—
Chief wage earner				
Employee		1082	647	21%
Self-employed		198	122	21%

History of claiming in-work benefits

While family credit has a reasonably stable constituency, there is also considerable turnover (Ashworth and Walker, 1992). We were interested not only in the proportion of families who were currently receiving benefit, which was covered in the preceding section, but also which groups had had contact with this benefit, either now or in the past, and had been turned down for family credit (or for FIS).

Table 3.8 shows that families with a self-employed main wage earner were less likely than employees to have had contact with family credit in the past. Among couples the majority of employed families had had some contact with either family credit or FIS. Among self-employed families, 58% had not applied for either benefit. The reason for this difference is not a greater number of successful claims by employees. The proportion of employed and self-employed families who had received one benefit or the other were about the same (38 per cent). However, one quarter of employees, but just over 10 per cent of the self-employed, had been rejected for family credit or FIS. These figures suggest that the self-employed enjoyed a higher success rate than employees.

Table 3.8   Contact with FIS and family credit

Column percentages

| | Chief wage earner by marital status | | | |
| | Lone parents | | Couples | |
	Employee	Self-employed	Employee	Self-employed
Weighted base	492	39	1082	198
Unweighted number	373	23	647	122
Contacts				
Has received	53%	39%	39%	38%
Has been rejected	16%	14%	23%	11%
	%	%	%	%
Some contact	60	43	42	42
No contact	40	57	48	48
Total	*100*	*100*	*100*	*100*

Low income families in and out of work: a summary

This and the previous chapter have shown that, apart from their low incomes, low income families are different from other families in a number of key aspects:

- The lowest income strata 'capture' most of the lone parent families; nine out of ten of them. Nearly *half* of our sample of low income families were lone parents. Two-thirds of these lived on income support, sometimes doing a little part-time work. They remained on income support for a long while, typically twice as long as IS claimant couples. The barriers they faced entering work were familiar but intractable: little education, training or work experience; a lack of really suitable jobs; a lack of affordable childcare; a lack of regular maintenance payments; and a loss of all income support on earnings above £15 a week that debarred lone parents from a gradual increase in working hours as their children grew older. They needed full-time hours or very few.

- But lone parents are not low income families just because they are lone parents. Most of them are women, so the one third of lone parents who get paid jobs tend to be offered lower wages. A quarter of low income lone parents work full-time and nearly four out of ten of these in full-time work have incomes low enough to qualify for family credit (compared with 4 per cent of all couples and 16 per cent of low income couples), even though they have fewer children than couples have.

- Couples, on the other hand, are found among low income families when only one of them works full-time, when the main earner's wages are low (though not necessarily the lowest, by any means) and when the children are young. A couple's route out of low income is to become a two earner family.

- However, wives in low income couples face similar disincentives to work to those that conspire to keep lone parents at home: similarly low levels of education, training and really suitable jobs. They too are offered wages that would pay for little childcare if they needed to. If it does, they will soon find going out to work becomes unrewarding financially. They have an advantage in being able to ease themselves into work more gradually, increasing their hours as children grow. But if they are on family credit this advantage all but vanishes. The wives in family credit couples have similar problems as have lone parents on IS. True they lose 'only' 70 per cent of family credit (though more if they are on HB & CCB too) for each pound they earn, but they get no £15 a week disregard as do those on IS. The fixed six-month term of FC awards cushions this disincentive a little, but nearly all of the 1 in 6 low income couples getting family credit were one earner families - though some of them are women full-time workers.

- A surprising number - 1 in 6 of working low income families - were self-employed.

- Thirty years ago, when families had two parents and one job, a survey of low income families would have placed unskilled manual work at the fore of any social construction of their position. No longer - the growth of out of work lone parenthood, and higher unemployment generally has seen to that. True, a fifth of lone parents who work had the poorest jobs in cleaning and catering, but the rest worked in junior non-manual, retail and personal service jobs. The same is true of wives. It is even true of their husbands, still less than half of whom are manual workers. Our definition of low income leaves the field open to many moderately paid non-manually employed families, especially if they have more than two children. But the emphasis has shifted from work to benefits: 59 per cent of low income families claimed means-tested benefits; another 8 per cent were entitled to them but did not claim; only 33 per cent relied solely on earnings and non-means-tested benefits.

- What is true among all families is true even among low income families: there is a close link between low pay, claiming benefits, having larger numbers of younger children, and social tenancy. These links create a fault line dividing low income families. On the one side are those who claim means-tested benefits and live in council accommodation. On the other are those who are owner occupiers and do not claim means-tested benefits. Work and income are also important, but the first split among *low income* families, is the coincidence of means-tested benefits and housing tenure. An exploration of family composition, social security and labour market participation, such as follows, looks first to these signposts, later to others.

This then, is the social construction of low income families in and out of work, claiming or not claiming benefits. The task for the remainder of this volume is to analyse the patterns of families' experiences of work and social security benefits. The aim of this analysis will be to show the influence of social security benefits on low income families' opportunities to work, or not, and to show the effects of these processes on their well-being.

We will be especially interested in the effects of family credit. Even more so than child benefit, family credit is a life cycle benefit. The gap in earning power 'caused' by having children occurs at the point of greatest family needs. Family credit is most likely to be claimed by two kinds of family moving through a quite narrow band of time in their life cycle as they bring up young children. It tends to be a benefit useful to lone parents whose children are old enough to look after themselves, and for couples whose children are not.

The constituency for family credit is created by the squeeze on income and need as working families pass through this gate in the family formation cycle. Before 1971, especially in the period from 1945 to the 1960s, opportunities for dual earning families were historically at a low point. There was considerable normative pressure against working mothers and few part-time jobs for women. The 'rediscovery' of family poverty in the 1960s was, in retrospect, a little like tripping over an elephant.

There might have been a number of ways of dealing with this problem. A number of possible solutions were considered, including increasing what were then family allowances. But a selective approach was taken with the introduction of means tested in-work benefits. The problems with FIS have been discussed. Their intended solution was family credit. How then is the new benefit working? What is it *doing* out there in the real world of families seeking or keeping work? Does the push-and-pull of influences between income support and family credit help float families into work? Does it really act as an 'up escalator', drawing families off sole dependence on benefits and, up through family credit, into the daylight of wage sufficiency? Or does it create a pool of long-term low paid parents; or deliver families into low-paid work only to have them soon return to income support; or even just cushion the fall of families who, for many reasons, find it harder and harder to keep decently paid jobs?

We will look at all of these questions, starting with the what to some is the most vexing: how many of those entitled to family credit manage to receive it?

Note

1. Not all families with children receive child benefit, but non-take-up is rare. Receipt of child benefit was a pre-condition for inclusion in this survey.

2. This was 67 per cent of *all* lone parents, including the higher income group that is not discussed in this report. This compares with a figure of 70 per cent found by Bradshaw and Millar (1991).

3. As with income support, the figures presented here are for summer 1991, the date of fieldwork.

4 The problem of take-up

Introduction: interest in take-up

Any social security benefit may go unclaimed. Research has found that levels of take-up vary between different *types* of benefit. The take-up of child benefit and retirement pension (ie universal benefits) is almost 100 per cent. The take-up of income support and especially family credit (i.e. means-tested benefits) has often been found to be rather lower (see Noble 1992, Craig, 1991; Dilnot et al, 1985; DSS, 1987).

Interest in the subject of take-up has concentrated on the take-up of income-related or means-tested benefits, since it is these benefits which are supposed to set a floor to the income received by each household. They represent the safety net through which people should not be allowed to fall.

A second motive for examining levels of take-up concerns public expenditure. Forecasts of spending on benefits will overstate the cost if it is assumed that everyone eligible to receive a benefit will actually receive it. If, for example, it was decided to introduce a rebate system for electricity payments, analysis of survey data would suggest a rather higher cost to the exchequer than would probably be the case, since many people would not apply for such a benefit.

Family credit take-up

Interest in the take-up of family credit adds a different angle to the take-up of safety net benefits like income support. Family credit cannot be regarded as providing a basic minimum in the same way that income support does. It is, for instance, possible to be better off as an eligible non-recipient of family credit than on income support. Families failing to claim small entitlements of family credit will still be better off than on out of work benefits. Chapter 8 examines the actual incomes of eligible non-claimants of family credit relative to other groups.

One purpose of family credit is to overcome the unemployment trap. Without a benefit for low income families *in work*, it will be possible for a family to be worse off working than they would be not in paid work and receiving unemployment benefit, and/or income support. More commonly, people would be only slightly better off working than they would be out of work: once work-related costs such as childcare and fares to work are taken into consideration, they may actually be worse off.

51

This discussion suggests a number of reasons why the take-up of family credit has become a matter of policy interest. First, there is the question of financial and material well-being. People at relatively low levels of income are likely to need all the sources of income that are available to them. Failure to claim a benefit for which they qualify will not promote family welfare and may leave it materially below the basic levels associated with claiming means-tested benefits. Second, governments will need to make projections of likely take-up in order to allow sufficient funds to be allocated to paying benefit. Third, in-work benefits are intended, amongst other things, to encourage families with children to enter and to remain in the labour market: to get and keep lower paid jobs in the hope and expectation of income improvement. Low take-up would mean that this process was not functioning as intended.

Previous research

Research on take-up has fallen into two main categories (Craig, 1991). Some researchers have sought to identify small numbers of people who either do or do not receive a benefit to which they are, or appear, entitled. Through in-depth interviews or group discussions, they have hoped to uncover the reasoning and decision-making processes that affect whether people receive benefits or not, or are prompted to apply for them. Such work may permit detailed checking of eligibility. It may even allow further observation of whether those interviewed go on to receive a particular benefit (Corden and Craig, 1991) hence providing some validation of status assessed by researchers, albeit on a small scale.

In another camp, economists and others have used existing large data sets to attempt to measure the level of take-up, and to document the factors that appear associated with the take-up of particular benefits. This investigation has involved multivariate modelling of take-up, seeking to untangle which of a myriad of factors are the most important in separating recipients from eligible non-recipients (Blundell et al, 1988).

Whatever the claims of this latter group, and the technical sophistication employed, this research cannot establish *reasons* for non-take-up of the same nature as qualitative research. It can associate various factors with non-claiming, such as having different numbers of children or lower entitlement, but cannot explain the reasons for these correlations. Nevertheless, the descriptions that emerge from this work can be used to corroborate or contradict various theories about take-up behaviour.

Being based on representative samples, such work can tell us the boundaries within which the true take-up figure is likely to lie. It can also identify those sub-groups of the population who are more and less likely to receive their benefit entitlements.

Nevertheless there are a number of clear weaknesses with this method, at least as it has been applied to date. Researchers have been forced to rely on surveys which were not conducted to measure eligibility for benefits, but instead to fulfil other objectives. The mainstay of UK researchers has been the Family Expenditure Survey (FES). As its name suggests, this survey is designed to measure spending, not income and certainly not entitlement to benefits. Data on incomes is collected, but not in the form that benefit agencies would require to assess a claim. In the FES, income data is collected largely for the time that the respondent was last paid. This figure may be higher or lower than normal, but there is little information about variability of earnings or other income. The FES has not collected savings data, other than in the form of income yielded from assets.

For family credit, at the time of the survey, the DSS assessed income over as long as a 13-week period for employees in order to establish normal income. Weeks that provided untypical data were liable to be excluded from the benefit award calculation. Moreover, at least for initial applicants, this data was provided by the employer and not the applicant. Since 1992, though, a fixed formula is applied to 6 weeks' wages and much greater reliance is placed on claimants' figures.

A further weakness is that surveys such as the FES will not ask all the questions that researchers would be interested in. For example, we do not have any history of claiming behaviour, so we do not know if a respondent is waiting to hear about the outcome of a claim, or whether they are an ex-claimant. At best we have a snapshot.

From both types of study, social policy analysts have identified the main explanations for non-take-up as a *lack of information*, *complexities* associated with the application procedure, and reluctance to take on the *stigma* attached to receipt of means-tested benefits (Deacon and Bradshaw, 1983). People will not apply for benefits where they are not adequately acquainted with the existence of a benefit, or do not realise that they are eligible for it. Even if these two conditions are met, application may not proceed if the application procedure presents problems. In the final analysis, people may simply not want means-tested benefits, because of the overtones of dependency and inadequacy that are part of the historical baggage of means-tested benefits.

An enhancement to these different explanations is to consider that their combined effects tend to reinforce one another (Deacon and Bradshaw, 1983). Thus, where a person associates a means-tested benefit with stigma, he or she will be less receptive to contrary information regarding that benefit. They may also tend to assume that the application process will present difficulties.

An unfinished debate concerns the manner in which these factors influence the claiming decision. A key question is whether they combine in an additive way, or present a series of thresholds. Scott Kerr (1983) has claimed that impediments to claiming may be represented as a series of thresholds: others have argued that there are a number of trade-offs that need to be considered so that a reluctance to cross one threshold as identified by Kerr may be counteracted by other factors.

Economists have tended to express these theories in the form of a costs to claiming approach. That is, the benefit of claiming is the cash value of the award, minus the value of time and inconvenience that is involved in the application process.

This study adopts the structured survey approach, but with a number of advantages over the FES or other existing data sets. First, the survey is designed to measure take-up as one of its principal objectives. This means that questioning may be structured to gather the right information, rather than relying on more general interview questioning. The interview schedule was also designed to investigate the possible reasons for non-take-up among an eligible population. We were able to include a range of questions that related to possible explanations for benefit claiming behaviour, and hence likely reasons for non-take-up.

Whatever the approach, on the other hand, there is a guiding principle in take-up research that should be borne in mind during the following discussion of our own results. Take-up is an estimate relative to the exactly eligible population at any one time. But no-one can measure the exactly eligible population at any one time. First, if measurements are taken from families over a period of time, as they have to be, quite rapid changes in people's circumstances will introduce changes, and errors in the estimates. Second, all measurements, however conscientiously taken, will be subject to errors. This is also true of researchers, and so eligibility will have been bestowed or denied wrongly in our estimates in a few cases. This is also true of the DSS staff at North Fylde who will have bestowed or denied awards to a few of our respondents on the basis of the wrong information. In our case, we have sampling variation to contend with too. That is to say, if we did it all again, our estimates would be a little different solely because we drew a new and different sample.

The take-up rate in the PSI/DSS study

It is customary to present results for take-up measured in two different ways.

- the proportion of families eligible for a benefit who actually receive it. The *caseload* measure.
- the proportion of the total money that could be claimed by the eligible population that is actually received. This is the *expenditure* measure.

The caseload measure allows us to infer how many people are not receiving money to which they are entitled. For family credit, it indicates, to some extent, how far it is acting as an incentive to take paid work. Previous work has tended to find a take-up rate, for FIS, of 50 per cent by caseload, and 65 per cent by expenditure (DSS, 1990). In this study, we found a take-up of 64 per cent by caseload, and 71 per cent by expenditure. Table 4.1 presents the main estimate. This is our 'headline figure' and, like others before us, does not include self employed families.

Table 4.1 shows how this calculation was done. First, eligibility was calculated for all respondents. This is because the take-up figure we need is the proportion of eligible families who receive family credit. And because families get an award of family credit unchanged for six months, some of them holding current awards drift out of eligibility as their earnings rise, or their hours fall below 24 hours a week, and so on. These are taken out of the total of eligible

Table 4.1 Take-up calculated from cross-section survey of low income families

	Claimants	ENC	Take-up Caseload	Expenditure
Basic calculation				
Initial totals	459	288		
Too few hours	-37	-		
Income too high	-55	-		
Subtotal	367	288	56%	63%
Refined calculation				
Recently applied for FC	+29	-29		
Self-employed	-32	-56		
Total	*364*	*203*	*64%*	*71%*

families. This calculation suggested an estimate of 56 per cent by caseload, 63 per cent by expenditure.

Next, as was done for all previous estimates, the self-employed were taken out of the calculation.

Third, we were able to transfer to the 'claimant' side of the equation 29 families whom we estimated were eligible and who had submitted a claim but had not yet heard the outcome. This has quite a striking effect, raising the estimate to the 'headline figures' of 64 per cent by caseload and 71 per cent by expenditure. This is, we believe, the first study in which this adjustment has been made. Most data sets do not have information on applications for social security benefits. Previous take-up estimates will have been biased towards too low a figure if there are perceptible delays in settling claims.

Recently, however, a number of changes have been made to the goverment's own take-up figures. These make an adjustment based on comparing initial caseload figures with final figures, for particular months. The latter figure includes so-called 'pipeline' cases: those where payment has been delayed, and backdated to a previous month. Government statisticians have calculated that: 'the effect of not using the pipeline information for 1988+89 would be to underestimate both expenditure and caseload take up by 5 percentage points' (DSS, 1993; page 44). Using information on applications which have yet to be successful therefore represents an important improvement on previous methods of calculating take-up rates.

It would, of course, be a useful check on the method used in this study to consider whether these applications turned out to be successful. However, to date, the only subsequent information that we have on the families is a follow-up of most of the lone parents interviewed. Only three lone parents who were assessed to be eligible non-claimants, awaiting the outcome of an application, were captured in this small group. All of them were receiving family credit at the follow-up, but of course this number is too small to carry weight.

These take-up estimates are rather higher than the FES-based estimates for FIS, and the only official evidence available for family credit. Official figures are rather lower, by caseload, but well within sampling error on the expenditure measure.

That, at least was the figure for the majority of families who were employees. The self-employed families are difficult cases to assess. North Fylde staff find it difficult too since it takes them at least twice as long, on average, to reach a conclusion about self-employed applicants compared to employed applicants. On the basis of the evidence gathered in this survey - evidence gathered in much greater detail than the FES - for example, take-up among the self-employed was 37 per cent. This figure should be treated cautiously because it is based on slightly fewer than 100 cases. Adding the self-employed to the employees reduced the 'headline figure' to 61 per cent.

Reliability of the take-up estimates
Survey-based methods of estimating take-up share a weakness. It may be that people who become eligible non-claimants are, more than others, people who do not like filling in forms or responding to official enquiries. They do not reply to surveys and they do not apply for benefits. As well as those with a distaste for forms, there are others who are simply not very good at them. The National Child Development Study, for example, estimates that up to 10 per cent of young British adults are functionally illiterate.

This is a special problem for this survey because it is based on an initial postal sift. It may have gained a lower response rate from those who do not like forms, who have trouble filling them in even when they have to, or whose first language is not English. These are three groups whom it is reasonable to expect would have lower rates of take-up of family credit, especially so since an application for family credit would be made by filling in a 12 page form and sending it in the post to someone they do not know.

Though it is not in itself an adequate defence of the method, it is worth pointing out that other sources suffer from the same problems. The Family Expenditure Survey includes only those households whose adult members *all* agree to a household interview and, each of them, to occupy the next two weeks keeping a meticulous diary of everything they buy. There are a number of possible reasons why lower take-up figures were found using the 1988 and 1989 FES. It is possible simply that take-up has risen in the intervening 2 years. Certainly, there was a sizeable increase in the caseload over this period. An alternative is that the FES does not provide as complete a picture as this survey. We may have been able to rule out more families found on the edges of eligibility, through more complete information on incomes, or perhaps by a more rigorous examination of savings. Quite possibly, we may be looking too hard for an explanation, when a significant proportion of the difference may be the result of sampling errors, given the relatively small numbers of eligible non-claimants in the FES.

A particular challenge to our figures comes from Noble et al (1992) who examined claims for non-income support housing benefit and community charge benefit in Oxford and Rotherham. The information required from HB/CCB claimants is very similar to that required of family credit claimants and allows an assessment of eligibility for FC among HB/CCB claimants. They found take-up rates of only 32 per cent in Oxford and 53 per cent in Oldham. On the other hand, the HB/CCB forms ask only if the applicant is receiving family credit, not if they had applied. New applications for HB/CCB from families typically come from those moving off income support and into low-paid work. Many would have claimed HB, CCB and FC all at the same time but would appear as eligible non-claimants of FC in Noble's figures. Noble also sent a postal questionnaire to HB/CCB recipients who filled the broad requirements of FC claimants (work, children, etc), and on the basis of their replies it seems that take-up rates of FC were 69 per cent in Oxford and 56 per cent in Oldham. On the other hand, if we had relied solely on our very similar postal questionnaire, we would have reported a take-up rate of only 37 per cent despite having a much higher response rate to the postal questionnaire: 70 per cent in our national survey compared to their 32 per cent in Oxford and 53 per cent in Oldham. Our interview survey found a take-up rate of 71 per cent among HB/CCB recipients.

There were other reasons for encouragement that our survey did not suffer unduly from the kinds of response bias that would seriously overestimate take-up rates. For example, the proportion of parents receiving family credit at the time of our sift survey was 10.9 per cent among lone parents and 3.8 per cent, according to DSS figures, among couples with children. In the sift results these figures were 9.8 per cent and 4.4 per cent respectively. Thus, if those who claim family credit are people more disposed to fill in forms than those who do not claim, they were not more inclined to fill in ours, even though it reached them from the same people - the DSS - who sent them their family credit. Indeed, it is possible to argue that non-respondents among claimants were more likely those whose incomes had risen sharply since their awards were made and they were nervous of losing their benefit, despite all assurances of confidentiality and PSI's good intentions. If so, this would argue that our take-up figures are *underestimates*.

So if distaste for forms is an unlikely source of bias, surely difficulty and ignorance will have contributed something? Perhaps it did, and we shall produce evidence later that even those eligible non-claimants who responded to the survey did not know very much about family credit. But neither did the claimants. And we argue that if ignorance explains non-take-up, knowledge does not explain claiming. We also show, in several places, that the eligible non-claimants who were found among our respondents were not, on average, less able or accomplished people than the claimants. Strangely, rather the reverse was true.

None of the above proves that our take-up estimates are not inflated by a class of people who avoid both benefits and surveys. But it provides sufficient confidence to say that the considerable resources put into this purpose - designed survey to measure take-up has provided the most robust-looking estimate so far.

What causes non-take-up?

1. The effect of small entitlements
We found, again as others before us, that the expenditure based take-up estimate was higher than the caseload measure. This means that larger entitlements were more likely to be claimed successfully, while smaller entitlements were more likely to go unclaimed, as you would expect. One method of displaying this is shown in Figure 4.1. It shows that the level of entitlement of eligible non-claimants is highly skewed towards smaller amounts, whereas there is a more normal distribution of awards among the recipients.

Figure 4.1 Claimed and unclaimed entitlements

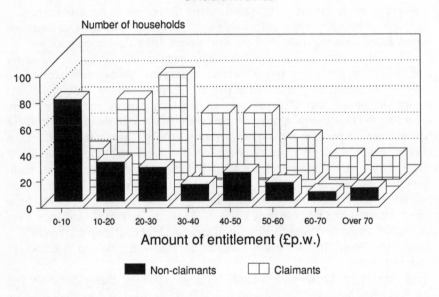

Amount of entitlement (£p.w.)

■ Non-claimants   ☐ Claimants

Table 4.2 shows how the take-up rate itself rises as entitlement rises. Or, rather, how take up rises sharply from the very low levels of take-up among those entitled to less than £10 a week to a peak of 82% among those entitled to the average amounts of award (£30-40 a week). It then falls back a little among those entitled to the very largest amounts.

Official figures show a caseload take-up figure of 66 per cent for entitlements exceeding £10 - almost identical to our figures.

Table 4.2   Take-up of family credit, by estimated amount of entitlement

	Take-up rate (employees only)	Bases (unwtd)
Amount of entitlement		
Under £10	29%	78
£10-£20	68%	74
£20-£30	76%	80
£30-£40	82%	55
£45-£50	69%	53
Over £50	70%	75

The variation by amount of entitlement is an important phenomenon, even though it needs to be treated with caution. But it does have some very interesting implications, both for the prior treatment and interpretation of take-up - what it is and what it means - and also for policy. For example:

One interpretation is that people estimate their entitlement quite accurately, but cannot be bothered to claim small amounts. £5 per week for six months comes to £130, and it would be surprising if people earning about £150 per week were willing to treat family credit in such a cavalier fashion, unless the process of claiming was really daunting.

A second and perhaps more realistic assumption is that people have rather inaccurate estimates of their entitlement, and that those whose true position is quite close to the threshold have a high chance of pitching their guess on the wrong side of it. There is much evidence later in this account of a wide scope for misunderstanding about family credit.

A third possible explanation for the observed relationship is, however, purely technical. Random errors of a few pounds in the earnings reported in a survey would create a pattern similar to that observed in Table 4.2. In fact, there was some evidence in our own data of a tendency to round answers to the nearest £5 or £10. For this reason, an *underlying take-up rate* of 67 per cent (ie the take-up rate among families entitled to more than £9 a week) is probably the most reliable figure. Above £9 a week, the figure changes relatively little.

Another important point about lower entitlements causing lower take-up is that the issue has a non-obvious relationship with income. The income and entitlements to family credit may be represented as in Table 4.3. We found that eligible non-claimants had slightly higher incomes than claimants, and so were entitled to rather lower awards. This means that eligible non-claimants are not quite as poorly off without family credit as current claimants would be if they too failed to claim.

Table 4.3   Income and entitlement, by occupational status of chief wage earner

	Eligible claimants	Eligible non-claimants
Unweighted Base	278	236
Weighted Base	368	288
Income assessed for FC	£	£
All	101.30	107.30
CWE employee	102.60	110.30
CWE self-employed	86.40	95.30
Amount of entitlement		
All	35.60	26.90
CWE employee	34.10	24.40
CWE self-employed	52.10	36.40

Put another way, family credit could have improved the incomes of those eligible by 31 per cent, if there had been 100 per cent take-up. That is, the average income counted for family credit purposes among those eligible was £103.90, and the average entitlement was £31.70. Eligible non-recipients would have had their incomes improved by 25 per cent if they had claimed, compared with a 35 per cent actual increase for the recipients, so their incentive to claim (unless, rarely, they were claiming housing benefit and community charge benefit) is somewhat lower, though hardly negligible.

2. Problems in assessing eligibility

Survey researchers have been calculating rates of take-up for some time. They all encounter a number of key difficulties, especially for family credit and similar benefits.

In assessing eligibility for a benefit, we may distinguish three sets of information. First, there is the question of whether a family really satisfies the benefit regulations. For family credit, do they have dependent children? Are savings below £8,000? And so on. The second is the information given to an interviewer in the context of a freely granted interview. The third is the information that is given to a Benefit Agency, in this case the family credit branch at North Fylde.

There are a number of differences between these three sets of information. First there is the problem of time delays between interview, application, assessment of earnings and so on. The effects of delay are examined in the next section. Second, there may be discrepancies of facts (numbers of children, hours of work, amounts of income, and so on) between information given either to benefit agencies or to social research interviewers - or either may misunderstand what is meant. Suppose for example that a claimant of family credit admits to an interviewer that they have savings of over £8,000, and that this level of savings has remained more or less constant. This should have ruled them out of entitlement. Were they exaggerating, did they mislead the interviewer, or the DSS, or was there some misunderstanding somewhere in the process?

Some of these discrepancies may arise from misrepresentation, and for this reason North Fylde officers check earnings with employers (though they do this much less since April 1992). But if there is misrepresentation in our data, it occurred well and consistently. There was a very close correspondence between our estimates of entitlement among claimants, and what North Fylde were paying them. (See Figure 4.2.) Misrepresentation would inevitably result in far greater differences between their sums and ours. This also has important implications for our measure of take-up. If we were as 'good' at measuring income and savings as were North Fylde for *claimants*, it follows that the same is true for those we calculated to be *eligible non-claimants*. North Fylde would take the same view of them and award them their eligible amount. To this extent at least our estimates are likely to be reliable.

Figure 4.2 Calculated entitlement compared to amount received

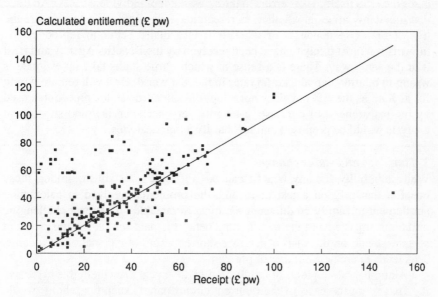

If there is a discrepancy, it is that there was some tendency for families to appear entitled to more than they said they received. Much of this can be accounted for by the difference between eligibility at the time of claim, and eligibility estimated at the time of the interview. Some claimants will have applied prior to the April uprating, and hence received less than if they had equivalent characteristics just a few months later. Also, at a time of recession, some workers may have lost overtime or bonuses that were taken into account at the time of claim, and which had since dried up. Nevertheless, the overall picture gives confidence in our calculations.

When an application for benefit is made, there is room for officers to use their judgement in deciding a claim. An example is in the choice of which income data is to be taken as representative of true normal income. Therefore it is at least possible for two identical applications to receive a different outcome. North Fylde conduct checks on the accuracy of decisions. For 1989-90, the Department of Social Security set a target of ensuring that less than 7 per cent of awards were in error by 50 pence or more: they achieved 8.4 per cent (NAO, 1991, p.23), and in the following year close to 7.8 per cent, or, as the DSS now prefer to say, an accuracy rate of 92.2 per cent against a target of 93 per cent. A test study by the National Audit Office found that 22 per cent of cases contained financial errors - including those of less than 50 pence per week - amounting to 6.1 per cent of expenditure.

Such checks, although valuable in providing details of errors within the DSS, can only be based on information received from claimants. We cannot tell how many of our respondents provided incorrect information, either through attempts to mislead or through misunderstandings. But we do know that in 7 out of 100 cases the DSS itself makes errors in the assessment of individual cases. An issue that inevitably arises is whether, as researchers, we should aim to measure the true status of respondents or whether it is actually better to reproduce the information most likely to have been received by the Benefits Agency and treat it in the same way. There is a sense in which a true status take-up estimate is wrong in relation to real take-up rates in the real world. Or it will remain wrong for as long as the Agency does not adopt the same true status procedures used by the researchers. In our case, a lengthy personal interview and subsequent analysis would be proposed, but it is hardly a practical idea.

3. Time lags and status changes

While eligibility for any benefit can be difficult to establish, among those benefits that rely on a test of means, the problems involved in calculating entitlement to family credit seem the most intractable. The most challenging problems emerge from the fact that the benefit is paid for six months, without re-assessment, on the basis of a rather shorter period of calculation of income. This tends to create a number of problems.

A number of recipients of family credit will appear to be ineligible to receive it. That is, on the basis of their current circumstances such households would not be entitled to receive family credit. This may arise from a change in circumstances between the time of applying for family credit and the time of interview. It may also arise from incorrect collection of data at either stage, or differences between information obtained by an interviewer and information seen by the Benefit Agency. While the Agency's application form is designed to be clear, in any series of questions there is scope for misunderstanding. An interview by a trained interviewer may be different even where the questions are the same.

At the same time, some respondents who do not currently appear to be eligible for family credit, and do not receive it, may have been eligible at some point in the recent past. For example, a couple may have been an eligible non-recipient of family credit three months ago, but since one of them has recently had a pay rise their income level would make them ineligible for family credit. Such a couple ought to be a recipient of family credit, but will not appear as an eligible non-claimant. This does not mean that a short spell of bad times leads to entitlement to family credit. When, prior to April 1992, DSS officers checked earnings with employers, they ask whether the information they have (covering a period lasting between 5 weeks and two calendar months) is a typical set of figures, or abnormal in some way. A request for the earnings of the previous 13 weeks might be made, so that eligibility could be established over a more representative period.[1] It is normal earnings that is the focus of attention.

Where a claim has taken some time to process, back payment will be made. Hence a future recipient, currently in the process of applying for family credit, could be classified as an eligible non-recipient by a cross-sectional survey. Such time delays would suggest that measured take-up would be unlikely ever to reach 100 per cent (Craig, 1991), at least when based on a cross-section survey. This possibility is not remote, as results from the survey, presented below, will show.

Many eligible non-claimants will go on to make a successful claim. If they claim within only a few months of realising their entitlement, but their fortunes pick up, again within a few months, they will not be any worse off in purely cash terms than if they had claimed earlier.

These dynamic features of the process of claiming and receiving family credit have been commented on before. Owing to lack of suitable data, the issues remain largely unexplored. One of the guiding principles of the exploration that follows is that there are windows of eligibility for family credit that open and close for individual families as their income and family circumstances change. A claim is triggered only when the window is open and the now-eligible family realises it is open. We have argued that the greatest problem in assessing eligibility is one of timing difficulties. Theoretically, it is possible that the problem of low take-up is *solely* due to time lags in applications from the eligible non-recipient population. If it should happen that *every* family eligible for family credit was eligible for a *single* 6-month period, but submitted a claim only after the third month of their entitlement, then the case-load measure of entitlement from a cross-section will be 50 per cent. Over the longer run 100 per cent of the available money would nevertheless still be taken up by all of the eligible families.

Matters are unlikely to be as simple as that, but it reminds us that a simple cross-sectional view of claiming family credit is liable to give misleading results. Unless, that is, the analysis is carefully controlled for period effects.

When measuring the take-up of family credit, it is usual to exclude those claimants who would be ineligible if they made another claim now, in recognition of the fact that a cross-section survey will exclude those who were entitled within the last six months but are no longer entitled.

This procedure would be correct for a similar benefit such as housing benefit or income support where entitlement was based on current circumstances, so that awards were re-assessed to take account of changes in earnings, savings, employment, and so on. However, if family credit were to be so based the rate of take-up could be very different. Families would then have an incentive not to drift out of eligibility, since this would have an immediate effect on the value of the award. It is those families who experience an improvement in circumstances - possibly assisted by the availability of family credit - that are currently excluded from the take-up calculation. If families on family credit manage to improve their financial position, by working longer hours or obtaining promotion, then this has a negative impact on the take-up rate. If, however, families remain on low pay for some time and cannot increase their earnings, then to that extent the rate of take-up is enhanced. Given these facts, the rate of take-up is scarcely a good indicator of the effectiveness of family credit.

On the other hand, were family credit to be more frequently reassessed, the incentive value of making a claim at all could be reduced. This is especially so where an early change in circumstances was anticipated. This might mean that fewer people applied, and remained part of the eligible non-claimant population instead. There are therefore a number of different biases to which the existing methodology of measuring family credit take-up is subject.

Take-up should be calculated as the proportion of families eligible for family credit over a period of the last six months, who actually received family credit. The formula analysed above, based on current status, is used because estimates of those who become eligible at a particular point over six months are not available.

We can also offer a small but important item of evidence for the effects of delay on take-up estimates. All the lone parents in the survey were sent a postal questionnaire six months after their interview. It collected information very like that collected by the original sift questionnaire; 83 per cent were returned.

There are a number of paths that might have been taken by eligible non-claimants between the two dates of collecting information. They may still be eligible non-claimants, they may have enjoyed increases in either earnings or another source of income that took them out of eligibility, or they may have lost their jobs and therefore be ineligible through not working enough hours (and then, perhaps, be eligible for income support). Figure 4.3 shows the statuses of the eligible non-claimants, based on their follow-up information.

Overall, 51 ENCs were contacted by the follow-up. Of these, 10 were actually receiving family credit at the latter stage, leaving 41 who might still be eligible. Changes in working patterns excluded another 3 cases (no longer working). Of the remaining 38 working non-recipients, previously identified as eligible non-claimants, 8 had incomes that placed them beyond the threshold for family credit, leaving 30 families who appeared to have remained eligible non-claimants (59 per cent of the initial total). We add the caution, based on our previous experience, that data from a short postal survey will tend to understate income compared to a full face-to-face interview.

Going further, we asked respondents about whether they were likely to apply (or re-apply) for family credit over the coming year. Of the remaining 30 ENCs, 7 said they were fairly certain to apply. A further three said they might apply. This leaves 20 long-term eligible non-claimants out of the original 51.

Figure 4.3 What happened to the lone parent ENCs?

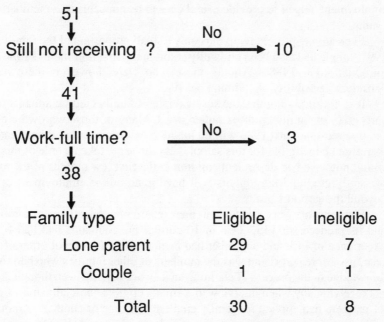

Family type	Eligible	Ineligible
Lone parent	29	7
Couple	1	1
Total	30	8

Of course, with such small numbers we cannot make general statements about the likely fate of all ENCs. In any case, these findings are based only on lone parents, and not on couples for whom non-take-up appears a more severe problem. From a policy point of view, the group that would cause concern (if it could be shown that there were an important number of them) is those who ceased working. Would they have continued working if family credit had been paid to them?

4. Claiming histories: receipt, rejection and application
While discussion of family credit has recognised the difficulties created by changes in people's circumstances over time, the discussion has been on a rather conceptual plane owing to the lack of appropriate data. One purpose of this study was to collect benefit-claiming data over a number of years, including rejected applications. This enables us to consider a number of issues related to the turnover of recipient and eligible populations (see Walker (1980) for discussion of such issues).

Apart from the follow-up of lone parents this study did not track a representative group of claimants from a particular starting point, as did Walker's study. We have a sample of current low income families whose histories on benefit - family credit in particular - may be traced.

At this stage it is as well to sound a caution that this data is based upon recall rather than on direct observation, and so will be subject to memory problems for respondents. However, detailed information was requested only for the relatively recent past and life events such as births of children and leaving/starting employment helped to provide useful cues to respondents in remembering such events.

Even among present recipients only a small proportion of the families in the 1991 sample had also been on family credit in the first four months following its introduction in 1988. Among those who were, however, there has been considerable stability of claiming behaviour.[1]

It is not surprising that the survival rate of family credit claimants from the early days of family credit is rather small. Many of those who were claiming family credit in April 1988 will no longer have dependent children, and would therefore be ineligible for this sample. By the same token, some of this sample would not have had dependent children in the first few months of the existence of family credit. Many others will have gone out of employment or moved beyond the earnings limits.

Respondents were asked about their record of applications for family credit and its predecessor FIS. One in 10 current FC claimants had had first hand experience of FIS, and a number had been rejected for one or other of the two benefits. More surprising was the numbers of other families who had first hand knowledge of the process of claiming an in-work benefit, even though they were not receiving any when interviewed. Among eligible non-claimants, as many as 41 per cent had applied for family credit at one time or another. Among those with incomes just above the family credit level, almost a half of lone parents and one quarter of couples had had previous contact with family credit.

This is an important finding. It means that lack of knowledge of a benefit's existence cannot explain non-take-up in a great many cases, since many apparently eligible non-claimants have had experience of applying for and even receiving the benefit. Of course, that still leaves 59 per cent who had no such contact.

5. Previous receipt of income support

In this section we consider only the extent to which *past* receipt of income support is linked to current benefit status for those in work. We found that recipients of family credit were more likely to be former recipients of income support than were eligible non-claimants. More than one half (54 per cent) of lone parents receiving family credit had received income support in the past. This compares with 36 per cent of the lone parent eligible non-claimants. Among couples, 36 per cent of recipients of family credit, but only 24 per cent of eligible non-claimants, had received income support in the past.

Table 4.4   Contact with family credit

cell percentages

	Out of work OPF	couple	FC Claimant OPF	couple	ENC OPF	couple	Moderate income OPF	couple
Weighted	1353	641	175	286	67	21	95	723
Unweighted	419	229	322	496	47	142	68	396
Family credit was received in the past	10%	17%	[100%	100%]	32%	24%	21%	12%
Claim for Family credit was rejected in the past	4%	11%	14%	14%	20%	26%	31%	19%
Some contact with Family credit either received or had claim rejected	13%	26%	[100%	100%]	41%	41%	46%	27%

For each family type, therefore, this provides evidence that claimants of family credit are on an upward earnings path to a greater extent than eligible non-claimants who, in turn, are more likely to be on a downward path. This is an important point and will be examined again later. That eligible non-claimants have not received income support to the same extent as family credit recipients strongly suggests that they have had less experience of being out of work.

6. Family composition and social characteristics

Various different types of family may have different rates of take-up. This information will be important to policy makers in determining which groups to target for their publicity. Perhaps the clearest difference in take-up between family groups is between couples and lone parents. The rate of take-up among couples was 55 per cent by caseload, compared with 71 per cent for lone parents. Put another way, lone parents represented 42 per cent of claimants, but only 23 per cent of eligible non-claimants.

One interpretation of this finding is that work is only viable for many lone parents if they claim family credit. Hence, the decisions to work and to claim family credit are taken concurrently. For couples, one parent is often available to provide childcare, and the routes into eligibility are more numerous and may be more complex, such as one partner ceasing to work.

Among couples, eligible non-claimants had been in relationships for longer than couple claimants, just over 13 years on average compared with 11.9 for claimants. They were also more likely to have been married to one another, rather than cohabiting.

We know that most lone parents have, in fact, lived with a partner at some stage of their lives. Those in work, not on income support, are more likely to be divorced or separated (rather than single, never married) than lone parents on income support (cf. Bradshaw & Millar, 1991: their survey did not include widows). Among the lone parents in our sample, there was no difference in the proportions of claimants and eligible non-claimants who had ever lived as part of a couple - 83 per cent in both cases. However, claimants had almost invariably *separated or divorced* from their former partner, whereas 10 per cent of non-claimants had been widowed.

We also found differences in the numbers of children in recipient and non-recipient families. On average, eligible non-claimants of family credit had smaller families than claimants. Among lone parents over half of non-claimants had only one dependent child: among claimants the most common number of children was two. Among couples, claimants are rather more likely to have families comprising four or more children -some 20 per cent of all couple claimants have families of this size. Over a fifth of couple non-claimants had just one dependent child. This is consistent with the finding that claiming is more likely, the higher the value of entitlement.

Age

The age of adults in low income families may have important consequences for attitudes to benefits, and may indicate different life history paths taken up to this point. In our sample, there was some difference between claimants and eligible non-claimants of family credit. Claimants tended to be slightly younger than eligible non-claimants. Among lone parents, eligible non-claimants averaged 38 years old but claimants 35. The corresponding figures for mothers in couples were 35 and 33. Partners were on average two years older than this.

Maintenance

At the time of the survey, maintenance payments were treated as income for all the means-tested benefits. That is, a lone parent receiving maintenance of £15 per week and £75 in net earnings would receive just as much family credit as a lone parent with the same family type with net earnings of £90 per week but no maintenance. Since April 1992, the first £15 of maintenance has been ignored (or disregarded) for calculating awards of family credit. This represents a significant increase in the attractiveness of working and receiving family credit for mothers receiving maintenance, compared with not working and receiving income support for which every pound of maintenance is counted against entitlement.

Further changes to the law on maintenance include the introduction of a Child Support Agency (April, 1993), both to set awards according to a specified formula and to collect money from absent parents. Taken together, these reforms are expected to lead to a rise in the number of maintenance awards made, and an increase in the average size of award.

Among lone parents in our surveys one third of both claimants and eligible non-claimants had a court order that said they should be receiving maintenance payments. A further 14 per cent, in each case, had a voluntary agreement. On average, claimants should have been receiving £19.20 per week: eligible non-claimants should have been receiving slightly more - £21.60. Around one quarter of both groups eligible for or receiving family credit did not always receive such payments on time.

In other words, neither receipt of maintenance, nor the amount of maintenance due, seems to be a factor in whether an eligible lone parent claimed family credit. However, the more important issue for this report and for policy makers is whether maintenance is an inducement to take paid work at all.

Housing tenure

Over the 1980s, the social and economic differences between families living in different housing tenures grew sharper and more significant. Many families, and for the first time lower income families, were encouraged to become owner occupiers. Amongst a number of changes, including an end to the mortgage queuing that had characterised earlier years, perhaps the Right to Buy represented the biggest change. This enabled council tenants to purchase their dwellings at a discount, often with the help of mortgages from the local authority. Meanwhile, the social composition of council tenants changed rapidly, becoming more homogeneous and available only to groups with 'special' needs.

There were marked differences in the tenure of the different population groups established in the survey of low income families. Claimants of state benefits, whether family credit or income support, were much more likely to be social tenants than the eligible non-claimant and moderate income groups. These latter groups were more likely to be owner occupiers, with mortgages. The upshot of these difference is presented in Table 4.5. The take-up rate was lowest, at 47 per cent, among owner occupiers. It was highest, at 77 per cent, among social tenants. Private tenants (69 per cent), and those in other types of tenure (59 per cent), had intermediate rates of take-up between these two extreme figures.

Table 4.5   Take-up by housing tenure

	Rate of take-up
Housing tenure	
All tenures	61%
Owner occupiers	47%
Private tenants	69%
Social tenants	77%
(Other tenure)	(59%)

This tends, to some extent, to contradict the proposition that there are frequent transitions between different low income groups. Owner occupation would probably have to be based on a period of employment and income stability, clearly denied to those on the margins of means-tested benefits. The significance of these tenure differences should not be understated.

How child benefit is received

Eligible non-claimants of family credit were more likely to have their child benefit paid into a bank account than were claimants. Among those paid by account credit transfer (ACT) the overall rate of take-up was 55 per cent compared with 62 per cent among those paid by order book. While this factor is of little importance in itself, it is a general indication, if not of affluence, at least of a well-ordered and salaried existence. This appears to suggest, as does other evidence including tenure, that eligible non-claimants had been rather better off in the recent past than our present analysis of income would suggest. Tentatively, this could lead us to suggest that eligible non-claimants may have been temporarily down on their luck, and that they normally enjoyed a rather higher income. That is, within the context of our cross-section survey, such cases were observed at well below their normal or long-run income. Over time, many of them may have been expected to drift upward out of eligibility. This is a key hypothesis that receives close scrutiny in Chapter 8.

Ethnic group

The position of ethnic minorities has tended to be a neglected area of social security research. Work from small-scale studies has identified a number of reasons why people from ethnic minority backgrounds may be less likely to receive their benefit entitlements. Our results, on the basis of self-ascribed ethnic group, suggested that there were some differences in the ethnic group of claimants and eligible non-claimants among couples (see Table 4.6). Among lone parents in particular there was some tendency for claimants to be white (95 per cent of cases) while eligible non-claimants were relatively more likely to describe themselves as belonging to an ethnic group other than white (10 per cent of respondents).

The result is that the take-up for whites - the overwhelming majority of the sample - was slightly above the overall average, at 62 per cent. This means that take-up will be lower than average among ethnic minorities as a whole, though there will be a large margin of error because there are few cases to analyse. Take-up was similar among Asians, at 58 per cent, but rather lower among those of other ethnic groups, including those who declined to answer the ethnic group question. However, the results for these last two groups are based on rather few cases, too few to be confident about whether there is any statistically significant difference between whites and members of other ethnic groups.

Table 4.6   **Rate of take-up by ethnic group**

	Rate of take-up	Base (unwtd)
Ethnic group		
All groups	61%	497
White	62%	426
Asian	58%	41
(Black)	(48%)	(13)
(Other/Refused/NA)	(36%)	(17)

Our results were derived, of course, from a predominantly English-speaking sample. Ability to complete an English postal questionnaire was a prerequisite for inclusion in the survey. For this reason, although the proportion of families in the sample from ethnic minority backgrounds was higher than the national average, we may well have under-represented groups from certain ethnic backgrounds for this section of the income distribution. It follows that there may be rather more ethnic minority ENCs in the population presently beyond the reach of both PSI surveys and North Fylde's best efforts. The DSS, though, is always careful to include non-white participants in their advertising and information is available in several languages.

Occupational factors

Are there any systematic differences between claimants and non-claimants in the types of jobs they do, their industries, variations in pay, and union status?

We saw earlier that the number of earners within the family was an important determinant of income. Among couples, only 12 per cent of claimants contained two adult earners and 17 per cent of the eligible non-claimants. Many of these are self-employed couples. For each group among the low income couples, the most common pattern of paid employment consisted of a non-working woman and a man employed full-time. This was especially typical of the eligible non-claimants (73 per cent).

Among lone parents, 50 per cent of the eligible non-claimants, but only 30 per cent of the claimants, were in white collar occupations and twice as many claimants as eligible non-claimants have unskilled jobs. For working women within couples the corresponding figures were 33 per cent for eligible non-claimants, and 20 per cent for claimants (see Table 4.7). These figures are another reminder that eligible non-claimants may not be a badly off group with low status on a number of dimensions, as is discussed in the following chapter.

One sixth of claiming lone parents worked in catering and cleaning, compared with only 1 in 20 of the eligible non-claimants (but none so much as the out of work lone parents, a *third* of whom last worked in cleaning and catering).

Table 4.7   Occupational distribution by claim status and position within household

| | | FC | | | ENC | |
	Lone Parents	Couples female	male	Lone Parents	Couples female	male
Weighted base	175	286	286	67	221	221
Unweighted base	322	496	496	47	142	142
	%	%	%	%	%	%
Professional, managerial	3	5	2	9	13	9
Junior and inter-ediate non-manual	27	15	10	41	30	21
Junior retail, personal service, direct selling	37	37	13	31	14	8
Skilled and semi-skilled	6	7	21	7	3	21
Unskilled	5	11	20	4	17	15
Catering, cleaning, agricultural	16	18	12	5	19	5
Transport and distribution	4	5	23	2	3	16
NA/Other	1	3	2	-	-	6
Total	*100%*					

There were similar types of differences among the males within couples. Only 12 per cent of claimants were in the two clear white collar types of jobs, compared with 30 per cent of the eligible non-claimants.

Size and type of company
One part of DSS publicity about family credit has been writing to companies to inform them about the benefit and its likely usefulness to their employees. In fact, DSS has written to all companies with more than 10 employees. There might be some suspicion that smaller companies, where each member of staff is more likely to know about each others' living standards, and the accounts departments may be rather informal, that the situation is less amenable to making a claim for family credit. On the other hand, small companies may provide a friendly supportive atmosphere in which claiming is made easier.

We found that recipients of family credit were, in fact, more likely to work for small firms than eligible non-claimants - see Table 4.8. Among lone parent claimants, one in three worked for a company with 25 employees or fewer. This was true of only 13 per cent of lone parent non-claimants eligible for family credit. For males within couples, those receiving family credit also tended to work for smaller companies. Eligible non-claimants were more likely to work for larger companies: 34 per cent for companies employing over 500 staff.

Table 4.8   Size of firm by claim status and position within household

| | Lone parents | | Couples | | | |
| | | | Women | | Men | |
	ENC	FC	ENC	FC	ENC	FC
Weighted base	175	286	286	67	221	221
Unweighted base	322	496	496	47	142	142
Number of employees	*%*	*%*	*%*	*%*	*%*	*%*
1-10	11	22	15	17	21	29
11-25	2	10	11	16	12	16
26-99	15	20	8	12	14	16
100-499	16	16	16	20	19	17
500+	55	32	49	35	34	22
Total	*100%*					

There were some differences in the types of company for which people worked. Eligible non-claimants were more likely to work for a local authority (or educational authority): claimants more likely to work for commercial companies. These differences were rather small.

Union membership
Taking male workers, within couples, union membership was higher among eligible non-claimants (41 per cent) than among recipients (28 per cent). The figures for lone parents, and the working females in couples, again indicated slightly lower unionisation of claimants relative to non-claimants.

Variability of earnings
It has been suggested that variability of circumstances is an important hurdle to putting a family credit claim together. That is, eligible non-claimants may face long periods of eligibility, but be thwarted by occasional increases or decreases in income. Or, they may not have a clear indication of their average. It was a strongly held hypothesis in the design of this study that variability of hours and earnings would go hand-in-hand with instability of employment and other things too, and that eligible non-claimants would be more marginal figures in the job market who find it difficult to establish themselves in steady work and become regular customers of family credit. It may as well be said now that we found precious little evidence for this idea and a lot to contradict it.

We attempted to measure fluctuations in usual income. For the lone parents, the variability hypothesis finds no support at all. As Table 4.9 shows, there were no discernible differences by claim status. For working fathers, however, 65 per cent of those identified as eligible non-claimants did not receive a usual wage all of the time but could be paid more or less, compared with 41 per cent of claimants. This is a significant difference and it must contribute something to a reluctance to claim. But it must also question the reliability of their status as eligible for family credit as well. They are the kinds of people who apply for family credit and find that the average of the last few weeks' pay pushes them just over their threshold even though they think of their usual pay as lower. Eligible non-claimants, remember, have higher earnings than claimants, so they, or at least the men among them, are more vulnerable than claimants to being pushed over the threshold in this way.

Table 4.9   Variability of Earnings by Claim Status and Position within Household

	Lone parents		Women		Men	
	ENC	FC	ENC	FC	ENC	FC
Weighted base	175	286	286	67	221	221
Unweighted base	322	496	496	47	142	142

Are you ever paid more or less than usual earnings?

	%					
Pay varies	42	39	45	51	65	41
Paid usual amts regularly	58	61	55	49	35	59
Total	*100%*					

Other variable factors such as hours of work were also examined closely. Eligible non-claimants are not noticeably more 'marginal' workers, in and out of work, working odd hours, working for multiple employers, and so on. If anything, their working habits are more stable than those of the claimants themselves.

Qualifications
Eligible non-claimants, at least for lone parents (71 per cent) and the mothers within couples (61 per cent), were more likely to have recognised academic or vocational qualifications than family credit recipients (whose figures were 54 per cent and 48 per cent, respectively). There was no difference for the male partners in couples, where just under half had some formal qualifications. These patterns are unsurprising, given the occupational differences already discussed.

Looking at the highest qualifications gained, lone parent claimants were more likely than non-claimants to have CSEs (21 per cent versus 14 per cent) or O Levels (29 per cent versus 11 per cent). Eligible non-claimants were rather more likely to have A Levels (13 per cent, against 4 per cent of claimants), and slightly more commonly had RSA awards (20 per cent to 15 per cent), City and Guilds certificates (11 per cent to 8 per cent) and nursing qualifications (9 per cent to 3 per cent). Similar differences existed for females within couples, but not for males where there were few differences.

The significance of these figures is that eligible non-claimants (at least, the ENCs in our sample) do not, on average, fail any literacy tests. They are not very well qualified but as low income families no-one would expect them to be. But they would take to the task of filling in family credit claim forms quite as many abilities as the claimants did; the lone parents among them would take more.

Attitudes
We also took very seriously the popular idea that eligible non-claimants are inhibited from claiming by a sense of stigma: that it is shameful not to be able to provide for one's family, *especially if you are in work.* This last emphasis bites keenly into the issues surrounding family credit. There may be a sense of special unease in the idea that families in work, paying taxes, paying mortgages even, could also qualify for means-tested benefits. That they could be one of 'them' when they are supposed to be one of 'us'. We asked people a number of quite searching questions on this point by asking them to agree or disagree with a series of contentious statements about work and benefits. Note that we asked respondents to do this by ticking answers to a self-completion questionnaire, so that husbands and wives would not interfere with each other's replies.

Perhaps the nearest question to this belief among those we asked was: 'People with jobs should not get social security benefits'. Very few people agreed with this statement. There were certain differences between claimants and non-claimants, but these can perhaps be termed differences of emphasis rather than important differences of opinion (See Table 4.10). Up to about a fifth of eligible non-claimants, and other families, were inclined to agree that employed people should not get social security compared with only about 1 in 10 among claimants. Though quite what these 1 in 10 meant is not clear: perhaps they felt they should not *have* to get social security benefits.

A widespread consensus among women that 'Every family, in and out of work, should be guaranteed a decent standard of living' and that 'No-one should ever feel badly about claiming social security benefits' was not shared so widely among husbands. Nine out of 10 women support these ideas, claiming FC or not, but these figures fell to two-thirds of claimant husbands and only a half of eligible non-claimant husbands.

Table 4.10   Attitudes towards claiming social security

	Claiming FC		Eligible non-claimants		
	Lone parents	Couples	Lone parents	Couples	All
Every family, in or out of work, should be guaranteed a decent standard of living			(Per cent who 'agree' or 'strongly agree')		
Respondents:	93	91	86	88	89
Partners:		65		52	64
No one should ever feel badly about claiming social security benefit					
Respondents:	91	88	88	83	89
Partners:		63		45	65
People living on social security benefits are not really part of society					
Respondents:	4	6	2	3	7
Partners:		5		6	8
If you live on social security benefits, everyone looks down on you					
Respondents:	27	30	18	30	27
Partners:		23		21	27
Only the very poorest families should be allowed social security benefits					
Respondents:	5	9	10	11	12
Partners:		6		11	10
If you live on social security benefits, you have to try to hide it from the rest of the family					
Respondents:	2	5	5	2	6
Partners:		4		8	6

People with jobs should not get social security benefits				
Respondents: 11	8	16	20	18
Partners:	7		15	15
People with mortgages should not get social security benefits				
Respondents: 6	11	7	13	12
Partners:	9		8	10

But these were the only noticeable differences and do not, in themselves, suggest that claimants had overcome widely held fears of social stigma in order to claim, and that the eligible non-claimants had failed to do so. Overall, as perhaps you would expect among a population of low income families, propositions that social security should not be available to those with mortgages, or reserved only for the very poorest, or that people receiving social security are not really part of society, or that claimants might have to conceal their status from friends or relatives, all drew scant support from anyone, claimant or not.

There was more division over the proposition that 'If you live on social security benefits, everyone looks down on you' which drew agreement from about a quarter of the sample as a whole, though again replies were not divided differently between claimants and non-claimants. It may well be that agreement among the minority arose not from feelings of stigma but from the simple observation that others do look down on claimants and, more shame upon them, they should not.

Does income support do better?
Income support is the key safety net benefit in Great Britain. It is designed to ensure that no family has an income below a certain specified level, dependent on size and type of family. It works by awarding families the extra income they need to bring them up to the level specified as a minimum. A small amount of earnings is disregarded for this purpose. Lone parents are able to earn £15 before any income support is lost, whereas couples on income support may earn £5 each until they have been unemployed for more than two years when they become entitled to the higher £15 disregard on their *joint* earnings.

We found that knowledge of such disregards was rather higher among lone parents. 77 per cent of lone parents on income support correctly identified £15 as the amount they could earn before losing benefit. The second most common response was Don't Know, representing 11 per cent of lone parents. By contrast 38 per cent of couples did not even attempt to guess what the disregard on earnings was; 18 per cent suggested £5 as the answer; just as many suggested £15.

For the sample as a whole, the take-up of income support was 88 per cent. This was split between 92 per cent for lone parents, and 80 per cent among couples. Generally speaking, as with family credit, unclaimed entitlements were lower than received entitlements as shown in Table 4.11.

Table 4.11   Amounts of income support entitlement

	Lone parents	Couples	All
Receiving	£75.80	£72.80	£75.07
Not receiving	£51.50	£65.60	£58.30

The expenditure based take-up figure was calculated to be 91 per cent.

As with family credit, eligible non-claimants of income support were much more likely to be owner occupiers: 40 per cent of eligible non-claimants, but only 17 per cent of recipients, were home owners. We found some differences in the ethnic group of claimants and non-claimants: 14 per cent of non-claimants were non-white compared with 8 per cent of (eligible) recipients. Recipients had slightly greater numbers of children, than non-recipients.

Free school meals
When a family is receiving income support, the children within that family are entitled to receive free school meals. However, unlike most other passported benefits, this is not available to families receiving family credit, although the rates of benefit are meant to include the cost of meals. To the extent that free school meals are taken up by income support recipients, family credit is less of an incentive.

Among recipients of income support, with school-age children, the take-up of free school meals was 82 per cent among lone parents, and 81 per cent for couples.

When asked why they were not receiving free school meals, 80 per cent said they didn't need them, very few were unaware of their entitlement. This may reflect a lack of willingness to differentiate their children's experiences at school from those of other families, although it may also mean that children preferred either to come home for lunch, or take packed meals instead.

How important is take-up?
While a high rate of take-up is important for maintaining the welfare of families, it need not be the main aim of policy to maximise the rate of benefit take-up. For family credit and other benefits, a move, say, to increase the size of the minimum available payment (fifty pence, at present), or to restrict the scope of the benefit in other ways, would be likely to increase the measured rate of take-up, but at the risk of failing to meet objectives of income security and sufficiency. While

take-up is an important issue, it should not be viewed in isolation from the other objectives of family credit, nor from other objectives of the social security system as a whole.

If most of the unclaimed entitlements are low, the caseload measure will tend to exaggerate the extent of the welfare problem. Generally speaking, families failing to receive a pound or two a week, whilst a problem, are of less concern than families failing to receive £40. Both count equally in the calculation of take-up by caseload. Hence the need to cite expenditure-based take-up figures as well.

A higher figure for the expenditure-based figure than for the caseload-based measure has sometimes been taken as encouragement from a policy point of view: ie that unclaimed entitlements are small. However, this has generally been based upon cash figures, and therefore will give a biased impression if take-up is systematically different for different family types. In practice, a couple with one child not claiming £5 may be viewed as needier than a family with four children not claiming £5. The former family will be missing out on a larger percentage of their potential income than the latter.[2]

No single measure of take-up, especially for family credit, is likely to be satisfactory on its own. There is a need to consider the differences between the various take-up findings, and to consider these in relation to the other objectives of family credit, including the improvement of work incentives.

Unlike income support, family credit does not attempt to bring each family up to the a fixed level of final income, relative to family size and composition. Instead it is designed so that higher earnings, while attracting lower state top-ups, still provide a higher final income to the family. Hence, a family failing to claim 50 pence of family credit will generally have a higher income than a family receiving a maximum award. Eligible non-claimants need not be any worse off in cash terms than family credit recipients and they would normally be better off than income support recipients. Given these circumstances, research and policy interest in rates of take-up needs to be rather sophisticated. For small unclaimed entitlements, welfare cannot be the whole issue. In addition, since the eligible non-claimant family is actually in work, the incentive issue is also rather clouded. Although family credit is not being received, the family *is* in work and, moreover, they can keep every new pound they earn in take home pay without worrying about its effects on their next claim for family credit. They have sprung their own employment trap, being in work and better off than out of work, and they have abolished their own poverty trap too.

Note

1. There are a number of problems created by the truncated nature of the sample. For the couples, we will not pick up former FC claimants who went on to join the high income population. However, this is not the case of lone parents - for whom we have a representative population sample - and we know from the analysis of the sift data that few ex-claimants of FC are to be found amongst the high income groups.

2.   The assumption is made that scale rates are correct, so that entitlements reflect true differences in the income needs of different family types.

5 How families take up family credit

Perhaps because, in previous studies, measured take-up appears to have been so low, attention has often been directed towards people's knowledge and understanding of family credit. A lack of information about family credit may contribute to families failing to claim their entitlements, which will give rise to concerns about family welfare. Lack of knowledge of in-work benefits may also weaken families' perception of what their total income would be in work, reducing their incentives to seek and take paid employment.

In this chapter, we consider a range of information on families' experience and knowledge of family credit. We examine the workings of the claiming process, families' decisions to apply, and their reactions to the outcome. What do these descriptions of the process of claiming tell us about the motivation and experiences of claimants? And what clues do they give to the behaviour of eligible non-claimants?

Sources of information

Families may find out about family credit from a variety of sources. There have been a number of TV and newspaper advertising campaigns, information is provided in child benefit order books, and leaflets are available in Post Offices. Family credit is well known to DSS offices, welfare rights workers, and Citizen's Advice Bureaux, any of whom people may turn to for advice. On a more informal basis, family credit (or a similar benefit) has now been around for more than twenty years, so the pool of people who have had some contact with it should be substantial. There can be left only a minority of low income families who have not claimed FIS or FC or who do not know another family who has.

Many families receive family credit for more than one six-month spell. For many current recipients the continuation of a previous claim will have been the reason for remaining on family credit.

We asked respondents: How did you hear about family credit at the time you put in that claim?, referring to their most recent *spell* of claiming. For 25 per cent of current claimants, but only 16 per cent of former claimants, their most recent claim was the result either of a transfer from FIS, or they had previous experience of receiving family credit. A hardy core of 10 per cent of current claimants were survivors from FIS. Advertising and various DSS information had reached 36 per cent of current claimants. 30 per cent of current claimants were informed by other people, usually friends or neighbours. For previous recipients, no longer receiving family credit, TV advertising and the notice in child benefit material were slightly more common sources of information. Table 5.1 provides a detailed breakdown of the sources cited by current and former claimants of family credit who had received an award and former claimants who had been rejected. The strength of *informal* sources is quite striking, at least the equal of official encouragement, though, of course, official sources may have been the original source of the informal advisors. (Perkins et al, 1992) But rejected claimants, particularly couples, were far more likely than current recipients to have responded to an advertisement, including those placed in their child benefit book. These latter cannot have been best pleased to have been turned down, recalling again Anne Corden's 'disappointed applicants'.

By way of comparison, the 1990 study for the National Audit Office found 32 per cent quoting television adverts, 25 per cent the Post Office or DSS, and 20 per cent friends and neighbours. The higher effect of TV advertising may be

Table 5.1   Sources of information about family credit

column percentages, respondents could give more than one answer

	Current claimants	Former claimants Received	Rejected
Weighted Number	462	146	116
Unweighted Number	818	194	205
Source of information	%	%	%
FIS transfer	10	7	1
FC before	15	10	2
TV advert	13	20	30
Newspaper	1	-	1
Other advert	*	1	-
Child Benefit book	7	15	20
DSS office	10	10	4
Post Office leaflet	5	7	8
Citizens Advice Bureau	1	3	1
Welfare Rights	*	-	-
Employer	1	1	-
Workmates	3	4	2
Relatives	4	2	6
Friends	16	10	9
Others	5	2	4
NA/Unsure	8	8	12

traced to a campaign of December 1989. These results correspond more closely to our findings for ex-claimants than for current claimants.

Deciding to apply

In addition to asking about sources of information, we asked applicants about their main *reasons* for making a claim. There are a number of causes that seem likely to trigger a family to claim, including starting a new job, losing overtime, reduced earnings, one or other partner losing a job, the birth of (another) child, or simply increased feelings of financial stress. Among the prompts to claiming (apart from one fifth who were transferees from previous awards) the most common explanation, provided by 31 per cent of all those who had ever made a claim (whether or not this was ultimately successful), was that they had only just found out about family credit. Getting a new job prompted more lone parents (24 per cent) than couples (15 per cent), while earning less money prompted a further 12 per cent and 15 per cent respectively. The arrival of a baby drew applications from 6 per cent of couples but from few lone parents, who instead were more likely to claim immediately following separation (15 per cent). Interestingly, far more rejected applicants gave other, idiosyncratic replies as their reasons for applying compared with successful applicants, past and present (16 per cent versus 6 per cent).

Encouragements to apply

The reactions of family and friends will be taken very seriously by many people. For a means-tested benefit, where stigma has often been mentioned as a deterrent to claiming, they could be crucial. In our pilot survey, for example, one claimant family living in a small village arranged to draw family credit at a post office a dozen miles from their home - this was so that workers in the local post office, fellow villagers, would not find out about their financial circumstances and their need to claim social security. We know from other research that some people do report feelings of doubt and difficulty about claiming. How common are they nationally?

Among those who had ever applied for family credit, 55 per cent had received encouragement to do so by family or friends. Lone parents received more encouragement than couples (65 per cent versus 49 per cent). Only 3 per cent had experienced any discouragement. This may indicate that very few adverse reactions to the idea of claiming are encountered. Alternatively, those who received scathing reactions may have simply given up before making an application, or, like our example, avoided any contact that was expected to be unfavourable. Whatever stigma may attach to claiming family credit, it does not come explicitly from their social networks.

Doubts about applying

With take-up being so much lower among couples than lone parents, is there something about being a two parent family that, of itself, discourages take-up?

For example, disagreement between the adults in married or cohabiting couples provides a possible source of non-application, or of delays in applying. We know that eligible non-claimants of family credit were more likely to have a male chief wage earner. It could be that working husbands feel that their earnings should be sufficient, and do not like the idea of state top-ups with their connotations of benefit dependency. By the same token, wives might hesitate to imply this by suggesting they might qualify for family credit. However, amongst those couples who had ever applied for family credit, three-quarters had agreed to apply quickly, as soon as they thought they might be eligible, without any long discussion of its merits. Even among those couples who did have some initial doubts, 84 per cent said that they found it easy to agree quickly. Male partners were only slightly more likely to express doubts than their female partners.

Where any doubts were raised - one quarter of couple applicants - the most common concern was uncertainty about eligibility (26 per cent) or the similar concern that they earned too much (15 per cent). Concerns about all the form-filling were rare. This seems further evidence that families, especially couples, who find themselves on the threshold of family credit, or think they are, still stutter into a claim and have periods of hesitation. This will add automatically to non-take-up rates of eligible families. This hesitation, however, does not have its origins in fears of the complexity of applications, rather in doubts about eligibility. Tellingly, such hesitation was twice as common among rejected couple claimants (33 per cent) than among successful couples, past and present (15 per cent).

Duration of job and delayed application
Although many respondents said that they applied for family credit because of a new job, it was common for families to be in a job for some time before getting around to claiming family credit. Over the sample as a whole, the median duration of the job prior to a claim was 12 months. There was considerable variation around this figure and, especially among couples, the duration in a job prior to a claim was either short, typically less than six months (33 per cent) or long, typically more than 5 years. There was a huge difference between prior successful and unsuccessful applicants in their duration in a job before using it as the basis for a claim, especially among couples: successful applicants had waited a median 5 months, unsuccessful applicants for 32 months. This, and much of the earlier evidence cited above, indicates that a lot of established working families tried a speculative application during the period of heavy advertising between 1988 and 1990.

This cannot be linked directly to the issue of rapidness of response to eligibility. A claim may have been made when a family was formed, or a partner left a job, or a partner left the relationship, or the introduction of short-time working, loss of bonus or incentive payments or overtime. In cases such as these, the job used to back up an application could be relatively long-standing, even though their entitlement to family credit was more recent.

We asked the more direct question: Did you put in your claim as soon as you thought you might be able to get family credit, or did you let some time go by before putting in a claim?. Three-quarters of the family credit applicants had applied as soon as they thought they were eligible. For those who did allow some time to pass, the median waiting time was two months.

A number of reasons were cited for this delay: in half the cases of delay respondents were simply unaware of their entitlement. Presumably they went on to take the view that submitting a claim would give them this information or they got supporting information from other sources. This is further evidence that delay is an important, though not the largest, component of non-take-up among eligible families.

Difficulties with the application form
In a preceding section, we found that few families cited excessive form-filling as an objection to applying. This tends to contradict the view that the complexity of application forms presents an important barrier against claiming. Clearly, an application form is essential to the postal procedure of family credit, a system preferred by some to visits to DSS offices (Corden and Craig, 1991).

Amongst those who had put together applications, few found problems with the application form. Less than one couple in ten, and fewer than one lone parent in twenty, experienced problems with the questions. By far the most difficult questions to answer were those on income. A number also experienced difficulty with questions on hours worked. By and large, respondents appeared to find solutions for these difficulties. Three-quarters of those reporting difficulties were able to supply the information eventually, usually with the help of their employer, their friends or relatives, the local DSS office, or on their own initiative.

None of this, of course, tells us anything about those who may have picked up a form, looked at it in dismay, and set it aside. It is possible to meet such families; often they are self-employed. We shall look for more such evidence later in this chapter.

Knowing how family credit works
We have described the various sources of information about family credit that people encountered. We have also considered their decisions to apply, and about any doubts that they might have had. In this section, we consider how far such publicity has contributed to an accurate understanding of how the benefit works.

Effect of family credit on other benefits
Family credit counts as income in the assessment of housing benefit and community charge benefit. This is rather different from income support, where benefit levels are set so that recipients receive maximum rebates. Family credit, plus earnings, will typically far exceed amounts of income support. Therefore, amounts payable towards rent and the community charge will be revised downward, indeed often extinguished altogether. An additional loss may be free

Table 5.2   'When you filled in the application form for your last claim were you able
to give all the information asked for, or were there some questions you
could not answer?'

column percentages

	Current recipients %	Former applicants	
		Successful %	Rejected %
Answered all questions	92	96	93
Some unanswered	8	4	6
Total	*100*	*100*	*100*

Some unanswered

Which questions were you unable to answer? (respondents could give more than one answer) %		%	%
Details of income	68	76	68
Hours worked	18	24	—
Other details	14	—	—
Can't remember/no answer	18	—	32
And did you ever manage to supply this information? %		%	%
Yes	68	74	76
No	25	26	24
Not sure	7	—	—
Total	*100*	*100*	*100*

school meals, available to children in families receiving income support, but not to those receiving family credit. Chapter 3 detailed the principal differences in the means-tested benefits that may be received in and out of work.

Overall, moving from income support to family credit will usually leave a family with higher net income. However, the net gain will be rather less than a simple comparison of income support against earnings plus family credit would suggest, given the loss of these other benefits. Of course, for those who receive family credit after being in work rather than on income support, any prospect of help with rent or the community charge becomes an ambiguous blessing because the amounts they receive from HB and CCB are lessened by family credit, and the comparison with income support passports becomes less appropriate. We look in detail in later chapters at what this actually means for the rates of all-benefit withdrawal for families in and out of work. Here we ask the families themselves what they know about it.

We asked families if there were any benefits they had expected to get while on family credit, but found they could not. A quarter said that they had been surprised by the loss of other benefits. For those who had faced this problem, 63 per cent mentioned free school meals and 23 per cent said they had expected to get housing benefit, but were unable to do so. This last figure was higher (36 per cent) among past recipients and this may indicate a certain amount of learning going on among family credit customers. However, for those who are surprised by their ineligibility for HB or CCB, Corden indicates that, for some families, this gives them a 'nasty shock' and causes major budgeting problems.

Changes in earnings

Increases in wages have no effect on family credit for the period of the award (six months), but may affect any renewal award. Of course, given that there is an uprating each year, and many people will receive pay rises, the exact relationship between income and awards may be rather obscure. We asked claimants if extra income affected their awards either immediately or for any subsequent award.

The majority of claimants knew that increases in income did not affect current awards. As table 5.3 shows, this was true of 71 per cent of lone parents and 57 per cent of couples. Couples were more likely not to know (16 per cent against 4 per cent of lone parents).

Table 5.3   **'If you get more money each week do you think it will have an effect on family credit?'**

column percentages, base: chief wage earners receiving family credit

	Lone parents	Couples
Weighted base	175	287
Unweighted base	322	496
	%	%
Will affect present award	24	24
Award will stay the same	71	57
Don't know	4	16
Not asked	1	3
Total	*100*	*100*

A follow-up question enquired whether extra money affected future awards. The overwhelming majority (94 per cent) of claimants knew that it would have an effect. Only a handful, as shown by Table 5.4, thought it would not. Only those few below the 'applicable amount' [£62.25] would have been correct.

The Taper

For each pound of net earnings, above a floor of £62.25, the size of a family credit award is reduced by 70 pence. Family credit awards usually last for 6 months,

Table 5.4   'If you get more money each week would this affect the amount of a new award of family credit?'

Base: chief wage earners receiving family credit

	Lone parents %	Couples %
Yes	94	93
No	4	3
Don't know	2	4
Total	*100*	*100*

no matter what the changes in circumstances. A pay rise of, say, £10 per week will be subject to income tax and national insurance but will have no effect on the amount of family credit that is received until a new claim is made, and even that could be at least partially taken care of in an annual uprating of benefit levels. Given this fact, it is not altogether surprising that knowledge of the family credit withdrawal rate was extremely limited. Over half of current claimants were not prepared even to guess at what the figure might be. Among those who did attempt an answer, the most frequent response was the right one -70p - but was given by only 15 per cent of those replying (only 7 per cent of all current claimants). Almost as many suggested £1 as the answer - a figure which would have been correct for income support. Given that economists are prone to discuss the disincentive effects of withdrawal rates as though everyone involved had perfect knowledge, this is an interesting result.

It is taken up again in Chapters 6, 7 and 8 when we discuss the incentive effects of this and other 'knowledge issues' such as awareness of thresholds of eligibility.

The information used in calculating family credit
The DSS takes a range of information into account in calculating family credit awards. We have emphasised net earnings. Other factors include the number and ages of children, savings, and number of hours worked each week. Respondents were asked which factors were taken into account: responses for claimants and eligible non-claimants are outlined in Table 5.5.

Overall, claimants of family credit were more likely to know what factors were taken into account when deciding a claim than were eligible non-claimants but the differences were not great. Claimants themselves rarely mentioned all, or even more than one or two factors used in calculating their benefit and sometimes included factors that are not taken into account. Also, lone parents were, on the whole, slightly better informed than couples, but not to the extent that would explain their higher take-up levels. In fact, lone parent ENCs are about as well (or ill) informed as claimant couples.

Table 5.5 'Apart from money, what other things do you think the DSS take into account when assessing an award?'

column percentages, respondents could give more than one reply

	Lone parents claimant	ENC	Couples claimant	ENC
Weighted base	175	67	287	221
Unweighted base	322	47	496	142
	%	%	%	%
Age of children	35	28	29	18
Savings	13	16	12	8
Other income	22	10	14	8
Number of children (and dependents)	7	4	6	4
Outgoings	5	6	4	3
Hours worked	1	-	1	-
Others	13	11	9	3
Don't know	26	40	35	52
{Not asked	5	4	8	13}

Reactions to the outcome

Employer reactions
The reactions of friends and families may cause someone to think twice about applying, or encourage them to claim. Our results indicate that many applicants received encouragement: few were discouraged.

However, one party that is usually involved in the initial claiming process is the applicant's employer, with whom earnings details are checked. Some applicants may be uncomfortable about this. Employers may use the existence of family credit to keep wages low - letting the government support low wage rates with means-tested assistance for certain workers. To this extent, employers will welcome the existence of family credit. On the other hand, employers might dislike the contribution they must make to the administration of the benefit. Yet another possibility is that applicant and employee will collude to make earnings look low - to the benefit of recipient and employer, but to the detriment of taxpayers as a whole. These issues might provide an important obstacle to the unqualified acceptance of in-work benefits.

Claimants were asked whether there had been any contact between them and their employer concerning their family credit claim. We asked a series of questions to investigate the possibilities that firms had been unhelpful or obstructive to applications, or that they had positively welcomed applications as a means of subsidising their wages bill. The questions were as follows:

Have your employers ever spoken to you about your claim for family credit?

(If yes) Did they appear in favour of your claim, or against it, or did they have no view for or against?

Have your employers ever suggested to you that you go without a pay rise, or without promotion or without something else that might increase your pay, because you get family credit?

There had been contact between employer and employee, concerning the claim for family credit, among 19 per cent of those claiming. Where discussion had taken place between the two parties, 41 per cent said that employers had appeared supportive. Only 5 per cent said that employers had seemed against it. In the majority of cases (54 per cent) respondents said that employers appeared to have no view either for or against.

In-work benefits give rise to the possibility that employers will adjust wage levels in line with their knowledge of the benefit received by an employee. However, in only 5 instances out of nearly 750 claimants had employers suggested to respondents that they should go without a pay increase or promotion because they received family credit. This does not rule out the possibility that the very *existence* of certain jobs is owed to family credit.

Understanding rejection

The success rate of first time applicants for family credit is just over 50 per cent, around 80 per cent for renewals. When applications are rejected, details of the reason(s) are sent to families. In this section, we consider how far people are able to remember and understand the reasons why they failed to receive family credit or, in the past, family income supplement.

There are a number of ways in which a family may be ineligible for family credit. They may have too much in savings, or work too few hours. However, as Table 5.6 shows, the most common reason they remember is having too high an income. This was the reason behind 89 per cent of the FIS rejections we encountered, and was true of around three-quarters of the rejections for family credit.

The second most common reason was not working enough hours.

Overall, only a very small percentage (5 per cent) were unable to give a reason. By the time that a family has been rejected more than once, all knew the reasons why.

Amount of cash expected

Once the complexities of the application process have been overcome, applicants may be either pleased or disappointed by the award. A disappointing award, and successful awards may be as low as fifty pence, might act as a deterrent to further contact with the benefit, or with working itself.

Overall, however, the sample expressed some satisfaction with the size of family credit awards. This was more true of lone parents, for whom the benefit

Table 5.6   Reasons given for rejection for FIS and family credit

Column percentages, respondents could give more than one reply

	FIS (last rejection)	Rejection for: FC (1st rejection)	FC (2nd rejection)
Weighted base	100	432	45
Unweighted base	75	316	31
Reasons for rejection	%	%	%
Too much income	89	71	82
Too many savings	1	-	-
Too few hours	5	13	13
Children too old	-	*	-
Some other reason	-	8	6
Not eligible	-	3	-
Never understood/Don't know	5	5	-
No response	1	1	-

provides the same money as it would for a couple with similar earnings. Among the current recipients of family credit, 38 per cent of lone parents had got a larger award than they had expected. 15 per cent received less, while 46 per cent had guessed the size of their award more or less accurately.

Couples were generally rather less impressed. 29 per cent had received a higher award than they were expecting, 32 per cent less, while 37 per cent said that they had predicted the outcome of the benefit calculation more or less correctly. Many of those receiving more than they had expected may have found they lost all or almost all their housing benefit as a result - unless, of course, it was loss of housing benefit which prompted the claim in the first place, or they were completely unused to means-tested benefits.

Much of this difference in expectation and outcome is a function of the relationship between income and eligibility: lone parents earn less than couples so they have larger entitlements and so are more likely to be agreeably surprised by the amounts they get. They still end up with less final income, of course, but they do not share it with a partner.

Looking to the future

Would families claim again?

Having taken respondents through a series of questions about family credit, discussing the way it works, we asked all respondents whether they were likely to apply for family credit in the future. Those who were not going to apply, or re-apply, were asked for their reasons. Intentions, and the reasons given in their support, are sometimes a better test of the feelings that influence behaviour than are broadly framed social attitudes of the kind discussed earlier.

Not surprisingly, an overwhelming proportion of recipients of family credit proposed to re-apply - 91 per cent of lone parents and 86 per cent for couples (Table 5.7). This amounts to a substantial endorsement of family credit by its present customers, though one qualified by the fact that families who receive family credit re-apply because they need to.

Among the eligible non-claimants, 31 per cent of lone parents and 35 per cent of couples said they were likely to apply in the near future. This adds a lot to an earlier impression that a significant proportion of non-take-up is delayed take-up and is an important finding on this point. As reported in the previous chapter, a fifth of the lone parent ENCs went on to apply successfully in the six months after their interview.

Among those eligible non-claimants who were not going to make a claim, 76 per cent of lone parents and 53 per cent of couples said that they earned too much or simply that they were not entitled (Table 5.8). A quarter of couples, but no lone parents, said that they didn't need it. This provides important further support for the view that it is *perceptions* of eligibility for benefits that drives differential take-up, rather than lack of information about the existence of the benefits themselves, or the fear of social stigma.

Table 5.7   Whether respondents will put in (another) claim for family credit in the future

row percentages

Will they apply for FC in the future?		Yes	No	Can't say	No response	
Lone parents						
ENC	%	31	50	19	-	= 100%
FC claim	%	91	5	3	*	
Moderate income	%	14	78	7	-	
Not working	%	31	39	28	1	
Couples						
ENC	%	35	47	17	1	= 100%
FC Claim	%	86	7	6	*	
Moderate income	%	17	64	18	1	
Not working	%	27	38	34	1	

Moderate income respondents were the least likely to say they would apply. They correctly perceived that their incomes put them out of range of eligibility. For the other groups, a range of replies were given, as shown in Table 5.8.

One of the most interesting features of Table 5.8 is what is not in it. Respondents gave their reasons for not applying for family credit in their own words, and did so following quite a lot of detailed questions about the form and the procedures applicants have to go through. Yet no-one spontaneously mentioned 'form filling' or 'bureaucratic hassle' or an inability to understand what is needed as a reason for not applying. Instead they gave plausible answers that stressed the obvious: they had no job, they were sure they earned too much, or were otherwise not entitled, and so on.

About a fifth of the eligible non-claimants said they did not ***need*** family credit. Every one of them was a couple and every one of them was an owner occupier. Not one lone parent, nor one social tenant said they would not apply for family credit because they did not need it. This gives another clue to the social construction of families' perception of in work benefits. There is something about being an owner occupying couple in work that innoculates many of them from the idea that they ought to be claiming means-tested social security benefits.

Table 5.8   Why families would not (re-)apply for family credit

Column percentages, respondents could give more than one reply

	Eligible non-claimants	FC claimants	Not in FT work
Weighted Base	139	66	761
	%	%	%
Neither working	2%	14%	46%
Not entitled	25	14	20
Earn too much	34	28	4
Wouldn't pay to work	—	4	3
Don't need it	19	6	4
No childcare	—	2	7
Children too old	2	10	2
Lose other benefits	1	4	4
Other	15	10	6
Don't know	2	—	—
No response	4	13	7

Conclusions

The processes involved in claiming family credit have often come under close scrutiny, typically as an explanation for low take-up. Our results give some ground for cautious optimism, although lack of knowledge persists among many eligible or potentially eligible families.

Recipients had entertained few doubts about applying, and couples generally agreed quite quickly once they thought they were eligible. Delay is contingent on doubts about eligibility, not about the ability to claim, and delay remains a significant factor in non-take-up. Claimants were naturally more enthusiastic about the concept of in-work benefits than non-claimants, but the differences were of degree rather than of kind. When it came to handling an application form, few recipients had encountered great problems.

Respondents, typically, knew about family credit in outline but were rather sketchier on the details. It was a benefit for working families with children, and depended on your income and the size of your family. Most realised that additional earnings in the course of the award would not affect the amounts paid. When rejected, they could usually remember the reasons given. By contrast, knowledge of the 70 per cent taper was just about non-existent; and many had not realised that their family credit might reduce or remove their entitlement to other benefits (like housing benefit and free school meals).

There was little evidence of negative employer interference. What contact there was between employer and claimant tended to be either neutral or encouraging.

This chapter has reinforced the conclusions of the last: that fears of stigma and lack of clerical skills do not play much part in preventing people from claiming family credit. Knowledge and facility with social security processes are not commonplace among all low income families, *including the successful claimants themselves.* The problem, where it arises, lies in misunderstandings about eligibility. These are specific misunderstandings, related to income, age of children, hours of work, and so on. And there are general misunderstandings linked to social location and housing tenure.

Note

1. Unless, of course, the applicant happens to be self-employed. This practice has now changed and payslips sent by applicants are acceptable evidence of earnings in nearly all cases.

PART TWO

THE EFFECTS OF
FAMILY CREDIT

Part Two   The effects of in-work benefits on low income families

Introduction
The second part of this volume is an investigation of the effects of in-work benefits on the patterns of work and welfare of low income families in Britain. It looks particularly at the likely effects of family credit in increasing families' incentives and opportunities to work and its impact on the circumstances and well-being of different kinds of family.

This investigation is organised into five chapters:

1. Constraints and opportunities
A description of the main constraints upon families' opportunities to get and keep paid work at the lower end of the wage distribution. An earlier chapter showed how differing family structures (lone parenthood, a child under five, and so on) determine families' labour supply and may channel them into low paid work, or a need to claim social security benefits, or both. This chapter discusses in more detail the influence of the availability of childcare, the availability of the right kind of job, the level of work skills, and disability. All of these place limits on the likely effectiveness of family credit, or any other measure designed to increase the numbers of parents with dependent children in paid employment.

2. Beliefs, attitudes and intentions
An account of how lone parents and couples see the influence of wage levels and benefits and how these impressions may affect their choices and behaviour.

3. The incentive to work
An examination of the incentive effects of family credit seen in families' behaviour. Is what they *do* consistent with the design of the benefit in placing incentives to work before families whose earning power is likely to remain low?

4. Relative material well-being
An investigation into the effectiveness of family credit in contributing to the relative material well-being of families who claim it, compared to those who do not. This includes an analysis of how the welfare aspects of the working of family credit, compared to the parallel effects of income support, or higher incomes,

Families, work and benefits

reflect in turn on families' incentives to work, and to work and claim family credit.

5. Summary and Conclusions
A final chapter summarises all the main findings of this study and discusses their implications for employment and social security policy.

6 Family credit and work: opportunities and constraints - what are the prospects?

Introduction

Much of the material of this chapter concerns what economists see as market imperfections. The labour market does not function smoothly. The effects of the incentives to work provided by family credit are not simply to 'dial upward' the supply of labour from low income families. Every extra £100 of family credit that is available by entitlement does not automatically generate, say, an extra 100 hours of additional labour. However effective may be the *design* of family credit in providing, on paper at least, a positive incentive for families to get and keep paid employment, sooner than rely on income support, its effectiveness is constrained by wider influences on employment. We discuss below some of the problems facing parents who want to work. Are there jobs to be had, even at low wages, offering hours of work compatible with childcare? Are people able to work, that is, do they have even the minimum skills employers want? Are their problems increased by disability? What do they say about their prospects of paid employment, especially if they are presently out of work.

It is also worth bearing in mind that the survey was carried out at a time of rising unemployment which can reduce the scope for family credit to work. On the other hand, it can be argued that rising unemployment in a recession can create as many family credit claimants as it eliminates because it does away with large amounts of overtime. Workers who rely heavily on overtime to bring their wages up to acceptable levels find that, without overtime, their wages fall below benefit levels. If they have children and little other income and only modest savings, they can claim family credit. Thus, family credit can 'catch' people on the way down the income distribution as well as offering a lift up for those at the very bottom.

Two definitions:

1. 'Out of work'
This chapter, more than others, is concerned with 'out of work' lone parents and couples. By 'out of work' is meant 'out of full-time work' as defined by the family credit rules at the time of the survey: 'working less than 24 hours per week', though we know already that part-time working families tend to work far fewer hours than 24 a week.

2. 'Husbands and wives'
It is becoming difficult to describe couples, especially when it involves ideas about who is expected to seek work. The difficulty is knowing for certain who is the principal breadwinner. Among low income families, this is sometimes the female partner. Usually, when describing couples, care must be taken not to make assumptions about:

a.   the legal nature of their union, and
b.   the sex of the parent who is supposed to be responding to incentives, as the main breadwinner.

'Partner' is a popular word nowadays, though we would have to resort to devices such as '1st partners' or '2nd partners' to define principal breadwinners and their co-resident partners. In simpler cases, this has its advantages. But when reference is made, for example, to the 'partners of 1st partners' these advantages disappear. The solution, solely for clarity of presentation, will be to refer to 'husbands' and 'wives'. This is done remembering always that some of the 'husbands' are 'female principal breadwinners', just as hitherto, we have remembered that some of our lone parents are men, but have called them 'she' throughout.

Out of work families
We saw in chapter two that being without full-time work is a major component in family poverty. In our sample of families whose earned income was less than 125 per cent of their family credit maximum threshold, more than half were there because they were out of work: 18 per cent were couples out of work and a remarkable 38 per cent of them were lone parents out of work. So, together, 56 per cent of low income families had no-one in full-time paid employment. Exactly two-thirds of the lone parents had no full-time job and most of them lived on income support or unemployment benefit, usually IS. The remainder had part-time jobs and/or received enough maintenance to live on; 15 per cent had part-time jobs, some combining income from work and benefits.

Maintenance is another complicating factor for lone parents' incentives. It encourages them to work because it is rarely withdrawn in the way a benefit is withdrawn when they enter work, especially if it is for the children. But if their total income from work and maintenance leaves them in range of family credit, a disincentive arises because maintenance is discounted against an award pound for pound, just as it is against income support. At least, this was the case at the time of the survey. The new rules introduced in 1992 include a £15 a week disregard for maintenance. In this sample, 23 per cent of the out of work lone parents had an order, and 12 per cent an agreement for maintenance, usually for the children, though fewer than two-thirds of them said they are paid promptly, or at all. We will look at the implications of this in more detail later.

Fewer couples than lone parents who were out of work receive income support or unemployment benefit, or both, though they were still a majority: 71 per cent. The remaining 29 per cent of out of work couples made a living with part-time earnings and other, less clear sources of income.

The most important difference between the out of work couples and lone parents is in their orientation to the labour market. Among couples, nearly two-thirds of former main wage earners said they were 'unemployed and looking for work'. Most of the rest were sick or disabled. Among lone parents out of work, only 9 per cent said they were seeking work. Most of the rest (70 per cent overall) say they were at home looking after their children and only 2 per cent said they were sick or disabled.

Questions about work incentives, therefore, have a different meaning for lone parents and for many of them, not much meaning at all for quite a long time to come. More than half of out of work lone parents, after all, have at least one child under five and few of them have the kinds of skills (see below) that are ever going to command the kinds of wage that will pay for a lot of childcare if none were available free. In fact, 15 per cent of out of work lone parents have never had a paid job of any kind. The rest left their last job an average of five years ago but one in five left more than 10 years ago. Only 28 per cent have had paid work within the last two years and the majority of these have very young children, that is, they were reporting their last job before they had children. Some of them had relatively brief experiences in the labour market. They averaged only six and a half years work between them and one in ten worked less than a year.

Long term unemployment is not unknown among couples, of course. Whilst almost all the former main wage earners say they have had a job in the past, for one in five of them the past was more than five years ago. The average time out of work is nearly three years. But half of them worked in the past two years and most of these a matter of months ago. And of course they have much longer employment records too, averaging nearly 18 years paid work while most of those with less are simply younger. They are therefore, far more 'connected' to the labour market and so work incentives are a far more immediate and realistic idea for them.

Before going on to consider the more immediate prospects of the non-workers who are looking for work now, let us look more carefully at the orientation toward the labour market of two large groups who consist mainly of women: the lone parents who are not in full-time work and the wives of main wage earners.

Most of the lone parents rely on the state for their main income; most of the wives rely on their husbands, or do so usually. Their opportunities and constraints with respect to employment, on the other hand, are rather similar and are ruled mostly by the age of their youngest child. On the other hand, on entering employment, the first will lose their state income and the second will now participate, to one degree or another, in a jointly earned family income. So the incentive effects are quite different.

Within these two groups of women, the first group of interest are those with part-time jobs. Among the benefit families, these are:

- 13 per cent of the 'out of work' lone parents
- 7 per cent of the family credit couples, and
- 8 per cent of the out of work couples.

In most cases, working part-time costs them benefit money. So why do they do it? We asked them why they are working part-time and were told by eight out of ten that they worked '...for the money'. (What did we think they did it for?) Nearly half (45 per cent) of lone parents working part-time were carefully earning weekly sums up to their £15 a week disregard. This is a perfectly rational thing to have been doing. Additionally, significant numbers (about 4 in 10) of lone parents and out of work partners were glad to be '...out of the house' and '...meeting people'(10 per cent) but almost no-one was anxious that it should '...develop into a full-time job'(1 per cent). That could wait.

Most surprising, in a way, are the small numbers of partners in family credit couples who are working part-time. Whereas partners in out of work families may or may not get IS or UB, all these FC partners are losing up to 80 per cent of their earnings. What are their incentives? Again we were told '...the money.' On the other hand, it is true that, being below the tax and NIC thresholds, they can keep up to £3.00 of every £10.00 they earn and they may well value this. These few were also asked what effect their part-time earnings might be having on the amounts of family credit they could get. Out of every ten in this position, three did not know, three thought they got less (but were presumably glad enough of the extra 30p per extra pound earned) and the remaining four said they thought it made no difference to the amounts of family credit they could get. However, these last groups made up only 2 per cent of family credit couples overall.

In contrast to the benefit couples, 13 per cent of the wives in eligible non-claimant couples were working part-time as were 30 per cent among the moderate income families. This, together with a further 9 per cent of the moderate income couples who were both working full-time, is why they are moderate income families. Fewer of these were impressed with the advantages of being out of the house or meeting people. They worked for the money and, less tax, it is all theirs.

Most of these part-time workers saw their situation as continuing unchanged. Asked to guess what their position might be in a few months time, nine out of ten thought they would still be working part-time and the remainder divided evenly between those who might get a full time job and those who might no longer work at all. Ten per cent of the lone parent part-timers anticipated full-time work.

All of these part-timers, except those few anticipating full-time work soon, were asked whether there was anything actually preventing them from getting a full-time job at the moment. Unsurprisingly, childcare was said to be a problem: 40 per cent of the lone parents and about a fifth of the other families could not afford childcare and a fifth of all these part-timers said no childcare was anyway available. Some of these, and many others, said that, besides, they really did not fancy a full-time job while others again said positively that they wanted to look after their families. Only 6 per cent said that they were prevented from working full-time because no full-time jobs were available.

The majority of these out of work families have no paid work at all. The lone parents and the wives were also asked about their plans. So few were actively seeking work that it was hardly worth asking them questions about their incentives. For this reason, the prospect of work was broadened somewhat to allow a glimpse of their thinking about an eventual return (or, in some cases, an introduction) to paid work.

Most of the out of work lone parents and wives did look forward to getting a paid job one day. Most of the lone parents (83 per cent), three-quarters of wives in working couples, and two-thirds of those in out of work couples said that, yes, they hoped to get a paid job '...one day.' The remainder, who did not expect to work or were uncertain about it, gave their reasons for putting paid work out of their minds at the moment. Childcare did *not* feature very highly in their reasons. Even among lone parents, 9 per cent said they could not afford it and 11 per cent did not think childcare would be available to them. This does not mean that the rest think that affordable childcare would be plentiful if they changed their minds about work. It means they did not give it among their reasons. Their reasons included the desire to care for a family (17 per cent), general lack of attraction of the working life (26 per cent), the impossibility of finding a worthwhile job (6 per cent), but more than anything: disability (36 per cent). This is dealt with in more detail below.

But a job '...one day' is not '...unemployed and seeking work.' On the other hand, '...unemployed and seeking work' is too strict a definition to curtail questioning about constraints and incentives. We needed a position in between: optimistic about getting back to work quite soon, perhaps. When asked the direct question, 'When do you think you might look for a paid job?', 15 per cent of wives in out of work couples, 17 per cent of lone parents, and more than a fifth of other wives without paid work themselves, said that they were looking for a job when interviewed, even if they were not strictly 'unemployed and looking for work' down at the job centre. A further 10 per cent said that they intended to look in a few weeks' or months' time.

On the other hand, a quarter saw paid work as more than a year or two distant and the majority saw it as something still in the indefinite future. This last group was largest among the wives in out of work couples (57 per cent) and smallest among those in moderate income couples (32 per cent). Further questioning about incentives and constraints, therefore, was confined to lone parents and wives who had it in mind to seek a paid job within the next year.

Most of these who were thinking seriously of a paid job soon were thinking in terms of full-time work or a part-time job that would lead into full-time work later -though 7 per cent had little idea of what sort of hours they might work.

Among the lone parents, only 8 per cent said they would wish to work fewer than 16 hours per week and most of these mentioned hours that would probably keep them within or near their £15 a week disregard. Among wives, rather more were looking for fewer than 16 hours (19 per cent). In contrast, 55 per cent of lone parents were looking for full-time jobs (these remember are only 15 per cent of all lone parents who have no paid work at all), and so were similar proportions of wives among the family credit and out of work couples. Only about a third of wives in ENC and moderate income couples were looking for more than 24 hours a week. (Table 6.1)

Table 6.1   Hours sought by lone parents and wives intending to work within the foreseeable future

column percentages

| | Lone parents | Wives in couples who are: | | |
| | | Eligible non-clmts | Family credit | Moderate income | Out of work |
	%	%	%	%	%
'No idea...'	8	10	8	1	4
1 to 8 hours per week	3	3	3	1	-
9 to 16	5	31	11	22	17
17 to 24	29	26	19	38	24
25 to 32	23	7	4	16	9
34 or more	31	24	53	21	46
Total	*100*				

This leaves a band of 29 per cent of those lone parents and wives who said they were seriously thinking about a paid job looking for hours in the 16 to 24 hour range. This is the new admission range for family credit under the April 1992 changes and below the lowest qualifying 24 hours a week still in force at the time of the survey. Is there, therefore, any connection between the prospect of the change in rules and the hours sought by lone parents, or, for that matter, others?

Earlier in the interview, all respondents were told of the change of rules and asked to guess (and guess is probably the right word) whether or not this would make them more likely to apply for family credit, following the alteration in April 1992. Among out of work lone parents, 35 per cent thought that it might increase their likelihood of applying for family credit. This of course can be interpreted as no more than an expression of interest. The increased likelihood might as well be an increase from 'no chance' up to 'well, perhaps'. It did however also catch the interest of 18 per cent of ENC lone parents and 21 per cent of the out of work couples.

Comparing these responses with their later ideas about when and how much they might work, those who felt that the reduction in hours might make it more likely that they would apply for family credit were more likely to be actively on the lookout for a paid job. Half of those seeking work within the next year said that the new hours rule would encourage them to include family credit among their options in their plans for employment. (Table 6.2).

Table 6.2   The possible impact of changes to the qualifying hours for family credit

row percentages

		Lone parents			
		The change in hours rules will make a claim for FC:			
		More likely	No difference	Don't know	
		unweighted base			
Looking for work now	%	(152)	51	39	10	= 100%
In a few weeks or months	%	(95)	53	39	6	
In a year or so	%	(243)	47	43	10	
Sometime in future	%	(385)	19	70	12	

Skills

Another major constraint faced by out of work families is a restricted range of employment skills. The out of work families selected for the sample need not, of course, have been 'recruited' to unemployment from among those working families who were defined as within range of family credit. They may well have fallen into unemployment from the ranks of those who were once paid much more than 125 per cent of their family credit maximum threshold.

A great deal has been written about the relationship between training, skills and employment (see for example W.W. Daniel, 1990). For the purposes of this report, we wish to make only one point: the 'skills profile' of the out of work families far more closely resembles that of the family credit families in work than it resembles the moderate income or even the eligible non-claimant families. This is especially true among the husbands in two parent families reporting a last full-time job. For example, about one in nine out of work and FC couples are or were non-manual workers (excluding junior retail and personal service workers), while a third of the ENCs and moderate income couples have non-manual jobs. Among lone parents more work in non-manual jobs but the contrast between groups is just as great: 50 per cent of ENCs and 61 per cent of moderate income lone parents are non-manual workers, but 30 per cent of the family credit claimants and only 19 per cent of the out of work lone parents previously had non-manual jobs.

Not that manual work is invariably unskilled, but among low income families, it tends to be. It is particulary telling that the former main wage earner in out of work couples tended rather more to report an unskilled job than even the family credit couples. This is not to say that there is no demand at all for unskilled work. There may be a wide variety of equally poorly paid jobs from which to choose, if 'choose' is the right word. But the unskilled have fewer choices of occupation and so fewer opportunities to get a suitable job. Possibly their problem is keeping their jobs since employers have less motive to retain them compared to skilled workers.

The point is that the coincidence of unskilled work and wages that qualify a family for family credit, imply a drag on recruitment into the kind of work associated with claiming family credit. This changes talk about incentives, with or without family credit, to talk about opportunity. In extreme cases, for example, Eithne McLaughlin's attempt to replicate in Northern Ireland her York study of work incentives and constraints for families on income support, questions about incentives to get a job were greeted with cries of: 'What job? We have 50 per cent adult male unemployment around here!'

Nevertheless, given reasonable assumptions about local labour market opportunities, these findings imply that the out of work families are potential family credit customers more often than not. They did the same kinds of work as family credit recipients did, many of them very recently. More than that, they contained more among them, especially the men among couples, who had lately done the kinds of unskilled jobs that pay the least and so attract the largest entitlements to family credit.

The problem of childcare

Family credit is not designed to compete with parenthood. Official social security policy takes a neutral view of lone parents with respect to work: they are not required to be 'actively seeking work'. The DSS has recently strengthened its policy towards the payment of maintenance by absent fathers for the support of children and their lone mothers. Equally, though, the DSS does not mind if lone parents do seek work and advertises family credit as one measure intended to make a choice to work a little more realistic for them. Policy takes no view at all of the wives of couples working or not (except to withdraw benefit if they do) and it is only (usually) the fathers within benefit recipient couples who are required to show willing in the labour market.

Also, in discussing the need for childcare as a constraint upon the opportunity to work, it is as well to acknowledge that 'constraint' is not quite the right word for behaviour that in many cases is the outcome of long cherished ambition - to look after small children for a while.

Nevertheless, for most families, the absence of need is the presence of work. Work is still at the centre of life for those of childrearing age and the route out of poverty means someone getting a job. For the low income families in this study, their routes out of poverty mean, for lone parents, their getting a full-time job, and a reasonably well paid one if they can, since as we saw in chapter 2, part-time work is not very much good to them. Then they move up into the family credit families and, they may hope, beyond. For among couples, going up the income distribution means both of them working, she often part-time.

But if children are of dependent age, especially under school age, the familiar problems of childcare arise and their effects have already been charted in earlier descriptions of families' patterns of work. The result is, for example, that among lone parents and wives who do not work, the same proportion, 64 per cent, have a child under five and only 12 per cent and 16 per cent respectively of these are looking for a job. Even these tend to be those whose children are rising nursery or school age. It is a familiar pattern and often has little to do with wage incentives or in-work benefits. When the children reach school age, so the majority of their mothers look for a paid job. Full-time work tends to come, if at all, when the youngest reaches secondary school. In our sample, for example, half of mothers without paid jobs, but whose youngest child was over ten, said they were actively looking for a paid job. But some families do work while overcoming the problems of childcare and what they do has an interesting relation to both patterns of work and claiming benefits.

The national picture was examined closely in an analysis of data from the DSS/PSI sift (see Marsh and McKay 1993). This suggested a large volume increase in the use of paid childcare, possibly expanding by as much as four and a half times over ten years. This has been caused by increased participation in the labour market by women who have young children.

Nevertheless, the most common forms of childcare were unpaid, in the form of help from partners, grandparents, and other relatives, working only school hours or having children who could fend for themselves after school. Overall, 23 per cent of working parents paid for childcare, paying an average of £30.70 a week. Among those working more than 24 hours a week, 31 per cent of couples and 34 per cent of lone parents paid an average of £36.80 and £27.30 respectively. Those using 'professional' care as their sole method of looking after children while they were at work paid an average of £42.40 a week. Working families who paid for childcare paid an average of £1.10 for each hour that the mother worked and this accounted for a quarter of her earnings; lone parents paid less at 81p/phw and 22 per cent of earnings, and couples more at £1.18phw and 26 per cent of earnings.

The conclusions suggested that relatively few women could afford to take a job if they had to pay for childcare. Those who did tended to place a limit on the amounts they paid relative to the amounts they earned. Amounts paid for childcare rose as earnings rose but stayed at a fairly constant 25 per cent of take home pay. This suggests that in evaluating a likely job mothers might mentally deduct tax and national insurance, and travel to work and clothing costs, and then childcare costs, and then, if they are left with less than half the amount offered, they wonder seriously whether it is worth going to work at all. The exception to this appeared to be mothers, especially those with partners, working in part-time jobs who appeared to be willing or able to accept a much higher 'childcare tax' of between a third and a half of their earnings.

If this is the national picture, among all families, how is childcare tackled by the low income families in the interview sample, which permitted more detailed questioning, including what out of work families did when they were working?

The question is simplified by reference to the partners' interviews. None but the smallest handful of low income couples whose main wage earner was working, said they ever pay for childcare. Even among those families no longer in full-time work, only 1 per cent said they ever paid for childcare when they worked.

Some couples had had to pay for childcare in the past, but not many. Among those couples where the mother was not working at the time of interview, 13 per cent recalled having paid for childcare sometime during the previous three years or so. Interestingly, this figure is 27 per cent among ENCs couples whose female partner was no longer working. This may be another echo of the better fortunes we suspect they have enjoyed fairly recently, times when her job was sufficiently well paid to justify buying childcare if it was needed and none was available free from relatives or from the education system. In contrast, only tiny numbers of out of work couples recall paying for childcare in the days when they had a job between them.

But the overall picture for couples is clear: if a couple is to afford childcare where none is available free, then they need two decent wages coming in before it is worthwhile substituting (usually) her childcare with her work. Few low income couples need childcare; when they do need it they need free childcare, only a few pay for it and when they do they do not pay much.

The lone parents tell a different story. Among those interviewed, low income working lone parents, working any hours, 19 per cent paid for childcare. Among those working full-time, 27 per cent paid for childcare, paying an average of £21.50 a week. These figures are not far short of the overall figures from the sift data of 34 per cent of lone parent full-timers paying £27.30. It means, on the other hand, that lone parents rely on unpaid childcare by their own parents and other relatives - a few are cared for by a 'partner' who may well be the children's non-resident father. But the largest category, more than half of all currently working lone parents, said they work only school hours or their children are old enough to look after themselves.

A consistent one quarter of ENC, FC and moderate income lone parents paid for child care, but ENCs and moderate income lone parents paid more: (£27 and £29 versus £15 a week). Quite how a quarter of ENC lone parents managed to pay between £10 and £38 a week for childcare is another mystery we must contemplate about their position.

How did our potential workers see all this? It is their incentives we are mostly concerned with here. Those most distant from the labour market - who said they did not think they would return to work in the foreseeable future - said that childcare was not the issue. Those closest to the labour market - the part-timers who are hoping for full-time work soon - said that childcare was very much an issue - either none was available or what there was they could not afford. Between these were our group of lone parents and wives who said they hoped to get a job of some kind within the next year. What would they do about childcare?

The impression is very similar: most would look to unpaid childcare. Among wives, a quarter of those with working partners and half those with out of work partners, said their partner would care for the children. Most of the rest divided evenly between those who would mobilise other relatives, usually their own mother, and those who would work only school hours or whose children were reaching the age when they could look after themselves, or each other.

Some (17 per cent) thought in terms of professional[1] childcare, usually a childminder, and this was naturally more common among the lone parents (21 per cent) than among wives (14 per cent). These figures are higher than is actually the case among those who are working because those intending to start work have younger children than those in work now. A quarter of wives and 40 per cent of lone parents said they expected to pay for childcare -proportions similar to those working who have the youngest children. The amounts they expect to pay are also very similar to the amounts actually paid by their counterparts in work. This may be coincidence, but it suggests an interesting example of effective transmission of information from working to non-working parents.

Since only a minority pay for childcare, the problems of childcare that keep lone parents out of work, and keep couples as single earner families, may be problems of the reliability of childcare arrangements. Instability would certainly deter lone parents from settling into the kind of longer-term job that typically attracts family credit.

Those intending to work certainly agreed that stability was important and nine out of ten of those expecting to make any arrangement with another adult for childcare said they expected to be able to rely on them more or less every day they were needed. Half of them said that they also had back-up childcare available at short notice, usually a relative or friend, and only 10 per cent of these expected to have to pay for back-up care.

Those who are presently working also gave a picture of considerable stability and reliability in childcare arrangements. The same nine out of ten of those who have arrangements involving another adult said they could rely on them more or less every day. The average duration of present arrangements was nearly two years and eight out of ten said they had never been obliged to change their childcare arrangements. Two-thirds had back-up care they could call upon at short notice - the usual mix of relative and friends. Only 12 per cent (but a quarter of full-time working lone parents) said that they have to pay for back-up care.

This picture of stability was fairly uniform across different kinds of family. Interestingly, it is the ex-workers among the lone parents and couples who have used childcare in the past who report the greater stability in terms of daily reliability and free back-up. So there is no evidence here that lone parents and wives are shaken out of employment by unreliable childcare.

Disability

Former main wage earners were much more likely to say that they had a 'long-term illness or disability' than were working couples of all kinds, and those who did say this were also more likely to say that it was severe enough to limit their opportunities for employment.

Fewer than one in ten of working couples said they have a health problem that '...makes it harder to get and keep a paid job' and that '...affects the kind of work' they could do. Among out of work couples, three times that number (29 per cent) said this, though half of them said they were nevertheless looking for work. For them, it may now be less family credit and more the new disability working allowance that will improve their incentives to enter work.

Looking at the problem of disability the other way about, people without paid work (mainly the out of work lone parents and the wives of single earner couples) were asked whether they intended to look for a job one day and, if not, was there anything preventing them from seeking work.

Only about one in ten lone parents said they did not expect to get a job one day and a majority of these (64 per cent) gave illness or disability as their reason. They were 6 per cent of all lone parents presently out of work, who were effectively sealed off from financial incentives to work.

This question about future work, and likely barriers to be faced, was asked in the section of the questionnaire concerned with the future. It was asked of the member of the couple who was *not* likely to be the principal breadwinner. Most were wives, some, nearly one in ten, were husbands. In some cases, the husbands' disability had turned wives into potential breadwinners.

These families, having a disabled male parent who was unlikely to seek work, were 9 per cent of all out of work families. Almost all are receiving sickness or disability-related benefits. Family credit provides these families with an interesting prospect. If it is possible - that is, if care of the person with the illness or disability allows it - the female partner can work in a low paid, and now part-time job while the family income from disability benefits would usually remain unaffected.

At the time of the survey, 4 per cent of family credit couples were in that position. They had a claim for family credit based on the wife's full-time job and had a husband receiving disability benefits. What is particularly interesting is that when some couples do this, the combination of her earnings and his disability benefits takes their disposable income well beyond that of other couples on family credit, since benefits for severe disabilities are disregarded for calculating entitlement.

Summary

This chapter has suggested some limits to the incentive effects of family credit. These of course are limits common to all work incentives but they take on a special character when related to families and family credit and they work very differently on lone parents and couples.

For lone parents:

The majority of lone parents do not work and most of them are resigned to that position for the while, family credit or not.

At the margins of work, as their children start school, the availability of childcare is crucial to whether or not they can move into range of family credit. There is a fine balance to be struck. That is to work enough hours to be able to claim but few enough hours to fit the available childcare. The reduction of qualifying hours to 16 will make this balancing act easier in the sense that less childcare will be needed, though they are still going to have to be 16 rather well-paid hours to bring their incomes up over the levels of out of work benefits they are getting now. More likely it will free more lone parents to work something like 20 to 24 hours if they have primary school aged children.

For those lone parents dubious of ever returning to work, it is less a problem of childcare, far more a problem of disability.

For couples:
Whereas some lone parents are kept out of range of family credit by the lack of childcare, such lack keeps some couples within range. It redoubles the disincentive to work common to all wives in benefit families. It is disincentive enough for many to lose 70 or 80 pence in benefit for each pound earned. To pay fares to work and cope with difficult childcare arrangements is a greater disincentive. To pay for childcare as well is an indication that the motive to work has nothing to do with money.

Again in contrast to the lone parents, disability in couples can create opportunities to claim family credit. If the husband is disabled the wife might be able to work. This is especially true if his disability is sufficient to keep him from work but not so severe as to need constant care or even for him to provide childcare. As a woman, she is more likely than a man to have a wage within the family credit threshold. If he is receiving disability benefits of the kind not counted against FC entitlement, a considerable incentive is created.

For many kinds of low income family, on the other hand, the continuing barrier to a smooth transition into work, across the stepping stones provided by family credit and up into average wage levels or better, is a narrow range of employment skills. This weakness in their labour market position may leave many low income families drifting back and forth from one kind of benefit to another, from income support to family credit and back again. It is to some extent a characteristic of the moderate income families and the eligible non-claimants that they have additional employment skills to sell that keep them more distant from the business of claiming benefit, perhaps also reducing the expectation of being a claimant, even in those times when their income dips into eligible levels.

Note
1. 'Professional' is used here to include formally paid childminders of all kinds, solely to distinguish them from relatives and friends who might also receive money in exchange for help.

7 Family credit and beliefs, attitudes and intentions

Classical approaches to understanding the effect of incentives upon the supply of labour assume more or less perfect flows of information between those offering work and those seeking it. This is not a very well justified assumption even in the most open of local labour markets. The introduction of social security into the equation that balances the choice to accept a job, or not, undermines this assumption further.

Family credit is supposed to increase the supply of labour from one particular social group: parents who have dependent children and whose earning potential is low. The effectiveness of the initial incentive depends in part on parent-job-seekers knowing all about it: how it works, what total income will they get in work, will benefit be taken away at once if they get to earn more, and so on. Equally, the *dis*incentive effects upon extra work among claimants, especially upon entry into work by the second member of claiming couples, will also be weakened if people are unaware of how the withdrawal of benefit against earning is actually applied.

We have seen already that people's knowledge of the rate of withdrawal of family credit is scant, even among current recipients. On the other hand, it is possible to argue, as economists do, that people's initial state of knowledge is not very important because, if they respond to an incentive that does not exist, they find out soon enough that they have made a mistake and revert to their initial state. If, for example, they find out that they are getting less money in work than they got on the dole, the tendency will be to revert to unemployment. Perhaps this is true, but we want to learn more about people's knowledge of how family credit works, if for no better reason than the DSS has spent £8 million telling them. More than that, it will be important to know what role is played by knowledge and by attitudes in influencing the behaviour of eligible non-claimants. It will also be valuable to know something of how people's conscious intentions about work and benefits reflect the incentives and opportunities they are designed to create. If they do not, it may suggest ways in which a better connection may be established between what people believe and what their opportunities really are. The better the connection, the more effectively family credit will work.

Reservation wages and the role of family credit

How much family credit is enough to create an incentive?
Economists tell us that workers' decisions to work are conditional on them being able to achieve a certain wage level, known as the reservation wage. This is analogous to the reservation price at an auction - the seller will want to get as much as possible, but will not sell at all if the price fails to reach a certain level, the reservation price. Likewise, potential workers will accept a job only if the wage they can receive is above a certain minimum 'reservation wage'. The reservation wage will be influenced, among other things, by the income a person can receive when not working, the costs of working (like childcare and travel), and any other, perhaps non-material advantages to working. Family credit should act to reduce the reservation wage. That is, people will be prepared to work for lower wages than if there was no family credit, since additional income is available from this source.

Various benefits are available both in and out of work whose value changes according to earnings and circumstances, such as housing benefit and community charge benefit. Different benefits apply to different ranges of hours worked (income support now up to 16 hours, family credit at 16 hours and beyond). In addition, national insurance and income tax are payable at relatively low hourly rates of pay. This means that the calculation of what total income would be in work is made very difficult for those not working. Remember too that work is offered at gross earnings, so there is national insurance and income tax to consider, whereas family credit, housing benefit and community charge are calculated from net earnings. Just about the only thing parents can rely on without recourse to a calculator is child benefit - the one constant in the equation that acts as a standing incentive to work since it is not withdrawn against earnings.

Given that considerable uncertainty is attached to each of these sources and deductions from income, some have suggested that the idea of a single reservation wage is in need of some qualification (McLaughlin, Millar and Cooke, 1988: Jenkins and Millar, 1989). It has been argued that it is reservation *income* that is important, rather than the reservation wage level. This is extremely plausible and it makes the decision to work much more a family decision, which is what it probably is in most cases.

It has further been suggested that the certainty or uncertainty of each of these sources also enters into people's decision-making processes; that families have a kind of 'reservation security' as well as a reservation income. This can take two forms:

- the security of the in-work income package: what they will really get in additional income from earnings and from in-work benefits, the rate of withdrawal against increasing earnings or changed family circumstances, and so on, how certain they feel about all this, and,
- how secure the job might be.

A family on income support may perhaps be poorly informed about benefits that are available in work. But they do know for certain that they will receive a familiar amount of money each week in income support, and that their housing costs will be met. This sum could easily exceed £100 each week. To take a job at around £100 each week, with the knowledge that some passported benefits such as free school meals will be lost, and uncertainty as to whether they will still receive assistance with rent and other costs, might not be rational. Even with information about the existence of family credit, it is a further step to being clear that the family will be better off overall - if there are no significant work-related costs.

For couples, however, continued refusals to take jobs offered - even if they would make them worse off - may lead to benefit sanctions. Their choices are to that extent less 'free' than those of lone parents.

The problems of how people may or may not experience the incentive effect of family credit include getting a realistic measure of what information people have. Respondents were asked a number of questions about the sort of wage level that they were looking for, or would be looking for. They were also asked about family credit - did they know at what levels of earnings it would no longer be available?

Knowledge of the family credit threshold

Leaflets describing family credit emphasise the relevant earnings levels or 'thresholds' for different types of family, below which family credit is payable. All respondents were asked what they thought was the upper limit for their family type.

This information is, in principle, readily available to families. The relevant amounts are printed in their child benefit order books, and they accompany details for those paid by credit transfer. Nevertheless, when asked this question, only 4 per cent of families thought to look up the amount in such a source and still only half of these got it right.

Nearly half (44 per cent) said they had no idea what their earnings limit might be (Table 7.1). Happily, the group least likely to say this were current recipients of family credit, but not by much; still more than a third of them could not guess what were the maximum earnings at which they passed out of range of family credit.

Among those who ventured a reply, lone parents provided a lower figure than couples did, and correctly so because, as a group, they have fewer and younger children than couples. The median amount guessed by lone parents was just less than the maximum that may be earned by a lone parent with one child aged less than eleven. Hence, it is rather lower than the true median threshold level for lone parents.

Among couples, the guesses were rather higher. They are broadly in line with the true figure for a couple with two children aged under eleven. But those not in work guessed a very low figure. At earnings of £130, every single one of those families would have been eligible for family credit (given sufficient hours, not too high savings, and so on), and half of them guessed a lower figure. Many of these couples would still be eligible if they earned far more than this. Thus there will be a tendency for the out of work couples to discount the likelihood of a claim for family credit since they believe that entitlement vanishes at extremely low incomes.

Recipients of family credit gave the highest figures among both couples and lone parents. They have had the most opportunity to discover that, especially for larger families, family credit is available for families whose incomes can approach £200 a week. Broadly, the median of the figures that they gave was more in line with the true figures for eligibility.

Overall though, respondents were unlikely to guess a figure that was too high. Two-thirds provided a figure that was too low. About one fifth guessed too high, and 12 per cent were spot on.

However, it would clearly be unreasonable to expect respondents to know their family credit earnings limit to the nearest £1. In any case, what we are really interested in is whether families had a reasonable grasp of the sort of incomes for which family credit would be available. Or, do they think it is restricted to very low earnings indeed. With these factors in mind, we allowed respondents to be within £5, either way, of the correct answer in order to be labelled as correct. The pattern of responses is shown in Table 7.1.

Table 7.1   Perceived maximum earnings before ineligible for family credit

column percentages

| | Lone parents | | | Couples | | | |
	ENC	FC	Mod Income	ENC	FC	Mod Income	Not in work
	%	%	%	%	%	%	%
Made a guess	51	61	58	38	51	37	42
Had no idea	43	33	33	48	36	51	44
Missing/NA	6	6	9	14	12	13	14
Total	*100*						
Median (£ pw)	123	130	126	141	144	139	130

Percentage of those actually guessing a figure who were:

	%	%	%	%	%	%	%
Correct (within £5)	33	40	26	54	29	21	28
Too low	59	49	61	38	54	57	63
Too high	8	11	13	9	17	22	9
Total	*100*						

Of those who were prepared to guess at a figure, the percentage who were within £5 of the true figure varied from 21 per cent of moderate income couples, to 54 per cent of couples who were eligible non-claimants of family credit. Where families provided inaccurate responses, they tended to give figures that were too low.

In other words, respondents tended to believe that family credit, for them, would run out at lower earnings than is, in fact, the case. These families would be eligible for family credit at higher earnings than they realised.

This would associate receiving family credit with being on a low income, when in fact a family can be eligible earning take home wages rather higher up the income distribution.

The position of eligible non-claimants was especially interesting. They were the least likely to offer a guess, consistent with their lack of acquaintance with family credit, though hardly more reluctant than other non-claimant groups. But those ENCs who guessed were able to gauge with some accuracy the highest earnings that would allow them to receive family credit. If psychological factors do play a part in discouraging claims, it is not because they are strikingly more ignorant of the rules. However, they were also the least likely to guess too high, supporting the view that some of them see family credit as a benefit available only for people on quite low earnings.

Reservation wages

The above findings are of some importance to this analysis. Many families appear to believe that family credit is only available to those on the lowest earnings, and do not realise that it is available at the relatively modest earnings to which they might reasonably aspire. This means that they will not be aware of their potential living standards in low paying jobs, since they will not add in the family credit to which they may be entitled. So they will underestimate the total incomes they would receive when in work. Hence, the incentive to work that is provided by family credit will pass them by.

Many will take jobs anyway, or those in work will not go to the trouble of giving up work or looking for other jobs - the employment stability of eligible non-claimants tells us that much. Others may go on to take jobs and be pleasantly surprised that extra income is available. However, for a sizeable number it will fail to enter their calculations of how well off they will be in work.

There is an alternative way of expressing this. In order to achieve a given reservation income a family may think that it needs a given wage - say £140. In fact, it could achieve that income by taking a lower paid job and topping this up with family credit. If they do not realise this, they may fail to take up the lower paid jobs that may be on offer to them. Much of the remainder of this chapter will be taken up with discovering how this information is understood by respondents and what effects it has on their labour market behaviour.

Target wages, acceptance wages and family credit

First let us look at what the out of work families feel they might earn in work. Respondents were told to disregard any amounts they may or may not get in family credit and suppose that they were looking for another full-time job. They were asked:

'How much money would you need to be offered in a new job before you felt it worth taking?'

The problem with such a question is that it invites answers that are a mixture of aspiration and expectation, of hope and reality. Moreover, the use of words like 'worth taking', though unavoidable, are open to the interpretation of a job that was really worth having rather than the sort of job people usually end up doing.

Given the importance of this measure, respondents were also asked to say how easy or how difficult they felt it might be '...to get a job around here paying that amount?' And they were then asked:

'Do you think you might in the end have to take a job paying less than...'(Interviewer reads out the amount given in reply to the first question.)

and then:

'How much a week do you think you would end up accepting?'

In this way we obtain two kinds of reservation wage:

* a 'target wage': the amount they would think worthwhile;
* an 'acceptance wage': the amount that, realistically, they say they might end up having to accept.

What we have called the acceptance wage is probably closer to what economists understand by a reservation wage. But asking the first question first removes a degree of aspiration from the second and focuses the respondents' attention on the idea of a very minimum wage that could actually be accepted.

These questions were asked of three distinct groups of out of work and part-time working families:

* lone parents;
* the member of couples who was the present main breadwinner or the one, usually the male partner, nominated the most likely to get a full-time job. These we shall persist in calling 'husbands';
* the other member of single earner couples (or the one in out of work couples NOT nominated as the likely main breadwinner) who also said that they were hoping to get a job in the next year. These are usually women, whom we shall persist in calling 'wives'.

Lone parents were exceptionally modest, not to say pessimistic in their view of their likely earning power. A quarter of them could not offer a guess about what they might expect. Since some of them have never had a job, this is not in their case surprising. The rest had a median target wage of £112 a week. Some figures were so low as to suggest that they surely had mis-heard the question's reference to a full-time job. Only 37 per cent of them looked for more than £120 a week; only 26 per cent for more than £140 a week. Even so, the great majority thought that such an ambition would be 'quite difficult'(39 per cent) or 'very difficult' (42 per cent) to achieve. So much so, in fact, that only 19 per cent would definitely hold out for their target wage and 71 per cent said that they would doubtless have to settle for less. 'Less' was a median of £86 a week; only 18 per cent realistically expected to exceed £100 a week, a third settling for £80-100 a week, the rest for less.

The replies given by the relatively few job-seeking wives were very similar: a target wage of £99 a week, great pessimism about getting it, and an acceptance wage of £81 a week.

The replies given by job-seeking husbands were very different. Their target wage was a median of £163 a week. Almost all looked for more than £100 week, nearly half looked for £100 to £160 a week, a third for £160 to £200 and the rest to over £200.

Though larger, husbands' target wages proved unexpectedly more fragile than those of lone parents and wives. There was pessimism about the likelihood of finding a job paying a wage that they felt was 'worth accepting'; twice as many (63 per cent) thought it 'very difficult' and 16 per cent 'quite difficult' to find such a job locally and only a quarter would hold out for their target wage. Those asked to think again came up with a median figure £126 a week, or about 45 per cent of the national average male wage in April 1991, or more realistically perhaps, about 60 per cent of the average wage for male manual workers.

These two measures may now be combined into a single reservation wage: the target wage of those who said that they would stick to it, regardless of the difficulty of getting such a job locally, and the acceptance wage of those who felt they would have to settle for less than their target wage.

This calculation enlarged the numbers who, in the end, could not provide a reservation wage. About a third of out of work families who were seeking work said either that they could not guess their target wage or that they could guess but thought it unlikely they would get it and went on to say that they could not guess at what they would have to settle for instead. This suggests that for these families, the value of a new job would have to be assessed first by intuition and later by trial and error. They would have to be intuitively sure that they could manage on the offered wage and would need early confirmation of a balanced budget to stay in work. For such families, the decision to work is, therefore, a risky one.

For those who could provide a reservation wage, median figures of £88 a week were given by lone parents. Since one in five of them gave a figure less than £60 a week they must surely have been thinking in terms of part-time work.

Even so, only 22 per cent looked for more than £100 a week. Among husbands, a median figure of £149 was given; 83 per cent would settle for not less than £100 a week, half for not less than £140 and 23 per cent looked for more than £200 a week.

Out of work families' reservation wages tend to be quite strongly related to their previous earnings, except among lone parents, few of whom have worked at all during the previous three years.

Surprisingly, reservation wages, when given, are not related to the size of family. Either families have in-work benefits at least half in mind when they quote a reservation wage, and so compensation for size of family counts for them both in and out of work, or, more likely, they focus on that aspect of the question that asks them to judge what they would have to settle for. This is more a judgement about what employers might offer them than what they think they could get by on. This is a very important point. Families' out of work incomes are strongly related to the number and ages of their children. If their reservation wages were adjusted to their out of work incomes, then they too would vary by family size. But they do not.

More light on the nature of this judgement is shed by the replies given to a follow-up question which asked whether such a job might be taken at the acceptance wage as a 'stop-gap job just for a few weeks' or whether it would be accepted longer term. Four out of ten lone parents and couples alike said that they would accept such a wage only on the shorter-term basis, half thought they could manage on such wages in the longer term and the remainder were unsure what they might do.

Fewer thought they could tolerate insecurity in a better paid job. Three-quarters of both the out of work couples and lone parents said that such a job, taken at their target wage, would have to be '...secure for as long as I wanted it...' and half the remainder looked for at least a year's security of tenure. So those of them who said that they would be prepared to accept less money for a shorter time were not saying they were actually looking for such a job, only that they would be prepared to put up with the lowest wages if they really had to, but not for long.

What they want is what most people want: a secure job at a realistic wage. Joining the 'flexible workforce' holds few appeals for people with dependent children to look after, at least for those of them who are main wage earners. This evidence seems to support the view that out of work families do have a 'reservation security' as well as a reservation wage. This was first suggested by McLaughlin's depth interviews with out of work families, who said that *security* in work was as important as money, as an incentive to get a job. Life on income support is basic and without luxury; but it is predictable. Getting into work, paying set-up and travel costs, re-budgeting to cope with a differently structured income, all present difficulties and uncertainties. The likelihood of making such an adjustment only to be flung back on income support after a few weeks can be a threat. It is a threat that people know about and it is a major disincentive to work among those whose families attract levels of income support only a little less than the net rewards their labour would command in work.

What then is the relation between these reservation wages among out of work families, when they were given, and family credit? The best question to ask is: what would be the benefit status that would result?

A little over half the couples (54 per cent) who got a job at their reservation wage would find themselves below their maximum earnings for family credit and, if they satisfied the other conditions, they would be eligible to claim; 46 per cent would be beyond their family credit limit. Among lone parents, 89 per cent would become eligible to claim family credit, only 11 per cent would be beyond their limit. It is hardly any wonder that lone parents fall so easily into claiming family credit as they start work. On the other hand, no more than a third of working lone parents are actually eligible for family credit, so either those out of work now are intending to 'start at the bottom' - and they may be, of course - or they are under-estimating what they really might be paid.

There is, however, a tendency for people to see their family credit limit as lower than it really is - that they believe FC is only for the very poorest among working families. A few guess their own FC limit accurately, while others place it higher than it really is. Among out of work couples who are looking for work and who gave a reservation wage, 56 per cent thought their limit lower than it really is, 8 per cent got it more or less right and 36 per cent thought it higher than it really is. The first group, who thought their limit lower than it is, tended to give a reservation wage that was within what they believed was their limit - they tended to pitch their bid for wages downward into the believed family credit zone. Those few who guessed right and the 36 per cent who thought they could still claim FC on earnings higher than they really could, tended to give a reservation wage higher than their believed FC limit -they pitched their bid for wages well over the family credit zone. (Table 7.2)

What this probably means is that wage expectations are affecting people's ideas about family credit earnings limits, rather than the reservation wages being pitched with one eye on family credit limits. Families with low wage expectations tend to be those with experience of income support and benefit level incomes and so associate benefit limits with subsistence incomes. They do not readily believe that means-tested benefits may be had at what may seem to them like decent wages. Those with high expectations, on the other hand, are those who tend to have very high expectations - many look for wages of at least £200 and often more than £300 a week. They tend to nominate a figure for their FC limit that is too high because they cannot conceive of themselves, or many other people, being paid what to them seem like below subsistence wages.

Perceptions might have changed following the advertising campaigns in 1991 which drew attention to a message printed in families' child benefit order books. The personalised message gave the level of income a family can receive and still qualify for family credit. The DSS believe that the campaign was successful in raising awareness of this point.

Table 7.2   Believed thresholds (compared to actual) FC thresholds and reservation wages

	Family thought their own family credit limit was:		
	Lower than it really is %	What it really is %	Higher than it really is %
Reservation wage is **within** their believed limit	65	(24)	11
Reservation wage is **beyond** their believed limit	35	(76)	89
Total	*100*		
Weighted bases	130	18	82

Much the same effect is seen when their expectations are compared with their actual family credit limit, as follows:

Table 7.3   Believed FC thresholds by reservation wages

	Family thought their own family credit limit was:		
	Lower than it really is %	What it really is %	Higher than it really is %
Reservation wage is **within** their actual limit	71	52	16
Reservation wage is **beyond** their actual limit	29	48	84
Total	*100*		
Weighted bases	144	67	20

Nevertheless, the main conclusion must be that out of work couples do not engage much in working out the relation between what they might earn in work and what they might get in in-work benefits. A third of them could not guess what they might earn. Another third had no idea of their FC threshold and they divided exactly evenly in pitching their reservation wage above or below their FC limit. The remaining third usually guessed wrongly but tended, nearly two to one, to pitch their reservation wage below their actual FC limit. The lower they thought their limit was, the more likely they were to be real potential customers.

This last finding appears paradoxical but it suggests, narrowly, that those out of work families who are more aware of FC, and who are more prepared to engage their minds in thinking about its limits and effects, are also those who are more likely to become its customers: to become low income working families earning low net wages. Most especially, they are lone parents, 89 per cent of whom pitch their reservation wage below their entitlement threshold compared with 54 per cent of couples.

The next step was to put these questions to families who were in work.

In-work incentive effects of family credit

Current recipients
Often the best approach to understanding a complicated problem is to start by asking a direct question of those most involved in it. The present family credit recipients were asked:

> 'If for some reason you were unable to get family credit would you continue in your present job, try to get another job, stop work for a while, or what would you do?'

Half would continue in work, nearly a third would try to get another job, one in ten would stop work, five per cent had no idea what they might do. These figures are similar for lone parents and couples. It is striking that, out of nearly 500 couples who were interviewed, only three suggested that their partner might get a job. It implies that for family credit couples, this is not an option. If it were an option, they would have taken it by now and they would no longer be family credit families. Those for whom it became an option, took it and are no longer on family credit. This is part of the evidence for the dis-incentive effects of family credit on married women re-entering the labour market.

More than a third of those who said earlier in their interview that they could not manage at all without their family credit, no matter what economies they might practise, went on to say later that they would continue in their present job without it. For many of them, however difficult it might be, continuation would be their only possibility. They would still be worse off out of work. The previous point about married women also applies: if there were a better job available, they would have taken it by now. Presumably some might try to do more paid overtime, or ask for a rise. But it is harder to see how many of them would manage, especially since it is those with the larger awards who say they could not manage without their family credit. This in turn is evidence that family credit, at least in the judgement of its customers, meets need. These are the type of working families who, 25 years ago, were found by Townsend and others to be unable to maintain adequate living standards.

Those with the smallest awards were more likely to say they would carry on in their jobs regardless. And it is only among those who have awards above £40 a week who are significantly more likely to say they would stop work; more than a quarter of the lone parents getting more than £50 a week say this. Yet still about a third of those with awards of more than £40 a week say they would continue in work without family credit even though, in many cases, this would leave them with incomes near or even below those they would get out of work. Probably they would try to carry on at work for the time being and look for some other solution to their problem.

These results give a strong impression of attachment to the labour market among FC families. This is an important point. It means that, whatever may be the wider incentives to work provided by family credit, it is the *sole* incentive for only a minority of current recipients. Only those with the poorest paid jobs and the largest families said, in effect, that only FC was keeping them at work. They would give up work without it since, presumably, they had little confidence in getting a better paid job anywhere else. They are 13 per cent of FC lone parents and 7 per cent of FC couples.

Like the out of work families, all those with jobs were asked to say how much they would need to earn in a new job, before they felt it worth taking. Families in work showed the same pattern of naming a target wage that was somewhat more than their present earnings (why else take a new job unless forced to?), but showed great pessimism about obtaining such a job and a readiness to accept, if they had to, a job paying about £30 less, on average. Still only a quarter of the moderate income couples, for example, would hold out for their target wage.

Other families

It is difficult to compare the incentives of different kinds of family in this survey. The recipients, the eligible non-claimants, the out of work and the moderate income families all approach the question from different positions.

It may be helpful first to compare the reservation wages of all types of family; these are the median values:

Table 7.4   Reservation wages by type of family (median £ per week)

	ENCs	FC	Mod. income	IS/UB
Lone parents	£130	£107	£148	£88
Couples	£146	£130	£153	£149

The first impression is that, whatever else is keeping lone parents out of a job, it is not excessive wage demands. Their expectations fit most closely to likely large awards of family credit if they do accept work at those levels. They may be a little out of touch with what present wage levels actually are. Out of work lone parents' reservation wages are substantially lower than even those of the lone parents currently in work and claiming family credit. These in turn are substantially lower than the ENC and moderate income lone parents. Among couples, the out of work families clearly aim, on average, to join the moderate income group if they can, though as noted earlier there is a very wide spread of ambition among them.

Again, though, it is the family credit families who expect the least in a new job and who would settle for less if they had to. The differences are not great but they do reflect an adjustment on behalf of those receiving family credit to lower earned income. In fact, their shortfall in median values compared with the moderate income group is about £28. This is not much short of the average award of family credit in 1991.

This adjustment is also seen in the relation between families' reservation wage, when given, and their actual and believed family credit earnings limits, as follows:

Table 7.5   Relation between reservation wage and earnings limits

	ENCs	FC	Mod. Income	IS/UB
Lone parents				
Percentage with res. wage within **believed** FC earnings limit	42%	73%	31%	-
Percentage with res. wage within **actual** FC earnings limit	66%	87%	41%	89%
Couples				
Percentage with res. wage within **believed** FC earnings limit	60%	69%	35%	42%
Percentage with res. wage within **actual** FC earnings limit	60%	78%	39%	54%

Among lone parents there is a clear pattern of adjustment. Current family credit recipients pitched their reservation wages accurately within their own earnings limit and most of them knew that they did. Very few of the out of work lone parents asked for more than their FC limit. The ENC and moderate income lone parents were far less likely to settle for less than their FC limit, though rather more of the ENCs did so than believed they did.

Among couples the pattern was a little different. A majority of the FC couples thought they asked for a sum within their earnings limit and more (nearly eight out of ten of them) actually did so. Six out of ten of the ENCS did likewise. So, again, there is no really clear evidence that ENCs are people who expect, or even look for rapid improvement in their earnings, even though four out of ten were more ambitious than family credit rules allow their customers to be. The moderate income families were more ambitious still, but even four out of ten of these said they would be prepared to settle for what are actually benefit level wages if they had to. Though again, in half of cases, not for long.

Incentives and intentions

It is worth remembering that the above conclusions rest on only about half the cases in some types of family - most particularly among ENCs and moderate income couples. They are what political scientists call 'an issue public' - those who are really prepared to give thought to what they might earn, what they might get in family credit, and so on. The rest contribute little to the debate.

To gain a wider glimpse of what our respondents thought they might be doing in the future, even what outline plans they might have to work or not, or to claim family credit or not, all families, regardless of their present activity or status, were asked:

> 'Taking everything together, what do you think is the most likely thing to happen for you and your family over the next couple of years?'

Lone parents were asked to say whether they were likely to be working full-time or part-time and whether or not they would claim family credit. Couples were also asked about claiming, but were asked to say whether one and/or both would be working either part-time or full-time.

Only two per cent of families said they could offer no guess at all about what they might be doing over the next two years or so. Couples achieved a very high degree of agreement between partners - and doubtless quite a lot of collusion in reaching a joint view, separately expressed to the interviewer. What differences there were seemed to hinge around definitions of part-time and full-time.

About a fifth of the out of work couples and more than a quarter of the lone parents saw no prospect of a return to work over the next two years. Those lone parents hoping for a return to work divided two to one in favour of a 'part-time' job. (Here, respondents were allowed to determine for themselves what was a 'part-time' job.)

Five per cent of out of work couples, but twice that figure among working couples, saw a future in terms of both partners working full-time. The remainder divided fairly evenly between one partner working full-time and the other either not working, or working part-time. Family credit couples were more likely to lean toward the traditional pattern of a full-time worker with a non-working partner rather than introduce part-time work for the other partner (49 per cent versus 32 per cent). A non-working partner taking up part-time work would conflict with continuing to claim family credit. This being so, it is perhaps surprising that as many as a third of current claimants did look forward to doing some part-time work and this places in perspective the disincentive effect of family credit upon wives working. It is clearly there, because the two groups unaffected by the withdrawal rate of family credit (ENCs and moderate income families) are more likely to add a part-time working partner over the next couple of years, but only by a margin of 45 per cent compared to 32 per cent. And the numbers intending to add a full-time partner are the same: about one in eight or nine. (Table 7.6)

Table 7.6   Combined working intentions

row percentages

In the next two years, we intend: One partner working: & the other working:	FT FT	FT PT	FT No work	PT PT	PT No work	No work No work	
Couples:							
Eligible non-claimants	11	45	40	-	2	1	(=100%)
Moderate income	14	46	34	*	3	4	
Current recipients	13	32	49	3	2	2	
Out of work	5	27	34	3	9	23	
Lone parents: working	FT		PT		No work		
Eligible non-claimants	79		18		2	(=100%)	
Moderate income	91		9		0		
Current recipients	57		41		2		
Out of work	24		45		31		

It is interesting to see that about one in six of the eligible non-claimants appear not to have given up on family credit altogether and expected to work and claim sometime over the next few years.

Working lone parents gave a clear reply: nearly all would continue to work full-time, except for four out of ten family credit lone parents who seem to think of their 24 hour-plus a week jobs as 'part-time' and resolved to continue to do them. The out of work lone parents who saw some prospect of work in the next two years, some of whom already have part-time jobs, said they favoured part-time rather than full-time work (42 per cent part time, 22 per cent full-time). This also qualifies earlier findings. No more than 31 per cent of out of work lone parents said definitely that the most likely outcome for them will be to remain out of work in a couple of years' time. This prefigures quite a strong intention to get paid work, if they can.

Respondents' intentions toward claiming family credit were also very clear. Among eligible non-claimants and moderate income families, lone parent and couples equally, the majority say they will *not* claim family credit. Among the out of work families, a third of the couples and half of the lone parents say they will claim. Among family credit families, two-thirds of the couples and eight out of ten of the lone parents said that they expected to remain on family credit. As in so many other things, the best predictor of future behaviour is past behaviour. The apparent exception among a third of the family credit couples who do not expect to remain on family credit is largely accounted for by those families who intend to become two earner families.

The shape of families' imagined destinations can be seen better if these two pieces of information are brought together: working and claiming. There are a number of ways of looking at this. For example, by examining the joint distributions of working and claiming (eg what proportion of couples plan to have one partner work full-time, one part-time and NOT claim family credit?). Another is to look at what proportion of each predicted work pattern attracts family credit. Table 7.7 brings together and simplifies as much as possible the main points of this analysis.

The table shows the proportion who say they will be likely to be claiming family credit two years' hence and shows this separately for the three commonest combinations of *working* intentions for couples:

- both working full-time,
- one working full-time/one part-time,
- one working full-time/one not working

And for lone parents who say they will work full-time or 'part-time'. Since we know a large proportion of them think of 24 hours as 'part-time', the more so will they think of 16 hours as part-time.

The table then further divides these families who have different employment plans into their present status as eligible non-claimant, claimant, moderate income or out of work families. Thus, we have in outline an account of where families start from now, where they think they are going and whether or not their destination in work might include a claim for family credit.

The account given by lone parents could hardly be clearer. Nearly all of those who get family credit now and saw the future as continuing 'part-time work' said they would remain customers of family credit. So did most claimants intending to continue to work 'full-time', except for about a quarter of them who thought their full-time work in future will carry them beyond the reach of family credit. Most of the out of work lone parents expecting to return to work in the next two years also included family credit in their plans. These included two-thirds of those intending to work full-time and nearly all of those out of work lone parents intending to work part-time. In contrast, relatively few moderate income lone parents expected to look to family credit. On the other hand, many of the eligible non-claimants who thought they might claim turned out to be lone parents intending to work full-time.

The important finding here is to reinforce earlier suggestions that lone parents coming off income support look naturally to family credit as part of their personal job-start plans. Although no more than a third of full-time working lone parents claim family credit, this means only that the majority of them did not spend time on income support. They always had a job, or maintenance, or both. For the majority of lone parents who remain on income support, family credit is seen by most as essential to a return to work. For the majority of them, it probably is.

Table 7.7   **Proportion who will claim FC in future, by what families may do in the future, by what they do now**

cell percentages

Couples one partner: & other partner:	Work FT Work FT	Work FT Work PT	Work FT Not work
Eligible non-claimants	-	13%	21%
Weighted bases	(12)	55	54
Family credit claimants	19%	46%	89%
Weighted bases	54	128	223
Moderate income families	0%	5%	14%
Weighted bases	62	217	140
Out of work families	0%	25%	51%
Weighted bases	23	97	111

Lone parents	Work FT	Work PT
Eligible non-claimants	27%	-
Weighted bases	35	(9)
Family credit claimants	75%	94%
Weighted bases	210	170
Moderate income families	12%	-
Weighted bases	72	(7)
Out of work families	67%	82%
Weighted bases	232	474

A large and important group of intended part-timers were the majority of lone parents who saw a return to work as likely in the next two years. This suggested strongly that there is a large constituency among presently non-working lone parents who associate *part-time* working with an opportunity to claim family credit. In fact, out of work lone parents who were intending to work part-time AND claim family credit were nearly a third (30 per cent) of *all* lone parents currently out of work. This is strong confirmation that the change in the hours rule, introducing family credit at 16 rather than 24 hours work a week, ought to have wide appeal among lone parents.

The picture given by the couples was a little more complicated and these complications hinged around the likelihood of dual working partnerships.

The moderate income families sent the clearest message: very few intending that both partners will work would ever trouble the staff at North Fylde with a claim for family credit. A few of those intending to be single earner families might claim (14 per cent).

In contrast, the current recipients of family credit who cleave to the traditional one-worker family intended to remain loyal customers of family credit. Half of the claimant families who were intending to add a part-time worker hoped to continue in scope of family credit. Few of those who expected to turn into two-full-time-worker families also expected to hang on to any entitlement to FC.

Half of the out of work couples who intended to become one-worker families also had family credit in their sights, but only a quarter of those intending to add a part-time worker to the team expected to claim family credit and none at all of those intending to become two-full-time-worker-families expected to claim.

Again, few of the eligible non-claimants would claim, though a fifth of the ENC couples intending to have only one worker in the family persisted in thinking that it might be worth a try.

What then was the connection, if any, between these intended working patterns that may or may not involve a claim for family credit, and our earlier discussion about reservation wages? Most important, did those who gave reservation wages within the scope of family credit go on to see the future in terms of being a claimant family? And did those who would seek wages higher than their family credit limit go on to see themselves as working in jobs that would not attract family credit?

Table 7.8 provides the necessary information by dividing the sample first into lone parents and couples, then into the same key 'intention groups' described in the previous Table 7.7, and then into those who:

* had earlier given a reservation wage that left them WITHIN scope of their actual family credit earnings limits,

and those who

* had earlier given a reservation wage that left them BEYOND scope of their actual family credit earnings limits.

Again, the lone parents' message is clearest. Those who saw the future as a full-time worker clearly sensed the connection between the wages they might expect to earn in a new job and their opportunities to claim family credit. Those among them who looked for wages within scope of FC were four times more likely to expect to claim FC while doing such work than are those whose ambitions take them beyond the scope of FC. Claiming FC alongside them will be found most of those lone parents intending to work part-time, regardless of the relation between their reservation wage and their entitlement to FC, because they were asked for full-time reservation wages, not part-time ones. They nearly all sensed that their intended part-time jobs would leave them well in scope of family credit and most of them might well have been right. If they were not right then, they are probably right now because most people would define 16 hours as part-time.

Table 7.8   **The proportion intending to claim family credit by intended working patterns, by whether or not families' reservation wages left them in scope of family credit**

cell percentages

Couples one partner : the other partner:	Work FT Work FT	Work FT Work PT	Work FT Not work
Reservation wage **within** range of FC	8%	25%	64%
Reservation wage **beyond** range of FC	6%	14%	36%
All couples	*7%*	*20%*	*53%*
Lone Parents	Work FT	Work PT	
Reservation wage **within** range of FC	64%	88%	
Reservation wages **beyond** range of FC	15%	73%	
All lone parents	*46%*	*87%*	

The couples who corresponded closest to the lone parents were those intending to have a sole full-time worker. Among these, the ones who earlier gave a reservation wage within scope of family credit, were twice as likely to see themselves as claimants in the future as were those placing themselves at more ambitious wage levels (64 per cent versus 36 per cent).

Otherwise, relatively few couples looked toward family credit in the future, except for about a fifth of those expecting to have one full-time and one part-time worker. Significantly, perhaps, the proportion intending to claim family credit among such couples was unaffected by the earlier relation between reservation wages and entitlement levels. The likelihood of a successful claim would depend entirely on the extent of part time work intended for the second partner. It rarely takes much to raise them swiftly out of eligibility. Only a small minority of present claimants had both partners in work, beyond the fewest number of extra hours per week.

Conclusions

What does all this really say about the impact of family credit on the incentives to work? It appears to say three things most clearly:

- low income families do not have a very clear picture of the rules of eligibility for family credit, nor of their value on the labour market. Neither means that they cannot function rationally as choosers of work and claimers of benefit, but it does mean that the perceptions that influence their behaviour are likely to be more intuitive than calculated.
- family credit attracts a conscious 'loyalty' from its customers. This is a *dual* attachment both to FC and to the chance to work in paid employment. From those who are not customers it attracts most interest from those most likely to benefit from it. More of this point will be explored in the next chapter.
- there is a broad connection between the way different types of families position themselves in the labour market, the extent to which this position increases their entitlement to family credit, and the extent to which the families themselves include family credit in their view of the future, even if they have no work at the present.

These three points seem to be consistent with the general conclusion that family credit can improve the incentive to work among low income families and that the families themselves are to some extent aware of it, both in and out of work.

It works best for lone parents, whose take-up is highest, *provided they are free to work.* Most of them are not free until their children grow older. For couples, these connections between beliefs about work and benefits are less clear, mostly because their options are always more complicated.

A difficulty with these data is that it is easy to confuse the incentive to work with the incentive to claim family credit, or to do both, or neither. The next chapter looks more closely at what people's options really are, where their advantages or disadvantages really lie, and what they do.

8   Benefits and families' incentive to work

Introduction
The first of these three chapters on incentives dealt with the relationship between families' social and economic constraints and their employment behaviour. The second dealt with the relationship between their beliefs, attitudes and intentions. This third and last deals with arithmetic and behaviour. We estimate what the gains and losses to families in and out of work really are - what economists recognise as incentives - and what they appear to do in response.

The unemployment trap
Family credit is designed to fulfil a particular purpose. It deals with a problem that arises in all social security systems that pay cash benefit to people who are not in paid work. In the British system this problem is acute because the main out-of-work benefit, income support, is progressively removed pound-for-pound on the basis of increasing earnings above £5 per adult in two parent families and £15 for lone parents. Such benefits are lost entirely, *regardless of income*, for those who work more than 16 hours a week, since April 1992, though at the time of the survey in 1991 this limit was 24 hours. Therefore, without some kind of in-work benefit it is possible for the lowest paid families in work to be worse off than similar families out of work. Since families who have dependent children command considerably higher benefit levels out of work than other people, the lowest paid families can find themselves better off without work than they are in the lowest paid jobs. The larger the family, the greater this possibility. This would constitute a disincentive for them to work at low wages rather than claim out of work benefits.

This, then, is the unemployment trap mentioned earlier where moving from out of work and on benefits to being in work without benefits, results in only a small increase in income. Once expenses associated with working (travelling, childcare) are taken into account a family might be worse off in purely cash terms. As previous chapters have indicated, this is not a common problem among the general run of families. But it is a problem encountered among the lower paid parents of younger children. It is not that common among couples, but is more often found among lone parents.

As discussed in the introductory chapter, there might have been a number of possible solutions to this problem. Indeed, in a study focused on means-tested benefits, such as this is, it is easy to forget that child benefit is still by far the largest in-work benefit for families with dependent children, in both caseload and expenditure terms. Only 5 or 6 in every 100 child benefit recipients also get family credit and for every pound distributed to family credit recipients, £10 is paid in child benefit.

The principles on which child benefit operates are inherited from Beveridge's original scheme (published by co-incidence exactly 50 years prior to the writing of this chapter) whereby family allowances would be paid at the same rate in and out of work. This maintains incentives to work (unless benefit rates are huge) because benefit is kept intact on entry to work, and free of tax, and is merely added to earnings in the family's total income. Problems arose in the 1950s and 1960s when rising out of work benefits, on the one hand, and rising average earnings on the other, left larger and poorly paid working families in a trough of low net income that could be higher out of work.

In theory, the problem grew larger in the 1970s and 1980s through the rapid growth in lone parents whose earning power in work is usually low. As it happened, family income supplement was introduced before the increase in lone parenthood accelerated to present day rates. But, for example, large increases in child benefit, or any similar universal benefit for families, might have met this gap just as effectively for *poorly paid families*, but at the greater cost of paying the new amounts to all families. There would have been dramatically lower administration costs, but such savings would have been only a fraction of the overall additional cost.

The choice was made instead to target additional benefit first though the introduction of family income supplement and later by family credit. The wider terms of eligibility for family credit, from 1988, plugged the growing gap between further increases in out of work benefits for families and the slower growth (and a temporary standstill) in the amounts of child benefit.

It is worth remembering that the predecessor of family credit, family income supplement, was in 1971 still a relatively recent and novel addition to the social security system. A key idea of the Beveridge proposals was that there was an important distinction to be drawn between working and non-working breadwinners. Households with breadwinners in work were not regarded as requiring income assistance unless they had larger families. It was the out of work who required attention and they on an insured basis, rather than through means-tested benefits.

Over time the rising cash levels of benefits and the falling level at which tax became payable contributed to the unemployment trap, and the phenomenon known as churning where people both receive benefits and pay direct taxes (see Parker, 1989).

In addition to the pure cash calculation, for out of work benefits there are often associated passported benefits - such as free prescriptions, free school meals - that increase the effective income received by out of work families. These disappear along with the benefit as soon as someone in the family gets a full-time job. This can make paid work even less attractive.

There are some real risks involved too. If the new job lasts only a few weeks, for example, set-up expenses will have been incurred in vain, or the family's return to benefits might be marked by unmanageable gaps between re-claiming and getting benefit, or long-term benefit advantage received earlier might be surrendered, such as 100 per cent mortgage interest payments.

Discussion of the unemployment trap often considers the extent and effect of replacement ratios. The replacement ratio is defined as the proportion of in-work income that an income unit receives when out of work. So, a replacement ratio of 70 per cent means that a family whose net earnings are, say, £160 a week can expect to have an income £112 a week from benefits when they are out of work. Clearly, the higher the replacement ratio, the lower the cash incentives for low paid workers to stay in work, or for out of work families to look for low paid jobs in the first place. Without any in-work benefits, some of these 'replacement ratios' will be more than 100 per cent -families getting more in out of work benefits than they can earn. This typically occurs in large families whose incomes out of work are larger, especially if the children are older. Their financial incentive to work is correspondingly nil, or, in a rational world, it should be nil.

By providing top-ups to earnings that are geared arithmetically to families' entitlement to income support if they are out of work, family credit can usually provide a total income in full-time work which exceeds the total income they would get if they were not in full-time work. The main exceptions, as noted earlier, tend to be out of work families who have recently taken out large mortgages.

Family credit therefore acts to lower the replacement ratio and hence improve incentives to work, always provided that people get around to receiving the benefit at all. (The problem of take-up where families eligible for family credit do not get around to claiming it was discussed in Chapter Four.) Probably more to the point is not that in-work total incomes are raised above the levels of out of work benefits for a given family, but by *how much* they are raised. The improvement has to be visible and significant before it can be expected to have more than the smallest effect. In practice the gain from employment can be affected by mortgage interest payments, travel and (especially for some lone parents) childcare costs. So what is actually happening?

Table 8.1 compares the current incomes of family credit recipients in our survey with what they would expect to receive if the main earner became unemployed. To be consistent with earlier analysis, and to reflect more closely the real world, we have defined out of work as families having no-one working more than 23 hours a week. Therefore the calculations include small amounts of part time earnings, up to their appropriate income support disregards.

The figures are interesting. Our lone parents on family credit were apparently gaining around £30 a week from full-time work: couples less than £18. Not all of this gain is provided by family credit. Some of it is real gains from earnings that survive the withdrawal rate (see next section). These figures are for gains in net cash income. If the average costs of travelling to work, and the average cost of childcare spread over all family credit families, is taken into account, the net gains from work fall to £23 for lone parents and only £10 for couples. Since the average amount earned in part time work by couples out of full-time work is only £1 a week, the average gain from work among family credit couples corresponds almost exactly to the amount they could earn without loss of income support (£5 each) if they were out of work. Lone parents are only £7 a week on the favoured side of the same calculation because they can earn £15 a week without loss of income support.

There are three important points to note about these figures:

- They are average figures, so some families see quite large gains from work while others, usually couples, see none at all.
- The gain from work is not only smaller for couples than for lone parents, it is shared between two adults and their 1.9 children compared to one adult and her 1.7 children, on average.
- These figures are a large part of the explanation of differences in relative family well-being that are discussed in the next chapter.

It should also be borne in mind that, should family credit vanish overnight, but the rest of the social security system remain intact, then the lowest paid families in work would qualify for considerably increased housing benefits, if they were tenants, and all who qualify would get more community charge benefit.

This can put the lowest paid owner occupiers in a tricky position. Hypothetical examples would lead us to expect people with mortgages to fare rather worse than tenants in this comparison, since payments for mortgage interest, unlike housing benefit, are available only to families with no full-time worker. In fact, within our survey, those owner occupiers on family credit did at least as well as other family credit families who were tenants. Typically, they had small mortgages and so payments of mortgage interest were correspondingly small: typically less than £50 a week. In addition, they tended to have higher earnings than average. Had they been tenants paying the same rent as they currently pay mortgage interest, they would often not have qualified for housing benefit anyway. This does not, of course, mean that we should ignore concerns about work incentives for owner occupiers. On the contrary, this finding may strengthen such a concern. It is only those owner occupiers with low outgoings, and who can attain sizeable earnings, who benefit from being in work.

Similar observations apply to families paying for childcare. Again, these appeared to earn more than did family credit recipients as a whole. This seems to confirm the observations in chapter 6 that family credit functions best as an incentive to work for families with comparatively cheap forms of childcare, and who can earn more.

The poverty trap

So, if the real gains from entering employment and claiming family credit are marginal for many families, why not just raise in-work benefits to higher levels and improve incentives all the more? Better surely to pay more family credit than

Table 8.1   Average incomes of family credit recipients in and out of work

£ per week

	Lone parents	Couples
In work (actual)		
Net earnings	86.70	113.80
Maintenance	8.74	0.87
HB	5.60	3.60
CCB	0.90	1.60
Family credit	33.60	28.60
Ch ben plus OPB	18.23	19.70
Other income	0.90	4.30
TOTAL	*154.67*	*172.47*
minus Travel to work	4.20	5.90
minus Childcare	3.10	1.60
REVISED TOTAL	*147.37*	*164.97*
Out of work (hypothetical)		
Income support rate	61.07	87.59
Est'd mortgage interest	8.10	8.10
Ch Ben plus OPB	18.23	19.70
HB	32.80	30.50
CCB	4.00	8.00
Other income (disregarded for income support)	0.20	1.00
TOTAL	**124.40**	**154.89**
Average net gain from work	30.27	17.58
Revised average net gain from work	22.97	10.08

to pay income support? This is true for any individual family, but it would push the maximum earnings levels way up into the mass of families who earn what we have called moderate incomes and, past them, all the way up to average levels. The overall costs to the exchequer would increase. The only solution to this problem would be to take away benefit at more or less pound for pound, just like IS is removed against earnings above a few pounds a week. This introduces a new set of incentive problems because the existence of a benefit like family credit tends to replace one type of trap with another.

For those receiving family credit, each extra £1 of take-home earnings reduces benefit by 70p. Thus, family credit recipients can be said to have a 'marginal rate of taxation' or withdrawal of 70 per cent, more than twice the rate of tax paid by most better paid workers. For most of them, the rate is actually higher. For example, among the better paid FC recipients, once account is taken of income tax and national insurance payments, each extra £1 of earned income results in an increase in income of only 20p, or a marginal rate of withdrawal of 80 per cent. Among the lowest paid and largest families, it is likely that the family is also receiving housing benefit. Then 65 per cent of their 20 or 30 pence retained from each extra pound earned will also be withdrawn, and finally withdrawal of community charge benefit will raise their overall marginal rate of withdrawal of benefit against earnings to 96 per cent.

This situation, where higher earnings tend to result in only a small increase in income, is known as the 'poverty trap'. The level of income at which national insurance and income tax become payable is well within the levels of income at which family credit is available to families. Hence, most families receiving family credit will also be paying both income tax and national insurance. At the time of this survey, NI became payable at gross earnings above £52 per week, and income tax at £96.45 per week, while even the smallest family would be entitled to family credit at a take home income of £130 net per week. This casts an interesting light on the concern for the preservation of incentives that accompanies any proposal to restore a top rate of tax for the richest earners to a figure above its present 40 per cent maximum rate.

This situation may also provide another reason for a lack of perception of eligibility among some families because, in effect, the government is taking away income tax with one hand and giving back family credit with the other, to the very same family. To those not privy to the needs of national accounting systems - systems that typically find it easier to pay and tax rather than to apply graduated discounts - the situation may seem to them so unlikely as not to admit the possibility of *means-tested* taxpayers being eligible for *means-tested* social security benefits. If they are mortgage-paying, MIRAS-receiving owner occupiers too, the likelihood of qualifying for such benefits must seem very odd when they first encounter it, and is not easily accepted. This provides strong grounds for our earlier interpretation of people's views and beliefs about eligibility. It is much less an *affective* problem of unease or stigma, far more a *cognitive* problem of perceived rules of eligibility.

When designing a benefit like family credit, it is necessary to make a decision concerning the cash levels of the benefit and its likely impact on incentives and costs. By having a low rate of withdrawal, the costs of the system would be rather large, but the reduction in benefit for each increase in earnings would have a lesser effect on income available to the family. A low rate of withdrawal not only costs more, it increases the numbers of claimants who have rather high marginal rates of withdrawal. This is what happened when family credit replaced family income supplement.

A higher rate of withdrawal will reduce the overall cost of the scheme, restricting it to a narrow range of the lowest earnings (lowest at least, relative to the numbers of children in the family), but tend to increase the effective tax rate faced by families on low earnings. The most effective level of family credit would be one that produced the most incentive to work consistent with the least overall cost.

The following graph (Figure 8.1) illustrates the poverty and unemployment traps faced by a lone parent, with one young child. The particular figures do not apply to couples because they have a smaller disregard of £5 and higher out of work benefits, but the overall shape of the graph is very similar.

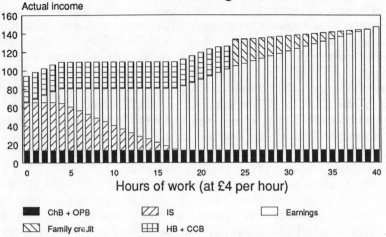

Figure 8.1 Composition of income at increasing hours of work

Once a lone parent starts work, she (or he) is able to keep each extra pound earned up to the level of the disregard (£15). After that, each extra pound is deducted one for one from income support. In other words, a lone parent on income support is no better off earning £45 per week than £15 per week (unless, rarely, she is a childminder). All the time that income support is received, extra earnings do not improve total income at all. As soon as the qualifying 24 hours a week are reached, there is an appreciable increase in income, in this example, about £5 a week, moving on to family credit. Once on family credit, especially if there is also housing benefit still being paid, the poverty trap lessens from 100 per cent, but remains at 90 per cent. It falls to 80 per cent when entitlement to housing benefit (and community charge benefit) is exhausted, and then to 34 per cent (ie 25 per cent tax and 9 per cent NI) when there is no longer any entitlement to family credit.

The effects are not quite as cut and dried as this analysis suggests. For example, higher earnings have an impact on family credit only when it is time to renew claims. Any increase in earnings is kept by the household until family credit is recalculated up to six months later. Housing benefit will also take some time to be altered following any change in circumstances, though it will be backdated to the date of a change in earnings.

The overall flatness of the graph is remarkable. A lone parent working 37 hours a week, is only just over £26 better off than she would be working only 5 hours a week. For lone parents receiving maintenance, which at the time of the survey all counted as income in the same way as earnings, changes to benefit rules in April 1992 mean that this gap will increase by a further £15 per week. This results from having a disregard on maintenance for family credit, as well as for housing benefit and community charge benefit when in work.

There is an important qualification to add to this analysis of the unemployment and poverty traps for families, one that qualifies our understanding of the incentive effects of the whole system: whereas families who receive family credit are in the poverty trap in the sense that they lose the lion's share of each extra pound they are earning when they renew their claim, *not all of them would be in an unemployment trap if they were not receiving family credit at all*. Typically, families who have larger incomes and smaller awards of family credit would find that the earned income remaining to them without family credit would still be more than they would receive on income support, even though they would still pay tax and may not get housing benefit either. So for them, family credit is not the sole instrument keeping them from walking out on their jobs to become voluntarily a burden upon the parish. In the previous chapter we saw evidence that families on family credit are actually aware of this and so would try to stay in work and within family credit.

Table 8.2   Marginal withdrawal rates faced by family credit claimants

row percentages

Tax and benefit combinations	Typical marginal withdrawal rates %	Lone parents %	Couples %
	Percentage who experience each type and amount of marginal loss of benefit for each additional £1 of income		
FC, IT, NICS, HB, CCB	96	6	5
FC, NICS, HB, CCB	94.5	2	2
FC, IT, NICS, HB	93	6	9
FC, NICS, HB	90.5	9	3
FC, IT, NICS, CCB	83.2	4	10
FC, NICS, IT	80.2	39	41
FC, NICS, CCB	76.8	2	2
FC, NICs	72.7	17	8
FC, CCB, HB	0	4	2
FC, HB	0	3	3
FC, CCB	0	2	2
FC only	0	5	9
Total		*100*	*100*
Others	n/a	5	3
Median marginal withdrawal rate (excl. others)		80	80

Before 1988, the combination of family income supplement with taxes and other benefits sometimes meant that a claimant's net income could actually go down if his or her earnings went up; in terms of Figure 8.1, the line sloped downwards. Family credit virtually eliminated that absurdity, at the cost of extending the range of earnings over which income remains virtually constant. Although the notional 'taper' is 70 per cent, the combination with tax and national insurance makes the typical marginal withdrawal rate 80 per cent. For families claiming rent rebates and community charge benefit, it is 96 per cent. An increase from 24 hours to 36 hours provides an extra £48 of gross income. However, after taking into account changes in benefits, the overall gain is just £8.45. This equates to a marginal tax rate of a little over 82 per cent. Put another way, each additional hour of work yielded an extra 70 pence in disposable income - for a worker normally paid £4 per hour. Official estimates show that while marginal withdrawal rates in excess of 100 per cent have virtually been eliminated, the number of earners among families with children losing more than 70 pence in the pound has been doubled (Hansard, 1987).

Table 8.2 illustrates all the marginal withdrawal rates created by various combinations of taxes and benefits and shows, separately for lone parents and couples, the proportion of each who are facing each combination. The most common combination is family credit, after income tax and national insurance have been deducted, giving a marginal withdrawal rate of around 80 per cent. However, some very low earning workers (the self-employed, for example) face a deduction of zero for every pound earned. Zero marginal withdrawal rates exist where the taxable income lies below the national insurance lower earnings limit which was £52 for 1991/92. Over this range, maximum amounts of family credit and other means-tested benefits are payable, and are not withdrawn. It really is quite surprising to find 14 per cent of lone parents and 16 per cent of couples in this very low income 'pre-taper' position.

Summary
This analysis of the actual position of low income families in and out of work has shown the scope offered for incentives to work in terms of increased total incomes in work. However, the introduction of tapered benefit weakens the links between earnings and disposable income. This has three potential disincentive effects:

• The most obvious one is for the *main earner* whose income is being assessed. He or she would have to make a big improvement in earnings in order to enjoy a better standard of living - hence the term, poverty trap. This may discourage people from changing jobs, working for promotion and so on. (Note that among couples, a male worker would be discouraged only if he took a family view of income: he would retain a large proportion of any increase in his own earnings; the loss of benefit would be experienced by his wife.)

- Second, the offer facing an *unemployed worker* may increase net income typically by at least £20, but not by much more than that. The effectiveness of family credit is therefore highly sensitive to the judgement of the amount of income which would persuade a breadwinner to accept a job.
- Third, there would be little point in a *partner* of a family credit claimant taking employment, especially if it was part time. Among couples on family credit, only 12 per cent had a second earner. While family credit may encourage lone parents to go out to work, it encourages married mothers to stay at home and look after their children. If they take employment, they lose 70p in family credit for each pound they earn, even before counting in-work expenses.

The effects of these points have been seen fairly clearly in the data, especially in the low rate of labour market participation among the wives of family credit couples. Usually, any appreciable second income will extinguish eligibility for family credit altogether. This may well be a desirable long-term goal for the family, but it implies that wives in families on family credit need to get straight into full-time work. The customary route of building up from part-time work is not really viable for them.

Evidence for the incentive effects of family credit

Conclusive evidence for the incentive effects of family credit could be obtained only by conducting an experiment. Family credit would be abolished without notice and all other economic conditions would be artificially held constant. A careful record would then be kept of how many of its customers left the labour market, and how many of a carefully matched sample of people newly meeting the former eligibility rules either left or failed to join the labour market.

Denied these scientific opportunities, good evidence of the incentive effects of in-work benefits might yet be sought in observing families' behaviour, in a controlled and scientific way, *over time*. Even then, it helps a lot to ask them periodically why they are making the choices they are, especially if they appear to be making one at variance with what economic rationality would predict.

Here we are dealing with a single, cross-section survey and we must rely on inferential measures that might support the idea that people's reported behaviour arises from the incentives provided. Our best opportunities rest in reconstructing what they say of their recent past.

The first inferential evidence in favour of incentive effects is that people do it. Again, we must be careful not to confuse an incentive to claim with an incentive to work. But we have already seen considerable evidence that family credit is improving lone parents' incentives to work in lower paid employment. Provided they can sort out their childcare satisfactorily, their incomes in work and claiming family credit are substantially better than on income support. As a result, their take-up rates are far higher and family credit is clearly making an important contribution to lone parents' access to the labour market. We feel more confident in this inference because, at so many points in a long interview, they told us that getting family credit was important to their being able to work.

Over the three years of its existence, quite a large proportion - almost a third in fact - of our sample of parents who are currently 'in range' of family credit have had some experience of this benefit. More past claimants will have left the eligible population (and our sampling frame) as their children have grown up. Moreover, the people who stand to gain most from family credit, like the lone parents, are the keenest to claim it. Larger families with larger entitlements are more likely to work and claim family credit than those who would get only a few pounds a week.

But this point also illustrates the difficulties presented by these kinds of data in teasing out the underlying effects of incentives. It is possible to produce a table that shows that:

a) as families' entitlement to out-of-work benefits rise, the proportion out of work also rise, but,

b) the proportion of the remainder, who are *in* work and who also claim family credit, also rises.

This may appear to show a recruitment to an unemployment trap created by the higher benefit levels that larger families can get that is then sprung by family credit, if and when the opportunity for low paid work arises. But it may not. It may merely illustrate that IS and FC are arithmetically bound together and share part of their entitlement rules in common: numbers and ages of children. Moreover, parents with larger families do tend anyway to have lower earnings, increasing the association between larger families and claiming family credit. Almost certainly, both effects are present, but it is not possible to partition out the effects due solely to differences between final incomes in and out of work.

From another point of view, we know already that the incentive effects of family credit additions to earnings are entirely lost on a third of the families entitled to receive it. They do not claim it. Obviously they have an incentive to work because they are working. But their incentive is unaffected by the existence of family credit. Equally, they are unaffected by the *disincentive* to work provided by the levels of benefit they would receive out of work. Eleven per cent of eligible non-claimants of family credit *would* actually be better off out of work compared with their present incomes. But they remain in work.

The next set of evidence that we need to examine concerns movement. Over the past three years, how have different kinds of family moved between the different key states that frame the analysis of this study? In particular how have they journeyed between being in and out of full-time work and in being claimants or non-claimants of family credit? What can the patterns of these journeys tell us about the incentive powers of family credit, or otherwise?

One of the key issues surrounding family credit is the extent to which it *does* enable families to make the transition into work from having no job. If it only has a limited effect on encouraging movement into work, does it instead support lower paid workers for long periods of benefit dependency?

So far we have talked mostly about the incentive effects upon those without work, There is another, perhaps more subtle incentive effect that is attributed to family credit. This is the intention that families should not really remain on family credit forever. The optimistic idea associated with family credit is that it gives people a start, helps them establish themselves in a job at a smaller wage than they really need, and then allows them to improve their position steadily while receiving diminishing amounts of benefit support.

In the short run, there is a built-in incentive effect of family credit in that increased earnings of any size are not penalised at all for six months. Someone offered a 'trial' at low wages with the promise of a decent wage if successful would have an incentive to apply.

In the longer run their destination should be up into the higher income groups, either through increased earnings or to dual earnings. Some we know are 'on their way' in that their earnings are already above income support levels and are topped up only a little by family credit. Thus, for them, an award of family credit that has bridged them across the unemployment trap has not just set them down on the other side abruptly but has carried them on further up the earnings scale.

But all these issues are two-sided. These people have small entitlements, so they have the highest incentives to work and the smallest incentives to claim, and we know that their take-up is lowest at the smallest levels of entitlement.

We have seen some objective evidence for this 'upward incentive'. There are numbers of past family credit customers now earning much more money. Most of these are couples whose children have grown sufficiently for their mother to get into paid work without incurring unaffordable childcare costs, it is true. And lone parent past claimants tend overwhelmingly to end up back on income support, though this in turn says more about the employment opportunities offered to women generally, and their rates of pay in work, than it says about the incentive performance of family credit.

We may express these journeys in rather more precise hypotheses. Once on family credit, do families remain on it for long periods? Or, do they return to income support, or instead go on to higher earnings that make them ineligible for in-work benefits? Our aim in the remainder of this chapter is to discover the direction and magnitude of these flows, and to investigate the main reasons behind each type of movement.

The costs to the exchequer are also of interest. The cost of family credit to the government, in cash terms, will be greater the higher the proportion of family credit recipients whose prior status was working, rather than being out of work and/or on income support (or unemployment benefit). One method of judging the success of family credit is by its claimants not returning to out-of-work benefits.

The data
The data design for this survey involved collecting detailed information about previous employment and benefit claiming among currently low income families. This should enable us to consider movements between the different

sub-groups that we have identified, and may be backed up by re-analysis of the larger sift to track long range movements by former claimants. This will provide considerable evidence about the turnover of family credit receipt, moving in and out of work, and the destinations of former recipients of family credit.

Some of the issues we have raised have been considered before, and addressed within structured surveys. The 1991 National Audit Office Survey provided several pieces of information about job and benefit histories. The NAO survey interviewed 782 people who were receiving family credit in November 1989, almost two years prior to the fieldwork for this study. Amongst other findings:

a) Thirty-six per cent of claimants had previously received family income supplement (FIS), the forerunner to family credit. Of this group, two thirds had then gone on to receive family credit *continuously* since April 1988.

b) Seven per cent of current recipients had received family credit before, but then had a break (for some reason, such as a rejected application) before successfully reapplying.

c) Of those in work at the time of the NAO study, 52 per cent had started their jobs after April 1988. 42 per cent of these had been previously unemployed, the remainder had changed jobs.

Claiming family credit

Questions on applications for family credit, periods of receipt, and times of rejections, were asked about the period since April 1988. We also collected data on spells of employment for the same time span. More general questioning related to whether income support had ever been received, and recollections of applying for and possibly receiving family income supplement (FIS).

We divided up the period since April 1988 into spells of four months - ten time periods in all. Various pieces of information: whether the family was then receiving family credit, whether there was a failed application, can be dated within each period. This provides a means of considering changes over time, without being at so fine a level as to introduce greater complexity. For some purposes, a smaller dividing period would be more appropriate.

In the sections that follow, we consider the patterns of claiming family income supplement, and then of claiming family credit. We also consider the effect of being rejected for family credit. We know from chapter 4 that a rejection for family credit is more common among eligible non-claimants. We consider, below, how far rejection is a deterrent to making claims in the future. How long does it take people to re-apply after a rejection?

Receiving family income supplement

We can begin with receipt of FIS, the predecessor of family credit. It was introduced in 1971, with some speed (Deacon and Bradshaw, 1983), as a move against family poverty. It differed in a number of important respects from the newer benefit, but for our purposes the similarities are more important than the differences. While the take-up of FIS often proved a cause for concern, its impact on the public mind is still traceable by the considerable numbers of people who still use the name, just as child benefit is so often referred to as family allowance.

There will be a natural tendency for the population receiving child-related benefits to change as children are born, or the youngest grow up. Given that FIS had disappeared over three years before the fieldwork for this study, the maximum proportion of current claimants who could have received FIS is around 80 per cent. To the extent that FIS provided a launching pad for families to enter paid employment, its former recipients would not appear in this sample. If there is a fairly stable population receiving in-work benefits like FIS and family credit, then a sizeable proportion of family credit recipients would have claimed FIS at some time. If, however, FIS did not work too effectively, then families on income support will have the clearest memories of it.

Again, for the couples, the analysis can only be for low income families. Hence the *long-range* income movers will not be picked up. By contrast, the *whole population* of lone parents is present, so the overall distribution of former FIS claimants (to the extent that they are still within the population of families with dependent children) will be present within the data.

Of those receiving family credit, 29 per cent had previously received FIS. This provides evidence that there is considerable stability of claiming behaviour. As expected, this proportion is less than was found in the earlier NAO survey. Of course, those with only younger children will have had a low frequency of contact with FIS, or no contact whatsoever. Receipt of family income supplement was, of course, higher among those families with older children, especially those in the 10-15 age group.

Family credit since April 1988

The high proportion of family credit recipients who received FIS provides some evidence of a stable claimant population, especially since the wider scope of family credit means that many families' eligibility for family credit would not anyway have qualified for FIS. Using data on periods of family credit receipt, we may also track the destinations of those who have claimed family credit at different times in the past.

Within the sample of low income families with children, 225 families had received family credit in its first four months. Of this group, 45 per cent were still receiving family credit, or had got back on to it, at the interview stage, three years later. Thirty-six per cent were no longer in full-time work, while 12 per cent now had incomes just above the family credit threshold. The remaining 7 per cent appeared to be eligible non-claimants.

As we consider time spans closer and closer to the date of fieldwork, the tendency for families receiving family credit at that time still to be recipients gradually increases. For those receiving family credit in April to July 1989, 52 per cent were still on family credit when interviewed. Going forward to the same few months the following year yields a figure of 60 per cent.

Of current recipients of family credit, 17 per cent had been receiving this benefit continuously since April 1988. Among former recipients of family income supplement, a rather higher proportion, 40 per cent, had received family credit continuously since then. This is rather lower than was found by the NAO survey, but both figures indicate that there is a hard core of claimants who remain on family credit for a lengthy period of time. However, the group of families who received FIS and have received family credit continuously is down to 12 per cent of all family credit recipients.

The effect of rejection

Taking a job in the hope of receiving additional income from family credit may involve an act of faith. Many will be unsure of the amount of their entitlement, or even whether they will be eligible at all. They may also expect the continued receipt of certain benefits in kind. To take paid work, and then be rejected for family credit, may be an unsettling experience. It may also act as a deterrent to a further claim even if circumstances change for the worse. We found, in Chapter 4, that this was the experience of some eligible non-claimants of family credit.

Just as receipt of family credit is fairly common in this section of the income distribution, so is rejection. This corresponds with evidence from administrative statistics, where new applicants face a success rate of little better than 50 per cent.

Table 8.3   Receipt and rejection for family credit
(Base: All with complete information)

column percentages

	Have ever received family credit %	Never received family credit %	Total %
Have ever been rejected for FC?			
Yes	18	11	12
No	82	89	88
Total	*100*	*100*	*100*
Base:	877	2587	3464

Within our sample, 877 families had received family credit at some time since April 1988 and about half of them had experienced a refused application. Overall, lone parents were less likely to have experienced rejection than were couples. Only 7 per cent of the lone parents had had an application for family credit refused. This had happened to 17 per cent of the couples.

Table 8.3 shows that there was considerable overlap between the recipients of family credit and those who had encountered a rejection. Eighteen per cent of those who have ever received family credit have also known rejection. Among

Table 8.4   Number of rejections for family credit, where known

column percentages

	All %	Lone parents %	Couples %
None	89	94	87
One	9	4	10
Two or more	2	1	2
Total	*100*	*100*	*100*
Base	421	124	298

those who have not received family credit, 11 per cent have been rejected for family credit since its introduction.

It was unusual, but by no means unknown, for families to have had more than one rejection. As Table 8.4 shows, couples were slightly more persistent in applying and being rejected for a second time. It was very uncommon for a lone parent to face two or more rejections.

The fact of having few rejections does not, in itself, show that there has been a strong deterrent effect to re-applying. It is possible that many of those with few rejections went on to make a successful claim. On the other hand, it may have been some time before a further application was made.

Respondents were asked about the dates of any periods of receipt of family credit, and the dates of any rejections. This enables us to consider what applications were made, if any, following a rejected claim. It also allows us to measure the time that elapsed between a rejection and a subsequent claim, where any had been made.

As we mentioned above, 426 families had been rejected for family credit since its introduction. Of these, 73 per cent had not applied again since. 19 per cent had gone on to make a successful application. 7 per cent had tried again, unsuccessfully.

Only a very small number of families were rejected twice or more. Of this group, three-quarters have yet to trouble family credit branch since, although the remainder who did re-apply experienced a balanced mix of success and rejection.

Of those who re-applied for family credit after a first rejection (there are less than 100 of these cases) the median time that elapsed to the next application was 35 weeks. This may be interpreted in rather different ways. It may be taken as an indication that even for those bold enough to re-apply after a rejection, it takes almost nine months before they will re-apply. An alternative is that such a time span allows circumstances to change - for children to become older, for scale rates to increase, or for incomes to fall - and therefore represents quite rational behaviour by claimants.

Where do ex-claimants go?

There are three main methods by which a family eligible to receive family credit may cease to be so.

First, dependent children may grow older, so that the family is no longer eligible for any benefits for families with children. This ageing process will have important effects on the changing stock of family credit recipients. If we assume that the age of recipients' youngest child varies uniformly between one and 17 years', then about 6 per cent of families will stop receiving family credit each year purely because their children grow up. Within four or five years, under such an assumption, getting on for a quarter of families would disappear from the eligible population. At the same time, a group of those with new families would then become eligible. We see only the recent arrivals in our sample.

Families may also cease to be eligible for family credit if their income increases. If workers move to higher paid jobs, or have a sufficiently large pay increase, or (within couples) a second adult goes out to work, then income may increase sufficiently to move the family out of range of family credit. For lone parents (re-) marriage may have the same effect.

The third method of leaving family credit eligibility is ceasing to have a full-time worker. This could mean that a full-time worker loses his or her job (and the vast majority of the eligible population has only one worker) or moves on to shorter hours.

Fourth, most rarely, a family might remain eligible, but simply stop claiming. However surprising, some of our current eligible non-claimants were found in chapter 5 to be in this position.

We may be interested in the first type of flow. We do not know much about the incomes and well-being of former family credit recipients whose children have grown up. However, given the objectives of this study and the survey design, it is the balance between the second and third routes that is at issue.

Most of the analysis in this report relates to the interview survey with low income families. This does not provide the whole picture of the employment and income destinations of former recipients of family credit. However, the postal sift used to find the sample did identify ex-claimants. This enables us to consider how far ex-claimants go on to higher incomes, or instead move back to income support.

Table 8.5 divides the sift sample of over 8000 families into those who have had experience of claiming family credit since 1988 and those who have not. Some of the latter will have had some experience of FIS before 1988, but that was not asked. Of those with any experience of FC, 43 per cent of lone parents and 36 per cent of couples were currently receiving it. Although lone parents, consistent with earlier findings, persist as customers more than couples do, they fare worse if they stop claiming. Fewer than a third have jobs and nearly all the rest (64 per cent) go onto (usually back onto) income support. It is fair to ask: where else would they go? There may be a few among couples reporting experience of family credit that was actually gained as a lone parent, and who has now been joined by a new partner, but not many.

Table 8.5 The income and employment destinations of ex-recipients of family credit and others

column percentages

	Received family credit during the last three years?							
	Yes				No			
	Lone parent		Couple		Lone parent		Couple	
	%		%		%		%	
Still receiving family credit?								
Yes	43		36					
No	57		64					
Total	*100*		*100*					
Among those no longer on FC								
Out of work & on IS	64		28		72		7	
Not on IS	6		6		10		5	
a) Eligible non-claimant	18	58	22	32	4	21	6	7
b) Moderate income	10	32	17	26	5	25	9	9
c) Average income	3	10	23	34	8	45	36	41
d) High income	0	0	7	8	1	8	37	42
Total	*100*	*100*	*100*	*100*	*100*	*100*	*100*	*100*

a) Apparently ENC according to the sift, half were found by the interviewers to be ineligible
b) 1-25 per cent above Family Credit threshold
c) 25 per cent-100 per cent
d) Over 200 per cent

Far fewer couples leave family credit for income support (28 per cent) though this is four times the proportion of IS claimants among couples who have no experience of FC.

Among those who have jobs, their chances of earnings that will take them clear of what we have called 'moderate incomes' (more than 25 per cent above their FC thresholds) are influenced jointly by their experience of FC and their family composition. The great majority of couples who have no experience of family credit seem unlikely to have needed any: two-thirds of the whole group have at least average incomes, a third have more. Fewer couples with prior experience of FC achieve those wage levels, but 23 per cent of them reach average incomes (between 25 per cent and 100 per cent more than their FC thresholds) and 7 per cent higher income levels. It is this access to higher incomes that really divides ex-claimant and never-claimant couples, by a factor of more than 1 to 5. Among couples, the key to these higher earnings is dual earnings (Table 8.6). Among recipient couples, only 4 per cent have two full-time workers. This rises

Table 8.6   **Percentage of dual-earner couples, by prior experience of FC**

cell percentages

	Received family credit in the last three years?	
	Yes	No
Still receiving family credit	4%	NA
Among those no longer on FC:		
Out of work and on IS	1%	1%
Not on IS	11%	14%
Eligible non-claimant	22%	16%
Moderate income	50%	35%
Average income	76%	62%
Higher income	85%	77%

to 22 per cent among the *sift ENCs,* jumps to half of moderate income families and goes on rising so that most ex-claimants who break the low income barrier do so through dual earnings. A similar rise is observable among couples with no experience of FC, but one less steep, allowing for the presence of some very high income one-earner couples. The number of earners in a family is becoming, together with housing tenure, more and more the most important indicator of family living standards.

Given the pre-eminence of dual earnings in carrying couples up the income distribution ladder, especially among ex-recipients of FC, it follows that access to such income is denied to most working lone parents, but, for them, regardless of their experience of family credit. Almost none exceed average levels of income and relatively few get into average levels.

Comparison with couples is complicated by the huge numbers of lone parents out of work. Indeed, only 18 per cent of lone parents without experience of FC had a job of any kind. The summary given in Table 8.7 considers only those ex-recipients of family credit who had jobs, and looks solely at the proportion

Table 8.7   **Proportion of respondents who exceed the low income line of 125 per cent of FC threshold, by earlier experience of FC**

column percentages

	Some earlier experience of FC		No earlier experience of FC	
	Lone parent %	Couple %	Lone parent %	Couple %
Low income	90	58	47	16
Higher income	10	42	53	84
Total	*100*	*100*	*100*	*100*

Table 8.8   The characteristics of ex-recipients of family credit, by present status

row percentages

		Out of work	Eligible non-claimants	Moderate income	(Base) = 100%
Lone parents	%	80	10	10	(203)
Couples	%	43	36	20	(289)
All	%	58	26	16	(492)
Owner occupiers:					
Lone parents	%	54	19	26	(92)
Couples	%	23	26	51	(97)
Social tenants:					
Lone parents	%	89	7	4	(131)
Couples	%	54	17	29	(172)
Youngest child is:					
0-4 Lone parents	%	93	4	2	(62)
Couples	%	49	20	31	(181)
5-10 Lone parents	%	77	7	15	(90)
Couples	%	38	26	36	(79)
11-17 Lone parents	%	65	26	9	(38)
Couples	%	21	7	72	(29)

whose incomes remain below, or exceed the definition of low income set by the survey: more than 25 per cent above the family's own FC threshold.

Among couple ex-recipients *who have avoided unemployment,* it is interesting to see how nearly half do break into the higher levels of income, even though, as noted above, few get past middling levels. This though is still half the rate of couples with no experience of FC. Among the many fewer lone parent ex-recipients who avoided unemployment, their chances of breaking the low income line are 1 in 10. Those with no experience of FC have an evens chance of getting higher incomes, rather like the couples who *do* have prior experience of FC. On the other hand, it is worth noting now that having what we have called a moderate income need not imply a very low standard of living, as the next chapter shows.

Table 8.8 uses the interview survey to look more closely at the composition of ex-family credit recipients. The fourth exit noted above, however improbable, does occur: 10 per cent of the low income, ex-recipient lone parents became ENCs, and no fewer than 36 per cent of the couples did so.

The abiding influence of housing tenure is also visible in the destinations of low income ex-recipients, with social tenants twice as likely to end up on IS as owner occupiers, to the extent that social tenant lone parents are four times more likely to end up on IS compared to owner occupier couples. It is important to remember that the majority of current recipients of FC are social tenants and only a third are owner occupiers. Yet half of the ex-recipient families, couples and lone parents together, who have made it into the moderate income group are owner occupiers, compared with only 17 per cent among the ex-recipients who ended up on IS.

The table also re-emphasises that, even among low income families, lone parent ex-recipients are twice as likely to end up back on income support as are couples. The lone parents with pre-school children almost all go onto IS, but still two-thirds of those with only secondary school children do so. On the other hand, the majority of the (relatively few) ex-recipient lone parents who went on into the moderate income band also have children below secondary school age. This must count strongly in favour of family credit in relaunching them into paid employment and then on into improved earnings.

Parachute claimants

All this discussion about incentives, almost by the very nature of the word, assumes that we are talking about the pace of forward or upward progress: away from benefits, onward and upward to work and more income.

We have found evidence that family credit does work this way, though for many claimant families the journey through the poverty trap is not a comfortable one and real progress is not made until the big leap forward: becoming a two full-time worker family. This is not common among low income families until the youngest child goes to secondary school.

We have so far overlooked the possibility that some families are really going in the other direction. Relatively few wives of unemployed men, especially those with dependent children, have paid jobs. For what little most of them can earn and the smallness of the earnings disregard, it is just not worth it. But what happens when a two earner family loses the main earner's job? In most cases this means that he has lost his job and she is left in full-time work that does not pay very well. Suddenly they are a low income family falling towards unemployment and income support, because they are now in the position that their out of work benefits would exceed what she is earning. If he does not get a job soon, she will have to give up work, perversely, to increase the family's income. The temptation will be for her to hang on in work and hope for the best. She will have many other good reasons for wanting to keep her job.

If she has only a part time job, then she probably has little choice but to give up, or accept the fact that she is working for no return. But if she works 24 hours or more, or now 16 hours, there is an alternative: to claim family credit on the strength of *her* income. This offers a number of advantages: more money than income support or unemployment benefit, preservation of her job now and for the future, and the opportunity of a possible bonus that if he gets a job after all following an award of family credit, they will enjoy a few months of enhanced income. It anyway widens his short-term job opportunities because he knows that she will remain in work. An offer of low money now, more if it works out well, can be accepted without threat of hardship.

In this way, family credit can arrest the fall of a family from the relative comfort of dual earnings, like opening a parachute at the time when the descent into dual unemployment looks unavoidable. Even part time working women might have the opportunity to increase their hours over the 23 hours ceiling, and now it will be even easier to get above the new 15 hours ceiling, and so stay in work.

Is there any evidence from this study that this kind of thing is happening? We found two parent families on family credit whose claim was based solely on the female partner's full-time job. In fact we found a few more of them than the DSS statistic of 16 per cent. The proportion among the 657 claimant couples interviewed was 19 per cent. Half of these female claimants had male partners who were unemployed and looking for work, others were in full-time education, unwell, or just looking after the home. A third had the additional good fortune of a partner in full-time work, so they were either recent lone parent claimants who had lately found a partner, or more likely they have benefited from the six month rule and continue to receive FC even though he has got a new job. These are the ineligible recipients we had to take out of our take-up equation in Chapter 4.

Those female worker-claimants whose male partners are out of work are made up of two groups: the majority who say that the male partner's unemployment was recent (within the last year or so), and a minority whose partner either had never worked, some by reason of disability, or had been unemployed a long time, some more than ten years. Unemployed male partners were most likely to have lost their job to redundancy or the end of a fixed term job.

Thus, we do have some evidence of 'parachute claiming'. Probably fewer than 12 per cent of two parent families on FC, or no more than 6 or 7 per cent of all claims found in this March-June 1991 sample were prompted in this way. But, as unemployment figures have risen steadily over the past two years, it is likely to have become more frequent.

It has probably kept a significant number of two parent families from falling out of the labour market in pairs. It is an interesting inverted view of benefits and work incentives, and one that may be set to become more common.

9   What difference does it make?

The policy aim of family credit is to ensure that families with dependent children are better off working full-time - in terms of total income - than they would be if they were without work and receiving benefits. For this reason, the amount of family credit a family may receive owes more to arithmetic than to any assessment of need among working families.

But family credit ought to make a difference to families' living standards. If income support is sufficient, and no test of sufficiency is attempted here, then family credit is more. The amounts of family credit are geared to the income-support-plus calculation and are not what officials might judge to be the expenditure requirements of families. This is why lone parents have some built-in advantage in the way family credit is calculated since, unlike IS, the adult allowance is the same for a one- or a two-adult benefit unit. For lone parents, it ought to make more of a difference, even though they receive a premium added to their income support when out of work.

There ought to a measurable difference in the *relative* material well-being of recipients of family credit compared with those without work and compared with the eligible non-claimants. Family credit families should be relatively better off than similar families on income support, relatively better off than the eligible non-claimants, but relatively worse off than the moderate income families.

Since this amounts to asking whether families who have more income are materially better off than those who have less, it may not seem an urgent question. But, within a population made up entirely of low income families, there are some important factors at work that are not obvious. To take the simplest example: those who move from income support into full-time work can face set-up costs like new clothes, tools, and so on and then pay travel costs, typically perhaps of £5 to £10 a week. They might even have to invest in a car to get to work. They may face childcare costs, though these are more likely to fall upon lone parents. They may also face the re-activation of debts frozen during a period of unemployment, such as rent or mortgage arrears.

This kind of problem will transform an apparent financial gain into a renewed struggle to balance the family budget for many months to come, especially if a claim for family credit proves difficult to process and payments are delayed. Also, any support received from relatives during unemployment may cease on resumption of work. They will lose help with housing costs, school meals and similar 'passport benefits' that come with income support. This will reduce their ability to maintain material standards despite their new income.

Factors such as these, both in a family's own experience and in the reported experience of other families known to them, can also have important effects on incentives to work or to claim benefit. This chapter will examine differences in relative material well-being between different kinds of family.

Measuring relative material well-being

This analysis of relative material well-being is based on a set of indicators:

- the possession of property, investments or savings
- the extent of debt, especially 'problem debt' causing arrears
- the purchase of 'essentials': food, clothes, basic leisure, etc
- the ownership of consumer durables
- perceived hardship: the extent of hardship people say they experience.

Another important aspect of well-being is housing, its type and quality. But housing lies on a somewhat different dimension to the 'money and consumption' aspects that are shared in common by the indicators described above and it is these we will look at first.

Savings

Savings and investments are important measures in this survey because savings exceeding £3,000 reduce the amounts of family credit that may be received by claimants; savings of more than £8,000 reduce entitlement to nil. About 5 per cent of families placed in the 'moderate income' category had savings of over £8,000 but had earned incomes and family circumstances that would otherwise have entitled them to receive family credit, or had savings between £3,000 and £8,000 that took their otherwise small entitlements over their family credit thresholds. Even savings held in children's names can be important because, while not discounted against overall entitlement, children's savings or trust funds over £3,000 count against the amounts of family credit that may be received for that particular child.

For these reasons, questions about savings and investments took up quite a lot of space in the questionnaire. In contrast, they took up little time in the average interview. Seven out of ten low income families had no savings or investments of any kind. Those who did, had little. Only 13 per cent of the sample had savings of more than £250, most of the rest had less than £100 put by. A small number of the out-of-work families were found to have savings of several thousand pounds, which went some way towards explaining why some of them did not receive income support.

All respondents were asked to say whether their savings had increased or decreased during the past six months. About half reported no change which, for most of them meant that they have nothing now and had nothing six months ago.

It is fair to say that some of our respondents got a little impatient with their interviewer at this point - in just the same way that Corden (1991) reports that claimants sometimes get exasperated when filling in family credit claim forms. Though, to be fair, we were going much further than DSS claim forms which do not ask for details of savings of less than £2,500.

Just over a third of all respondents said that their savings had fallen over the previous six months while the remaining one in ten families said that they thought they now had more than six months ago.

Of those whose savings had changed, for better or worse, only about half could discuss their recent fortunes in any detail. Asked to say how much they had six months ago, half said they could not guess amounts or were unwilling to try. This left too few gainers for analysis. Among the losers, there was a sharp division between about half of them who had used up less than £500, most usually between £100 and £300, and those who had used up considerable amounts, half of these using up more than £2,000.

Following the family credit claim format, questions were also included about money saved or held in trust under children's names. Some families wryly asked if these questions were a joke in poor taste. Nevertheless, a perhaps surprisingly large number of such accounts were reported, though may have been created by relatives, typically grandparents perhaps. Overall a quarter of all low income families had money put by for their children.

Debt

Debt is defined, as it is in the recent Policy Studies Institute report on the subject by Berthoud and Kempson, as unmanageable repayments on loans and advances. Credit is the money people borrow, whereas debts are payment commitments *which are causing financial problems*. Questions were asked about mortgage and rent arrears, problems with paying household bills, getting behind on consumer credit (hire purchase, credit cards, catalogues) problems with overdrafts, money lenders and private loans and so on.

The PSI report (Berthoud and Kempson, 1992) found that the risk of debt was concentrated in low income families with dependent children. Debt was rare among households of retired people and among better-off families, but the majority of families with incomes of less than £150 a week (in 1989) faced debt as a normal aspect of their budgeting. Larger families had more and larger debts. The younger low income families who had several credit commitments, and who placed a low priority on keeping payments right up-to-date, shared an average burden of 1.5 debts per household, seven times the national average.

Rent arrears were common and the widespread use of consumer credit through cash advances from financial services and through catalogue sales was associated with many of the problem debts. Such problems, measured for example by the incidence of repossession actions, have been increasing sharply since 1989 and a special interest was taken in this survey of low income families in the extent of debt in 1991.

Housing debt

Mortgage arrears

In this sample, mortgage arrears among those buying their own homes were more common than the national estimated average of about 3 per cent being 6 months behind. Overall, 15 per cent of buyers were getting behind with their repayments. Mortgage arrears were far more common among the relatively few lone parents who were buying their homes (25 per cent 'getting behind') compared with couples (10 per cent) and as many as a third of lone parents buyers who were presently out of work had arrears.

Where mortgage arrears had built up, some amounts had grown considerably. Four out of ten families with mortgage arrears owed more than £1,000, half of these owed more than £2,000. Some of these amounts, owed of course by only a very few families, seem nonetheless to have grown well beyond the levels when lenders step in with repossession orders. It may be that this is what was happening and the family was riding out the last months of negotiations before having to depart.

Generally speaking, families are reluctant to allow mortgage repayments to slide into arrears to any significant extent because the amounts, averaging £200 a month, will quickly build up and be difficult to deal with. The threat of repossession is real and, at the time of the survey, was becoming topical: the Council for Mortgage Lenders' provisional figures for 1991 counted 75,000 repossessions. Among renters, in contrast, arrears of rent were far more common. At least they were common among social tenants; almost none of the smaller number of tenants of private landlords had arrears.

Rent arrears

Most of the social tenants were in local authority accommodation; more than a third of them had arrears of rent (37 per cent of the couples, 34 per cent of lone parents). In contrast, almost none of the private sector tenants had any rent arrears.

The median amounts owed by local authority tenants were just over £100. About one in ten families in debt owed more than £200 or about six weeks rent for those without housing benefit, far more for those receiving it.

Taken as a whole, these figures for rent arrears paint a strange picture. It seems not too fanciful to suggest that many low income families use their local authority housing department as a kind of reluctant bank that provides interest-free loans. Deferral of rent is the most efficient and reliable way to come by extra cash in a difficult week. No-one in a gabardine mackintosh any longer comes weekly to the door to argue or embarrass. This degree of volition in the manner of payment makes deferral very simple and, unlike mortgage arrears, fairly unthreatening. It is unlikely that families with children will be evicted by their council before rent arrears have risen to insupportable levels. The pressure on mortgagees is far greater, as noted above, even though they meet much larger weekly amounts, an average of £50 in repayments compared to £32 in rent, out of very similar incomes.

The position of the family credit families is particularly curious with respect to rent arrears. Actually the majority of them are social tenants, a far larger proportion than any other type of family in work. Half of them have arrears and between them they owe the largest amounts, larger than the out-of-work families in arrears who average about £230 with a lower median of about £100.

This suggests two things:

1. As Anne Corden points out, many of the family credit families who enter the labour market from a position out of work, are taken by surprise by the withdrawal of housing benefit and community charge benefit as earnings increase. It can be a particularly nasty surprise if HB & CCB take time to be cancelled and are suddenly recovered by the local authority as back rent. Only those receiving the larger awards relative to their threshold still get housing and CC benefit and they suddenly find themselves having to budget in a quite different way.

2. Many families may also have been floated off income support and into work on family credit, towing behind them a previously 'frozen' debt of local authority rent arrears. On income support, rent arrears are often allowed to rest at earlier levels while the regular weekly payments are met in full from housing benefit. Now, in work on family credit, they are struggling to pay off these arrears, some of them not very successfully, so they are maintaining the gap in earlier payments while still maintaining the arrangement of not letting the debt grow any larger.

The community charge

The survey was carried out in July and August 1991 which was a period of remaining uncertainty about how local authorities were responding to and coping with the changes introduced by the government at that time. Only two months earlier, community charge notices had to be withdrawn and re-issued. Some of our respondents remained quite uncertain about how much they would have to pay during that year. Others, about 6 per cent of the sample overall, had applications for community charge benefit pending.

All this likely confusion aside, it was still quite a surprise to be told by 43 per cent of the whole sample, including the moderate income families, that they were 'behind' with their community charge payments. Doubt as to whether these were mostly reports of families still making up their minds exactly what they ought to pay this year are raised by the average amounts owed: £190 for each family who said they were behind with their payments.

Household bills

Apart from rent, the most common household bill to cause problems was also housing related: 13 per cent were behind on their water rates. Problems with fuel debts were reported by a minority of families: 8 per cent were behind with electricity bills and more, 12 per cent , had problems with gas bills. Fuel debts were most common among the out-of-work lone parents: 12 per cent had problems with electricity bills, 16 per cent with gas bills.

Other kinds of household bill seemed for the most part well in hand in the sample as a whole. Fewer than 5 per cent had problems meeting their telephone bill (though seven out of ten families have a telephone), insurance premiums, television or video rental charges, or in making prompt repayments on their hire purchase or similar undertakings.

Although only a minority of the sample had problems with household debts, the amounts involved were often large, especially considering the levels of family income typical among those in debt. For example, the average gas and electricity arrears were both over £140. Amounts of water rates were also well over £100, on average, and overdue telephone bills averaged nearly £150. The 5 per cent of the sample having problems with hire purchase agreements were, on average, nearly £200 behind on their schedule of payments.

Set against total family net incomes that average £185 for the sample as a whole, and more like £150 for those families most likely to have problem debts, the term 'problem debt' is not lightly used.

Problems with credit accounts

As Berthoud and Kempson point out, credit is what people want, debt is what they hope to avoid. A neatly inverted glimpse of the relative financial position of our different kinds of family in this study is provided by their use of credit cards and store cards.

Among the moderate income families, 39 per cent of couples and 45 per cent of lone parents have active accounts on charge and credit cards. Among the eligible non-claimants, these figures are 36 per cent and 26 per cent respectively. Among the family credit families, only 17 per cent have such accounts and only about one in ten of the out-of-work families have, or, more likely, are allowed to have charge or credit cards.

Again as Berthoud and Kempson found, profligacy with credit cards is not a major cause of debt, even here among a sample of low income families. Only 4 per cent report difficulties with meeting the repayments asked of them, though of course the minimum payment required on an outstanding account is quite small relative to the principal, even though interest rates are high. Again, though rare, amounts of such debts can be large: average arrears (not the principal) amount to over £250 and the median amount is £150.

This impression of well regulated credit use is disturbed a little by the answers given to the question: 'Have you ever had a card like one of these and given it up or had it withdrawn?' Overall, 14 per cent said that they had, though this may also be linked to the introduction of annual charges by Access and Barclaycard.

The figures may reflect the quickness of the credit card organisations in restricting problem debt. Those with modest incomes (and families) who are prone to fall behind with repayments quickly lose their cards. Those with the lowest incomes (and families) are not given cards.

Financial services and personal loans

Among these low income families, credit and loans were more readily sought and obtained from traditional sources: from banks, and finance companies, from less formal sources like 'tally men', friends and relatives, and, among those on income support, from the social fund at the local DSS office. Loans and advances from one or more of these sources were current in the budgets of 44 per cent of families overall.

Again, credit from commercial sources was more readily given to those more likely to be able to afford the repayments. Overall 12 per cent of families had bank overdrafts, 8 per cent fixed term bank loans and 8 per cent finance company loans but these figures were much higher among the moderate income families.

Only small numbers of families had turned to money lenders or a 'tally man' for current loans: about 2 per cent overall though 5 per cent of the out of work couples had done so. Friends and relatives were the main source of informal advances: 15 per cent overall owed money to friends and relatives. The friends and relatives of lone parents were called upon in this way more often (18 per cent) than those of couples (12 per cent).

Among the 44 per cent of all families who ran loans of these kinds, about one in seven said they were having difficulties in keeping up the repayments due to lenders and were 'getting behind'. The meaning of 'getting behind' in some of these areas of problem debt, for example in debts to friends, or the use of an overdraft, is less clear compared with the more formal arrangements of a fixed term loan. In a different way, some customers of the DSS social fund maintain a recurring cycle of loans that keep them at the maximum advance and constant deduction level, so that it is difficult to say they are 'getting behind'; they are just permanently 'behind' and so are not really in debt according to our definition. Difficulties with loans of these kinds occurred in all kinds of family, but most often among out-of-work lone parents (21 per cent of those with such loans).

The amounts of arrears on these loans were often very large, so much so that it seems possible that some respondents quoted the outstanding principal, despite the care of the question, which asked:'How much do you now owe on these *overdue* payments?' (Emphasis in the original.) The average arrears were said to be nearly £600, though the median was far smaller, at about £100. Among the largest group of such debtors, the out of work lone parents, an average of over £600 was reported because about one in ten of them quoted very large four figure sums. The median amount was only £60, which is the sort of figure typically obtained from relatives or from the DSS social fund and which, for them, no present means was available to repay.

The total of debt

Even without considering the community charge, whose status as a debt remained ambiguous at the time of the survey, 39 per cent of the sample as a whole had one kind of problem debt or another to deal with. Exactly a third of couples had problem debts, 44 per cent of the lone parents did so. This difference is mainly a function of the much larger numbers of out of work lone parent families compared to out of work couples.

In terms of numbers - which is almost certainly an under-enumeration of the likely total of debts - the average number of problem debts among families who have any is 1.8. Like Berthoud and Kempson, this survey too has detected the problem of multiple debt in low income families, even with a much reduced count.

In terms of the amounts, couples and lone parents report similar levels of arrears: an average of £640 and £700, and median values of £200 and £195 respectively.

Domestic welfare: buying essentials

Domestic welfare is reflected in families' ability to pay for things that most people would agree are among what Robert Tressell's decorator philosopher called 'the necessaries of life'. Key indicators among these are regular and nourishing food, adequate clothing and footwear, being able to pay the costs of basic social activities and celebration, and increasingly nowadays, the possession of a range of consumer durables. Twenty-four items of these kinds were included in the questionnaire and respondents were asked whether, for example, they had fresh fruit available most days, a weatherproof coat for each child, a television, and so on. Those who had not were asked, for each item foregone, whether they did not want them or whether they could not afford them.

These are all measures that are known from other studies, for example the OPCS study of living standards in unemployment (Heady and Smyth 1989), and the two 'Poor Britain' surveys (Mack and Lansley 1985, 1992) to be important indicators of relative material well-being.

Examples of 'basic' expenditure were divided into three types of item: food (6 items), clothes (also 6 items) and minimum leisure spending (3 items). A list of the most commonly owned consumer durables was also included (11 items). The average numbers of these kinds of items found beyond their means were 0.7 food items, 1.7 clothes and leisure items, and 2.3 consumer durables.

Item by item, minorities of families said they did not have them because they could not afford them. These minorities were smallest for the food items: almost everyone got a cooked meal every day and no more than 10 per cent to 15 per cent forewent any other item because they could not afford them. More difficulty was encountered in keeping everyone in the family warmly clothed and soundly shod, especially the adults. A quarter were without a second pair of shoes for the children, a third could not have new, rather than second hand clothes when they were needed. Another quarter had no spare money for trips or holidays.

Consumer durables showed a wider range of ownership. Almost everyone had a colour TV, fridge and washing machine; about a fifth could not afford deep freezes, telephones, or central heating; a third could not afford a tumble drier; four out of ten families could not afford a dishwasher (few actually have one, by choice) or a car.

Respondents were also asked whether there were any other things that they needed to buy at the moment but they '...really cannot find the money for.' The question was in two parts: first, things for the children; second, things for themselves. Those who said that there were things they needed but could not buy, were asked to say, in their own words, what these needs were.

Forty three per cent of all families said that they had no pressing needs of this kind at the moment while the remainder divided evenly between 29 per cent who needed things for either themselves or the children (usually the children) and 27 per cent who needed things for both children and adults.

Most of these things, especially for children, were clothing, footwear, and schoolwear. Others could not afford new bedding, highchairs and similar equipment. Relatively few mentioned leisure items like sports equipment, toys or money for outings. The adults' needs were similarly dominated by clothes and footwear but also included household items like bedding, furniture, carpets and curtains, home improvements and repairs or replacements for electrical equipment. Only 6 per cent said they were in want of a car, 8 per cent of a holiday. This does not mean that, for example, 92 per cent got all the holidays they needed. It means that 8 per cent said they really needed a holiday and could not afford one. In total, the average number of needs mentioned was three.

Of a possible total of 28 items foregone because they could not afford them, the average score was 5.8. This average was significantly higher among lone parents (7.1) compared with couples (4.7). But this again was due to the much larger proportion of lone parents who were out of work, who forewent an average of 7.7 items, while out of work couples fared only a little better (6.9)

Perceived material well-being
Subjective measures of well-being are also important since they reflect the family's recent financial experiences. Respondents were asked to judge for themselves how well or ill they were managing on their money, whether they worried about their position, whether it was changing for better or worse, and so on. The point of such measures is not that, of themselves, they allow a lighter view of circumstances that seem otherwise grim, but that they are likely to reflect, in some cases, financial advantages or disadvantages that are not measured elsewhere in the interview.

Families were asked to judge how well they felt they were managing on their money nowadays; how often they found themselves worrying about money; whether or not they felt their situation had become worse or better during the previous six months; and how optimistic they felt about their immediate future: would things get better or worse, or just go on as they are?

Anxiety about money matters was widespread. Nearly half said they worried about money 'almost all the time' and a further fifth, quite often. Though it is fair to add that quite well off people worry about money too. In fact, most families were willing to give themselves the benefit of financial doubt; 45 per cent conceded that they were '...getting by alright' - a phrase used spontaneously by many in open-ended pilot interviews - while 19 per cent felt they were managing '...quite well' and 5 per cent thought they managed '...very well'. At the other end of the scale, 31 per cent felt they were in difficulties of one degree or another: 7 per cent felt they just '...did not manage very well'; 19 per cent had '...some difficulties'; and only 5 per cent thought they were '...in serious financial trouble'.

Financial anxiety was not confined to those with debts though it was clearly increased by debt. Those who worried about money '...almost all the time' were almost four times more likely to have problem debts compared with those who, more rarely, said they never worried about money (54 per cent versus 14 per cent). The proportion who said they had problem debts to deal with rose steeply as people's assessment of their position grew more gloomy from 6 per cent among those who were managing well, to 15 per cent of those managing 'quite well', 30 per cent of those 'getting by', 53 per cent of those 'not managing well', 75 per cent of those with some difficulties, to 89 per cent among those who, not without justice, said they were in deep financial trouble. The average amounts owed by those with problem debts rose in the same sequence from a few pounds to an average of nearly £1800 among those who said they were in trouble. Among low income families, if you are 'managing well', you are meeting your bills and are not getting behind on any repayments.

A little more than half the sample felt their situation was unchanged compared to 6 months ago, just over a third thought things had got worse, and only 12 per cent had seen any improvement. Half of those for whom things had got worse said they were having to manage on less money; about a third needed to buy more, and the remaining 18 per cent said they have both less cash and greater needs. The minority seeing improvements cited more money as the main reason, rather than reduced commitments.

With respect to the future, only a minority (16 per cent) expected things to get worse, nearly half (44 per cent) expected to continue much in the same way while 40 per cent said they expected improvements.

This then is the pattern of well-being, or otherwise, among our population of low income families. How does this pattern differ among our four types of family?

The location of financial and material stress
To achieve some clarity in comparing the relative material well-being of different types of family, we need to use summary measures of well-being. In the preceding section, the answers to over 70 questions were considered. Table 9.1 reduces these 70 to one combined indicator. A brief word first about the rationale for doing this.

The idea of a combined indicator of financial and material stress relies on the commonsense idea that things add up and, as people say, start to get on top of you. A family can cope well enough without savings, or with getting behind with a few small bills, or putting off buying shoes, or just going without things they know other families have, without their anxiety levels rising to insupportable levels. Taken one at a time, benefit level incomes can be managed to cope with any one of these kinds of problems, perhaps two kinds, for a while. Three kinds of problems, say, more than one problem debt, children needing new shoes, coats and other items that the family cannot afford, and hardship moves on to a different level. So, as well as providing the convenience of a single measure, there should be a 'scaling effect': the combination of *several different but related* aspects of a single underlying dimension, like well-being, provides a sharper distinction between families in differing circumstances.

A seven point index (lowest = 0, highest = 6 of relative financial and material stress was constructed, adding one point for each 'yes' answer to the following questions:

Does the family have:
1. Two or more problem debts?
2. Two or more items on the food list scored 'unable to afford'?
3. Three or more items on the clothing and leisure lists scored 'unable to afford'?
4. Four or more items on the consumer durables list 'scored unable to afford'?
5. Additional unmet need spontaneously listed for *both* the children and for the adults in the family?
6. *Both* the financial anxiety measures scored at the highest point ('Always worried about money' *and* 'In deep financial trouble')?

This scale ignores community charge arrears, overlooks entirely the amount of debts, does not count, in some cases, up to six items of basic expenditure scored 'unable to afford', disregards spontaneously-cited unmet need for adults if children's cited needs are met, ignores those who worry constantly about money unless they (only 4 per cent overall) *also* say they are in real trouble, and disregards the lack of any savings. This means that to get any kind of score on this scale means to experience some hardship. But, as the last few pages have shown, such difficulties are not that uncommon among low income families. So the scale is designed to pinpoint severe hardship. This is because severe hardship, at these levels, is the target of social security benefits. This is what it is hoped to avoid. Its successful avoidance is the keenest measure of the *relative* effects of being without work and on benefits, being in work and on benefits, and being in work without benefits.

Table 9.1 provides this comparison and draws attention to a rule of thumb measure of severe hardship: the proportion scoring 3 or more on the 7 point scale.

Table 9.1   Index of relative material hardship, by type of family

column percentages

| Number of problems | Lone parents | | | | Couples | | | |
	Out of work %	FC Clmt %	ENC %	Mod. Income %	Out of work %	FC Clmt %	ENC %	Mod. Income %
None	30	40	62	63	35	35	59	72
One	22	27	16	17	22	22	19	18
Two	18	17	11	14	19	18	11	6
Three	16	11	6	3	10	11	6	2
Four	9	4	2	1	10	8	4	1
Five	4	2	2	1	3	4	1	*
Six	2	0	0	0	1	1	0	0
Total	*100*							
Average number of problems	1.7	1.2	.8	.7	1.5	1.5	.8	.4
Percentage having three or more problems	30%	16%	11%	6%	24%	24%	11%	4%

Overall, one in five low income families met this definition of severe hardship: scoring three or more on the scale. Our hypothesis was that severe hardship of this kind would be most commonly found among out of work families. Among those in work, the moderate income families should report the least number of problems, the eligible non-claimants ought to report the most, and the family credit families should be somewhere in between.

As Table 9.1 shows, we were only half right:

We were right about the out of work families: they are worst off, especially the lone parents among them, nearly a third of whom reported severe hardship.

We were right about the moderate income families, they were best off with only 1 in 20 of them reporting severe hardship. So the scale 'works' in the sense of sharply discriminating between two groups of families whom we would expect to share differing fortunes.

We were wrong about the eligible non-claimants. They do report more hardship than the moderate income families, but not much more.

We were wrong about the family credit families. They report only a little less hardship than the out of work families; among couples, the same amounts.

Crucially though, we were most wrong about the relative standing of the family credit and eligible non-claimants families: the family credit families were significantly *worse* off than the eligible claimants.

Why? Why are the family credit recipients not further ahead of the out of work families than they are? And why do they lag behind the eligible non-claimants, who ought to be worse off than everyone else in work but who instead look more like the moderate income families?

Perhaps the better question is which kind of family is the one out of line? Are the eligible non-claimants 'too well off' on the well-being index, or are the family credit families 'too badly off' relative to what we should really expect? We expect that because income is related to well-being, and they have different incomes, their well-being will differ accordingly.

Since incomes within groups are so compressed, and since they are partly standardised on size of family in benefit families, it is actually quite difficult to analyse the independent effects of income on welfare within this group. And with the above results, the relation between income and well-being is seriously weakened by the family credit and eligible non-claimants trading places on the well-being scale. Put another way, a population composed only of out of work and moderate income families would show a very strong relationship between income and well-being. But a population composed only of families eligible for family credit would show a *negative* relationship because of the lower incomes and greater well-being of the eligible non-claimants compared with recipients.

Part of the problem may lie in our understanding of the incomes of the eligible non-claimants, for example:

- Some of the non-claimants may have under-reported their true income.
- The non-claimants may have had higher incomes in the past, and this may have put them in a position to ride out a period of low income with relatively little hardship. Economists distinguish between current income and 'trend' or permanent income.
- The non-claimants may have been drawing on resources which are not counted for benefit purposes, nor in the questionnaire (eg from their wider family, their businesses, home produce and so on).
- The non-claimants may have been more skilful than other people at managing on a given income, and avoiding hardship.

Whichever of these hypotheses may be true, the explanation has to include the reason why these families did not claim their benefit. The first hypothesis would explain that easily enough; if respondents understated their income, they may not have been eligible after all and their relative well-being is no longer a mystery. But why should they do this? No-one is going to take a benefit away from them if they let on about hidden income. They do not *have* benefits. And such a theory would also have to take on board the possibility -perhaps a stronger possibility - that claimants understate their income too. They have a better motive for doing so.

This would leave the puzzle back where it was. Why would the two types of family have a consistently different tendency to understate their income? Chapter 4 showed that the income stated by the claimant families in their interview was extremely similar to the income disclosed to the DSS. There is no obvious reason why the eligible non-claimants should have responded differently. They had earlier written down their net earnings on a form that had their name and address on it and sent through the post to a total stranger. This does not advertise them as people with something to hide. And it would be difficult for low income families to forget any significant income inadvertently.

The other three hypotheses would have to explain non-take-up on the basis that people who did not experience hardship did not feel the need to claim. But there was no direct evidence for such an explanation in what we have seen so far in this chapter. For example, the greater differences in items foregone were seen in week to week items like clothes and leisure, and not in ownership of consumer durables. And if they were such good managers, why did they turn away good money?

The first steps towards answering some of these questions will be to check that our assumptions are correct and to control these comparisons for other factors that affect well-being: income, tenure, type of employment, housing costs, and so on.

Income, type of work, and well-being

We know already that we are making the right assumptions about income.

The eligible non-claimants have more than the out of work families but they have lower cash incomes than the family credit families, £10 a week lower in the case of lone parents, £36 a week lower in the case of couples which, co-incidentally, is almost exactly the amount of family credit that the average FC couple got in 1991. So why are families who have less money to live on (and higher average housing costs) apparently better off on every aspect of relative material well-being than the family credit couples who have more money and lower housing costs?

The family credit families have, on average, net cash incomes that are much higher than the out of work families: 82 per cent more in the case of lone parents, 49 per cent higher among couples. Though we do know that loss of housing benefit and community charge benefit reduces these advantages down to about £30 a week for lone parents and less than £20 a week for couples. So we can sharpen our second question too: why does an increase in net income not produce corresponding improvements in relative material well-being?

We asked earlier if the eligible non-claimants had income that was not recorded. We have said already that this is unlikely to be cash income because every possible kind of cash income - earnings, benefits, pensions, grants and awards, fostering fees and many more - were all asked about in great detail.

If eligible non-claimants are getting extra help from somewhere, it is more likely to be income in kind or direct cash contributions from relatives, or in the case of the self-employed, from their business. Self-employed families are sometimes able to heat their homes, feed themselves, run their car, and so on, from their business activities. If this is making a difference then it should be visible when the data are analysed separately for people in employed or self-employed work.

On the other hand, the impact of self-employment on these findings is likely to be limited because the proportions who work self-employed are quite similar among both eligible non-claimants and family credit families. The proportions who work as employees are actually identical, but among the family credit families the remainder split into those who work self-employed and those who no longer have their jobs. The latter, about 7 per cent of the family credit families, are families who were working and getting family credit when selected for the survey. They subsequently lost their jobs, though still getting family credit and probably some income support too.

Table 9.2 looks at the proportion experiencing three or more problems among employees, the self-employed and out of work families.

Table 9.2   Proportion scoring three or more on the index of material stress, by type of family and employment status

cell percentages

	Moderate income	Eligible non-clmts	Family credit families
Working full-time:			
Employees	3%	12%	20%
Self-employed	3%	6%	26%

This table answers two questions. First, the apparently better material well-being of the eligible non-claimants is not solely due to there being more self-employed among them, especially more of those kinds of self-employed families who can transfer a lot of their domestic consumption onto their business accounts. Self-employed and employed families have quite similar levels of relative material welfare and this is true within each type of family. Their incomes are quite similar too. The problem is that the differences go the 'wrong' way. Self-employed ENCs are a little better off than employed ENCs. Self-employed family credit families are a little *worse* off than employed family credit families. So among the employees, family credit families are less than twice as likely to be in severe hardship compared to ENCs. But among the self-employed, family credit families are four times more likely to be in severe hardship compared to ENCs.

A sharper comparison between family credit and out of work families can be made by separating the 7 per cent recently unemployed family credit families from the 93 per cent still working, and separating the part-time working families from the genuinely out of work families. Some part-time working families are making a more than tolerable living: they are couples who both work part-time and lone parents who also receive maintenance for their children, and their index scores are correspondingly better than the families who have no work at all. The 7 per cent of family credit families who have lost their jobs, in contrast, already share the much higher levels of material stress commonly found among the out of work families, with more than four out of ten families in more than ordinary difficulties.

This opens up a gap in their relative material well-being between the family credit families and those out of work of about 10 points: 21 per cent compared with 31 per cent scoring three and above. And this is not due solely to differing numbers of lone parents and couples, but, as Table 9.3 shows, the gap is far larger in favour of the lone parent FC recipients over the out of work lone parents. They are half as likely to be in severe hardship. Among the couples the gap is still a mere 4 per cent.

Table 9.3 Relative severe hardship scores (percentage scoring three or more on index) of family credit families still in work, and families who have no paid work at all

		cell percentages
	Working and receiving family credit	really out of work
Couples	24%	28%
Lone parents	15%	33%

Thus we can say now that families working and on family credit are a little less badly off compared to those who are out of work and relying solely on benefits, especially if they are lone parent families. But they still lag behind the eligible non-claimants (11 per cent) and a long way behind the moderate income families (4 per cent).

Housing tenure and well-being

The next factor to introduce into this comparison is housing tenure which we know differs greatly between different kinds of family. Table 9.4 reduces this comparison to its simplest form. It gives the proportion scoring three or more on the hardship index separately for different types of family, further divided by owner occupiers (owners and mortgagees), social tenants (Council and Housing Association) and other kinds of tenure (private renters, living at home, with friends, etc..).

The recently out of work family credit families and the part-time working families have been excluded from Table 9.4. This factor (from Table 9.3), now further controlled for housing tenure, all but closes the gap in relative hardship scores between family credit families and eligible non-claimants, except for a remaining such difference among the minority group of owner occupiers. The effects of tenure on hardship are very strong. Social tenants are twice as likely to be in severe hardship compared with private tenants and three times more

Table 9.4   Proportion scoring three or more on the index of hardship, by family type and tenure, excluding all self-employed and part-time working families and FC families who have lost their jobs

cell percentages

	Moderate income	Eligible non-clmts	Family credit	Out of work	All
Owner occupiers	2%	7%	15%	17%	8%
Social tenants	9%	23%	25%	30%	24%
Private tenants and others	6%	(11%)	10%	15%	11%

likely compared with owner occupiers. Nearly all of the mysterious advantage in well-being held by eligible non-claimants over claimant families is associated with the greater proportion of owner occupation among them. The contrast with moderate income families who are not social tenants is the greatest. Such hardships, or at least such hardships as are measured by the index, are almost unknown among them. And these, remember, are families whose incomes are still below average.

Family size and well-being
Family credit families have more children than other low income families. For example, 37 per cent of them have three or more children compared with 27 per cent of the out of work families:

Table. 9.5   Percentage having three or more children

cell percentages

	Moderate income	Eligible non-clmts	Family credit	Out of work
Couples	30%	40%	48%	36%
Lone parents	8%	16%	14%	24%
All	28%	34%	37%	27%

There are in fact some wide compositional differences between the different types of family, for example: 43 per cent of the moderate income families have the 'model' profile of a couple and two children, among the ENCs, 31 per cent have this form, among the family credit families, 23 per cent, and among the out of work families, only 13 per cent. In contrast, 16 per cent of the out of work families are lone parents with three or more children; among the moderate income families, only 1 per cent.

It is true that families on benefits get more money for more children but the economies of scale seem to work against them rather than for them. Average hardship scores rose sharply in larger families, and rose most sharply among the largest. The very small number of families with six or seven children had a majority of them occupying the higher scores on the hardship index. Interestingly, though, none of this is true of the moderate income families.

Table 9.6 presents a selective comparison between the family credit and the out of work families. Again, only current employees are admitted to the family credit families, and only those with no work at all are admitted to the out of work families.

These employee or genuinely out of work families are then divided into owner occupiers and social tenants, putting aside other tenures. They are further divided between lone parents and couples and finally divided between those having one, two or three or more children. The distribution of family size is shown, together with the average score on the hardship index that is found in each cell.

Table 9.6   **Hardship scores by tenure and by family type, employees and out of work families only**

	Family credit		Out of work	
	Lone parents	Couples	Lone parents	Couples
Owner occupiers				
One child	1.4	.7	1.0	.5
Two	1.0	.9	1.1	1.1
Three or more	1.0	1.2	1.7	.8
Percentage who have three or more children:	14%	54%	31%	35%
(Weighted bases)	(125)	(186)	(177)	(147)
Social tenants				
One child	1.2	1.6	1.6	1.5
Two	1.3	1.7	1.9	1.7
Three or more	1.6	1.6	2.5	2.0
Percentage who have three or more children	20%	48%	25%	42%
(Weighted bases)	(196)	(272)	(796)	(347)

A cell by cell comparison appears to confirm more clearly what has been indicated in the analysis so far: if you are a lone parent, family credit improves your material quality of life (unless, oddly, you are an owner occupier who has only one child). Among owner occupier couples, the larger family credit families are actually worse off than the out of work families. Interestingly, these are the only families who stand a good chance of being worse off in work in cash terms because they lose the mortgage interest payments they get when out of work. Among social tenants, all the lone parents are better off on family credit but the couples are not, unless they have three or more children when there is, on average, some advantage.

These numbers may not seem large, but it should be borne in mind that a score of more than 2.0 implies about half the group in severe hardship, scoring three or more on the scale.

There are really too few eligible non-claimants to break down to this level of comparison, especially the lone parents among them, but among couples the same edge of advantage in relative material well-being lies with the eligible non-claimants over the family credit families, with one qualification: this advantage is much smaller among those with large families.

The advantage of the eligible non-claimants - expressed in apparently maintaining a better material quality of life despite lower incomes - still lies with their base in owner occupation. This is the modern base of advantage among lower income families and contrasts with the deteriorating base of social tenancy. Council accommodation, once described by Mark Abrams in the 1960s as 'The bastions of working class privilege', is now transformed into a large residue of the less desirable properties occupied by people whose rents are paid, one way or another, from public funds.

But why should it? Taken at face value, it does not make any sense. The ENCs *do* have lower incomes than the family credit families and, among the couples, higher housing costs too. Whatever advantage a minority of them may get from self-employment, its effects are very small. The problem may be that we are not looking at them at face value, but at past value. They are predominantly owner occupiers. Families who own or are buying their own homes, however modest many are, are the kinds of family who (like so many of the moderate income families) have in the fairly recent past been able to persuade a building society or a bank to lend them rather a lot of money. They found a deposit from somewhere too. Either they were higher earners then than they are now, or they inherited some money, or they were given some by supportive relatives, typically parents. On average, that was about six years ago. They still have their house and the things they were able to put in it. They probably still have their relatives too.

On the other hand, a fifth of the ENC couples and nearly a third of the ENC lone parents did have experience of receiving family credit in the past. So did similar numbers of out of work families and, even more surprisingly, so did 12 per cent of the moderate income couples and a fifth of the moderate income lone parents. What difference has this made? Table 9.7 investigates this.

Among families not in work, it made little difference: they were a little worse off having been solely on income support compared with those having had a prior spell on family credit. Among all the others, it made a considerable difference. *Both* the eligible non-claimants, and the moderate income families who had had a spell receiving family credit, were distinguished by proportions scoring three or more on the hardship index about three times larger than those who had no experience of family credit. The eligible non-claimants who had had experience of claiming family credit had levels of hardship that were the same as those who get family credit now (a quarter scoring three or more). Among the rest, these levels were low (7 per cent) - almost as low as the moderate income families (4 per cent).

Table 9.7 Percentage reporting three or more problems, by type of family and prior experience of FC

cell percentages

	Ever received family credit?	
	Yes	No
Out of work families	23%	29%
FC recipients	21%	NA
Eligible non-claimants	24%	7%
Moderate income families	11%	4%

Among the *lone parents* presently out of work, the proportion in severe hardship rose from 21 per cent among those with no experience of family credit to 31 per cent among those with any. It did not seem to make any difference how many spells have been spent on family credit, just whether any at all were reported.

You would expect hardship to persist, even to worsen, when a family goes onto IS from FC. But it seems more likely to persist in any new status, even among moderate income families, following a spell on FC, than if the family never claimed FC.

But is it family credit that is doing this, or is it income support?

Table 9.8 looks at hardship by prior experience of IS.

Table 9.8 Percentage reporting three or more problems, by type of family and prior experience of IS

cell percentages

	Ever received income support?	
	Yes	No
Out of work families	31%	9%
FC recipients	25%	17%
Eligible non-claimants	14%	8%
Moderate income families	7%	3%
All	28%	7%

173

Here we see that present FC recipients who have never claimed IS are, on average, somewhat better off than those who have. This again is especially true among lone parents. Elsewhere, we see a similar pattern but with wider differences among out of work and moderate income families, narrower among eligible non-claimants.

Table 9.9 puts past experience of FC and IS together and looks at the proportion reporting three or more problems among those with experience of both, of either, and of neither benefit. Clearly, avoidance of both benefits remains the clearest marker for the absence of hardship.

Table 9.9   **Percentage reporting three or more problems, by type of family, by prior experience of family credit and income support**

cell percentages

	IS, not FC	Both	FC not IS	Neither
Out of work				
Lone parents	33%	24%	—	13%
Couples	30%	25%	—	9%
FC recipients				
Lone parents	-	20%	11%	-
Couples	-	32%	20%	-
Eligible non-claimants				
Lone parents	(————	11%	————)	0%
Couples	11%	19%	21%	7%
Moderate income				
Lone parents	(————	3%	————)	5%
Couples	7%	11%	8%	2%
All families:	30%	23%	15%	5%

Among present recipients and among those who moved ahead into moderate incomes, persisting hardship is significantly more likely to be associated with IS than with FC. This is not true among eligible non-claimants, in fact rather the reverse seems to be true: it is prior experience with FC that is associated with persisting hardship, which may be another clue to why they are eligible non-claimants: apparently, it did not do them much good in the longer run.

The remaining majority of ENCs who have contact with neither benefit, have noticeably few reporting three or more problems: 7 per cent. This can be compared with the corresponding figure among present claimants who have come off IS, and with out of work families who have claimed FC in the past: 24 per cent in each case.

This finding underscores the main conclusion of this chapter. Contact with social security benefits, especially if it is associated, as so often it is, with social tenancy, is a marker for a greater than average chance of experiencing severe hardship. The absence of any contact, even among those receiving (actually or apparently) benefit level incomes, is a marker for lack of severe hardship. This is as true for past contact as it is for present contact. This association is stronger for income support than it is for family credit, unless this association is itself part of the explanation for why they no longer claim family credit.

What difference do they think it makes?

Finally in this chapter we return to our respondents to ask them to judge for themselves what contribution family credit makes or has made to their welfare. Obviously, this is a question that can be asked only of those who have experience of family credit, either receiving it now or having received it at some time since April 1988. As we have just seen above, these are the families in greater relative need and so should be well placed to see the larger differences.

Asked to judge how well they might manage if they were not receiving family credit now, the majority of the present family credit families said either they 'could not manage at all' (55 per cent), or that they could manage only by 'cutting down a lot' (26 per cent). This of course is strongly related to the amounts they received: three-quarters of those who said they could manage with only minor economies received less than £20 a week in family credit and the majority of these, less than £10. They were the family credit families with the highest total incomes or the fewest children or both.

The degree of perceived dependence on family credit is related to the index of relative material well-being. Only 13 per cent of those who could manage well without their awards of family credit scored three or more on the index compared with 41 per cent of those who said that they could not manage at all without it. These latter are the family credit families with the lowest total incomes and the largest families. Even so, nearly half those who said they depended heavily on their family credit, and a third of those who said they could not manage at all, were receiving less than the average amount of about £36 a week.

Those with experience of family credit in the past make the same judgements about its usefulness as those who receive it now, with substantial majorities saying that they could not have managed without it, or could have managed only if they had cut down a lot. Interestingly, this is equally true of those who have moved up into the moderate income group of families as it is of those who went out of the labour market and onto (probably back onto) income support. And it is also true of the eligible non-claimants. One must be cautious about an observation based on 50 families but two-thirds of them said that when they received family credit in the recent past, it made an important or an indispensable contribution to their ability to manage their budget. Which makes one wonder all the more how they are managing now. And the answer, in Table 9.8 above, is not very well, even compared to other ex-recipients of family credit.

Another glimpse of the usefulness of family credit - the difference it actually makes - is what they say they spend it on. When the National Audit Office survey asked recipients whether or not they spent their family credit on anything in particular, only 30 per cent said they did and they tended to name things for the children, especially clothes and shoes. This survey asked them to say in their own words simply what they spent their family credit on. Only a quarter said 'nothing in particular' or gave no reply and these tended to be those who received the smallest amounts. Reversing the NAO finding (and providing a wry lesson in the extent to which question wording can influence data) three-quarters named one, two or sometimes three items.

The largest specific use, named by 4 out of 10 families, was for food, or as many said 'extra food' they would otherwise forego if they did not receive family credit. A quarter named clothes, usually children's clothes and shoes, and a further quarter named a variety of household bills, usually fuel bills. Seven per cent said that they put their family credit directly into debt repayment, usually housing debt while, in contrast, many families with small awards (9 per cent overall) distributed their family credit, or some of it, directly to the children as pocket money.

The proportions using family credit to improve diet, buy clothes and pay fuel bills were the same among the ex-claimants and, again, this was equally true among moderate income, out of work and eligible ex-claimants. Yet we know that nowadays the eligible non-claimants are *less* likely to be going without food, lacking clothes and getting behind with bills compared with present claimants. Nor are those ENC ex-claimants who said that family credit was really important to them when they got it, any worse off now than those who said it did not make much difference.

A last test of the usefulness of family credit was also a simple one: what do people prefer? It is not reasonable to suppose that anyone would prefer to be on family credit rather than be a moderate income family. Nor is it reasonable to ask anyone if they somehow prefer to be an eligible non-claimant. The valid

Table 9.10   Preference for income support or family credit, by families who had experienced both

column percentages

	All %	Out of work %	FC families %	ENCs %	Mod. income %
Prefer FC	61	49	71	70	79
Not sure	12	13	11	16	9
Prefer IS	27	38	18	14	12
Total	*100*				

comparison is with income support. Interviewers first identified families who had experience of both family credit and income support over the past three years. They were then asked 'Taking everything into consideration, what do you think was best for you and your family: living on income support, or working and getting family credit?' Interviewers said that families regarded this question thoughtfully and couples usually reached a unanimous view.

One in ten families, including those receiving family credit, could make no choice and felt there was no real difference between FC or IS. For the rest, the choice went decisively to family credit. Among those still working, five families to one were in favour. This was so even among the ENC former claimants whom we suspect of having had a difficult time. Those out of work were more evenly divided: five to four in favour.

Table 9.11 looks more closely at the key actors in this choice: those who received either benefit and had experience of the other in the past, and does so separately for lone parents and couples. Table 9.11 looks first at the families who were working and currently receiving family credit and who have experience of income support in the past. Among the lone parents, 81 per cent said that family credit was what they preferred. The corresponding figure among couples was 62 per cent. This means that 26 per cent of the family credit couples who were once on IS said that IS is what they really preferred; a further 10 per cent saw nothing to choose between FC and IS. This at least was the view of the respondents, usually the non-working mother. Their partners were a little firmer in their preference for FC: 69 per cent for, 19 per cent against, 12 per cent not sure.

Table 9.11 **Preference for income support or family credit, by families who had experienced both**

column percentages

	Total %	Couples now on IS %	Couples now on FC %	Lone parents now on IS %	Lone parents now on FC %
Prefer FC	61	33	62	60	81
Not sure	12	19	12	9	10
Prefer IS	27	48	26	31	9
Total	*100*				

Table 9.11 also supports the view that family credit is good for lone parents: they like it and, compared with their incomes on income support, well they might. Though this is to say nothing of their relative position compared to what the average family can expect as a standard of living. This also confirms the trend that couples on FC are only marginally better off, despite higher cash incomes, than they were on income support. Two who have children cannot live as cheaply

as a lone parent. Now they have travel costs, housing costs, no free school meals, and other expenses that brings their discretionary spending power down, sometimes perilously close to the former levels on IS with the added insecurities and inconveniences of going to work every day. None of this provides a decisive explanation of why they are not better off than they are. But the legacy of hardships experienced whilst on income support, especially in accumulating debt, undoubtably plays a hidden role. It may act as a drag on improvement under a family credit regime.

Now let us look at those who are now on IS (that is actually receiving IS, not just out of work) and who have experience of family credit in the past. Among the lone parents, still a majority looked back to FC and said that FC was what they preferred compared to being on IS as they are now. But it is a much smaller majority: 58 per cent. Among the couples on IS, the most common view expressed by wives (51 per cent) was that being on IS is what they preferred. Only 33 per cent said they would prefer to return to a working life they once knew on FC. Their partners inclined more towards FC (42 per cent in favour) but still 46 per cent said that they too preferred income support.

What can this mean? Why should a third of the lone parents and half the couples bringing up children on income support who also say they have experience of working and getting family credit, now say that they *prefer* income support to working and getting family credit? Among the lone parents who say this, there are doubtless those who have made a decision to be at home for the children and others who are simply unable to find affordable childcare. But we asked what *was* better, not what might be better. So it seems more possible that it is the memory of these difficulties that is influencing their present view. Among the couples, childcare is not a problem with respect to family credit because as soon as wives take a job they both move a long way out of eligibility anyway. Something else is going on.

Table 9.12 Percentage scoring three or more on index of hardship, by preference for income support or family credit, by families who had experienced both

	Couples now on IS	Couples now on FC	Lone parents now on IS	Lone parents now on FC
Prefer FC	5%	28%	32%	19%
mean	1.3	2.1	1.8	1.3
Prefer IS	51%	38%	18%	23%
mean	2.8	1.6	1.3	1.7

We speculated earlier, that scores on the hardship scale tend more to reflect past income than present. Those who have been on low incomes for a long while tend to wrack up problems of these kinds. Those who have had better incomes in the past still have the welfare residue of better times. We know that half the couples on IS who have had FC in the past now say they prefer IS. Among this half there is a high concentration of families in severe hardship: 51 per cent of them score over three on the scale compared with only 5 per cent of those who prefer FC (Table 9.12). Again, there are only 70 families in this comparison and it must be treated with caution. But it aligns well with the earlier finding that those 7 per cent of family credit families whom we found sliding out of work and back onto IS, also had very high levels of hardship.

This finding is also of some importance. It means there is a small group of families, usually the lowest paid, usually couples, for whom family credit does not work. Equally, there are families for whom family credit does work, usually the better paid, often lone parents. We know that eligible non-claimants of family credit were much rarer among lone parents than among couples, both in numbers and in amounts of cash foregone. This and the previous chapter has shown, among other things, why family credit is more popular with lone parents. On average, it leaves them better off.

10 Summary and conclusions

The important advance when family credit replaced family income supplement in 1988 was the link established between in-work and out of work income-related or 'means-tested' benefits. The link was not entirely closed. The position of low income families who have mortgages and who receive support only when out of work, is the most obvious asymmetry. And the question remained open as to whether means-tested benefits were, ultimately, the best way to help low paid families both get and keep paid work and maintain their living standards. Arguments continued in favour of a more universal approach involving, for example, much higher rates of child benefit or some child related tax credit system.

But by replacing family income supplement with family credit, and aligning the rates of benefit to other means-tested benefits like income support, housing benefit and community charge benefit, a system was created that was intended to serve two main policy aims:

* to provide support for working families with dependent children; and
* to preserve families' incentives to work.

This study, carried out three years after the implementation of the 1988 reforms, had these aims:

* broadly to improve understanding of the processes associated with low income among families with dependent children;
* to examine the roles played in these processes by social security benefits, especially at the margins of work,
* to examine in detail the effects of family credit and, in particular, its effects on:
  — families' relative material well-being;
  — their work incentives;
* to estimate as accurately as possible the take-up rate of family credit and to study the factors associated with failure to claim among some eligible families;
* to examine the effectiveness of other administrative aspects of family credit;
* to consider the implications for policy.

The results have said a good deal about the circumstances of Britain's low income families but has focused on family credit itself. It provided evidence on the extent to which the new benefit met or did not meet the two primary objectives of support for families and the preservation of incentives.

This chapter summarises the most important findings and discusses their significance in terms of policy for in-work family benefits.

Families, work and benefits

The social patterns associated with low incomes among families are well known and were seen clearly in the data. They had their origins in the limits set by low earnings and uncertain labour market opportunities on the one hand and by the needs of young children, on the other.

Barriers to work were steepest for the growing number of lone parents. They are now one in six of all families but made up nearly half the families in this lowest quarter of the family income distribution. Two-thirds of them had no paid jobs and most of these lived on income support, compared with fewer than one in ten of two parent families. In fact, three-quarters of all families who received income support were lone parents and they had been on income support twice as long as couples with children.

Lone parents had low incomes not just because of their family structure, and the difficulties they have in going out to work. Most of them were women and, as women, they received lower wages than men even when they did manage to get paid jobs. It was noticeable that lone fathers were far more successful than other lone parents in raising their earnings in work.

Couples, on the other hand, were captured by the low income strata when the main earners' wages were low and the children were young. Women in couples faced disincentives to work wrought by three elements that eroded their likely profit from earnings: low pay for women; the scarcity of childcare that was either affordable or reliable; and the loss of benefit through the means-test. Almost all couples claiming family credit were single-earner families.

In this way, family credit was a 'life-cycle' benefit to an even greater extent than child benefit. Its constituency was created in a narrow range among lower-paid workers whose labour market participation was restricted by the need to care for young children. Paradoxically, perhaps, it recruited most of its customers from among lone parents whose children were of school age, and no longer needed full-time care, and from couples whose children had not yet gone to school.

The numbers claiming family credit have grown, to almost 450,000 claims in payment at any one time. On the evidence of the postal sift, as many non-claimants also have some experience of family credit during the past three years. Payments now average over £42 a week, each secure for six months from award, and bringing with them 'passport benefits' such as free eye tests. About half of claimants made use of these.

People who received family credit were much like other working low income families except in two key aspects: they tended far more to be unskilled manual workers and to live in social housing, especially council housing. In these respects they were very much like the out of work families and were unlike the moderate income families.

This was part of a wider pattern. There was a close link between low pay, claiming benefits, having larger numbers of younger children, and social tenancy. These links created a 'fault line' dividing low income families. On the one side were those who claimed income-related benefits and lived in council accommodation. On the other were those who are owner occupiers and did not claim income related benefits. Work and income were also important, but the first split among *low income* families, was the coincidence of income-related benefits and social housing tenure.

The problem of take-up

Low take-up has been a persistent problem of income-tested benefits. Family income supplement appeared to perform especially poorly; estimates based on the Family Expenditure Survey (DSS, 1991) and the Family Finances Survey (Knight, 1981) suggested that barely half of the families entitled to receive the benefit actually did so. No benefit could claim to be doing its job with a 50 per cent success rate. The ineffectiveness of this approach was one of the most serious criticisms levelled at the decision in 1985 to rely on family credit as the central plank of policy for low income families. Official estimates of the impact of the new benefit were based on the assumption that the success rate would improve, but only as far as 60 per cent.

When family credit was introduced in 1988, the DSS made a great effort to bring the benefit to the attention of those within its scope. The Department wrote to employers asking them to encourage claims from their low paid workers. Eight million pounds were spent in advertising to inform potential claimants of the new earnings thresholds. The threshold was calculated for every child benefit claimant, and printed on order books.

The number of families receiving in-work benefits has risen: there were 224,000 FIS payments in December 1987; this increased to 285,000 family credit payments a year later, and to 355,000 in July 1991 when this survey was carried out. Family credit, having higher payment thresholds, should reach more families than FIS; it is not clear how far changes in the number of claims since it was introduced should be explained in terms of higher take-up, or an increase in the size of the eligible population. Even the most recent figures are below the 470,000 claimants predicted by the Department at the time of the change, but the prediction itself may have been unreliable.

The standard source of data for estimating take-up rates has been the Family Expenditure Survey (Craig, 1991). The FES does not ask the specific questions required for assessing entitlement to benefits, and cannot therefore provide estimates as accurate as those in this study. The first FES estimates for family credit in 1988, the year FC was introduced pointed to a take-up rate stubbornly about 50 per cent by caseload, about 65 per cent by expenditure. More recent estimates, combining 1988 and 1989 FES data, raised these figures to 57 per cent and 67 per cent respectively.

It can be argued that no set of survey questions can provide a definitive answer, without submitting apparently eligible claims to the DSS for adjudication. There are often discrepancies between, for example, earnings reported by claimants and the details obtained from employers. Nevertheless, this study went further than most in investigating all sources of income, savings, and so on. We have also been able to take account of claims pending settlement.

The base-line estimate of take-up of family credit from this survey was 61 per cent. Even with a purpose-built questionnaire, there are a number of alternative ways of making the calculation, but the variants all lay within a few percentage points of this estimate. Previous estimates did not count self-employed workers; if these were excluded from our own estimate, the figure rose to 64 per cent.

It had been clear from FES-based estimates that the take-up rate of means-tested benefits varied with the amount of the estimated entitlement: small entitlements had a low take-up rate. It has been implicitly assumed that this was broadly a linear relationship - the larger the entitlement, the greater the take-up. In fact the relationship identified (for housing benefit) by Blundell and others (1988) was logarithmic. Very small entitlements had a very low take-up rate, but the effect became weaker and weaker as the amount of the entitlement grew. Our own estimate showed a similar pattern. The take-up of family credit entitlements of less than £3 was as low as 8 per cent; entitlements of more than £9 had a fairly uniform penetration of 67 per cent. This might be seen as the *underlying take-up rate*. It changed little as the size of entitlement rose further. This figure included the self-employed. If, as before, the estimate was limited to employees alone, it was 71 per cent.

Because large entitlements were more likely to get through than small ones, the take-up rate was higher if measured in terms of pounds than if it was based on people. Our estimate of the 'expenditure-based' take-up rate was 66 per cent; if self-employed workers were excluded, 74 per cent.

This variation by amount of entitlement is an important phenomenon, but it needs to be treated with caution. One interpretation is that people estimated their entitlement quite accurately, but could not be bothered to claim small amounts. But £5 per week for six months comes to £130, and it would be surprising if people earning about £150 per week were willing to treat family credit in such a cavalier fashion, unless the process of claiming was really daunting. After all, the majority of lone parents were ready to claim their £5.60 one parent benefit each week - though, to be fair, they only have to do this once.

One possible corollary of the non-take-up of small weekly amounts is that they might be picked up more readily if they were offered as lump sums. They were overlooked, possibly, by people who were also unaware that family credit was paid unconditionally for six months. A quarter even of those who had claimed seemed to believe that extra income would lead to an immediate deduction from their order books, as it is from income support. This could make small claims not worth picking up - why bother claiming three pounds a week if they might take it away in a few weeks time? A giro for £78 might be another matter. There is a parallel with the lump sums paid to people entitled to relatively small industrial injuries pensions. A lump sum for small amounts would also advertise the unconditional nature of all awards over six months.

A second hypothesis about the low rate of take-up of small amounts is that people had rather *inaccurate* estimates of their entitlement, and that those whose true position was quite close to the threshold had a high chance of pitching their guess on the wrong side of it. A third possible explanation for the observed relationship is, however, purely technical. Random errors of a few pounds in the earnings reported in a survey would create a pattern similar to that observed. There was some evidence of a tendency to round answers to the nearest £5 or £10, for example. For this reason, the *underlying take-up rate* of 67 per cent was probably the most reliable figure.

Another important component of non-take-up was delay. The average period of time in receipt of family credit, including renewals, among all families who had made a successful claim was about one year, or, in effect, two consecutive claims of six months. If it took each family three months before they realised their entitlement, that in itself would cause a 25 per cent shortfall in take-up, if measured by a cross-section survey like this one. The survey showed that many recipients did not in fact realise they were eligible for family credit at first. Some waited two months or so even after they realised they might be eligible. More evidence for this has been found in the first returns from a postal follow-up survey of the lone parents in the study. One fifth of those identified as eligible non-claimants in the July 1991 survey had actually become family credit recipients by March 1992.

So another way of looking at the problem is in terms of a range. A higher proportion than 61 per cent of those with any entitlement did make a claim sooner or later. But the proportion who received everything they were entitled to was lower than 61 per cent. The data do not allow us to provide precise figures for the upper and lower bounds of this range.

The number of families foregoing significant amounts was lower than was feared. But at least one in three eligible families were missing out and this cannot be satisfactory. Nor can we say with any great certainty whether take-up has increased, or whether we simply have a higher measure of the same true rate. The increase in the number of successful claims at least allows for the possibility that take-up has increased.

But why, despite much official encouragement, do about 170,000 eligible families still allow good money to go unclaimed? Qualitative research, especially Anne Corden's painstaking series of studies of FIS and family credit (Corden 1983, 1987; Corden and Craig 1991), identified the main problems of take-up as *lack of information*, *complexities* associated with the application procedure, and reluctance to take on the *stigma* attached to receipt of means-tested benefits.

Others have suggested that perceived need is important - that whatever people's incomes, they will not seek help unless they feel they are going without things they regard as necessities (Kerr, 1983). Another, more technical hypothesis, favoured initially by the present authors, was that non-claimants had unstable incomes - that their 'windows of eligibility' opened and closed too rapidly for them to submit reliable claims. Or that they stood a greater chance of rejection and so were more likely to become one of Anne Corden's 'disappointed applicants' who were discouraged from further claims.

This study certainly found that eligible non-claimants were different kinds of people compared with claimants. Their average earnings were higher than those of the claimants; a relatively high proportion were couples. (Lone parents' underlying take-up rate was 78 per cent.) More of them were skilled workers and owner occupiers; this was true even when lone parents and couples were examined separately.

So eligible non-claimants tended to occupy, surprisingly, the opposite side of the 'fault line' compared to the claimants. They had much more in common with the moderate income families. This at least was true of the never-claimants. Those, the minority, who had claimed family credit in the past looked more like present claimants: doing less skilled jobs, living in social housing.

Little evidence was found that eligible non-claimants feared stigma or criticism. Indeed questioning on this point showed that almost everyone who applied had found their friends and relatives either neutral or supportive. Often they were the source of information about the benefit. A series of questions on the desirability of benefits drew no sign either that there was any widespread stigma attached to claiming, or that this was something peculiar to eligible non-claimants.

Nor was unfamiliarity or ignorance a special characteristic of non-take-up. It was striking that four out of ten eligible non-claimants had some past experience of claiming family credit and almost as many said they intended to claim in the future. And on a whole series of questions concerning the administrative details of the benefit, non-claimants knew as much about family credit as the claimants themselves. Or, rather, as little: neither claimants nor non-claimants had a clear grasp of the details. For example, fewer than half the *current recipients* could hazard a guess about the rate of withdrawal against earnings (the 70 per cent taper) and most who guessed got it wrong. Ignorance may form part of an explanation for non-take-up but expertise explained few of the claims.

Few people cited the complexities of form-filling as a barrier to claiming. Those who did not claim simply thought, for the most part, that they were not eligible. A few who found the problems too great tended to be self-employed families in business on their own account who simply did not have the answers to questions about income. This is a problem that has received some attention lately. On the other hand, an 'eligible non-claimant' whose *accountant* cannot even find the information needed probably is never going to be in a position to claim.

Claimants themselves rarely cited serious problems with complexity or delay. Problems were encountered but were overcome without too much difficulty. This finding, though substantiated by quite a large number of observations, is different from the findings of qualitative research citing such confusion and complexity as a prime cause of non-claiming. In a sense, we find the same, most people having contact with family credit found it quite complicated *but this was equally true of successful applicants*. There is little evidence from any source that significant numbers of families sit down with the claim pack, start filling it in and later give up.

Very little evidence was found for the instability hypothesis. There was some tendency for eligible non-claimant couples to be paid varying amounts each week, but the effect was not great. On other measures of stability that might have affected eligibility, such as hours of work, they seemed more stable than the claimants, not less.

On the other hand, prior rejection was relevant. Controlling for the effects of other factors, significant numbers of eligible non-claimants recalled having been rejected in the past in a claim for family credit, some for FIS. This may equally cast doubt, of course, on whether, despite all efforts at accuracy, the survey had correctly identified them as eligible.

Does family credit improve the incentive to work?
Yes, it does. But it is a complicated issue. The main problem is that it improves families' incentives to *get* paid jobs at the expense of reducing the incentives of those with jobs to do *more* or better-paid work. And it operates rather differently for one- and two-parent families.

The survey evidence showed that lone parents were, on average, about £30 a week better off in work and claiming family credit than they would have been out of work and claiming income support. The net gain among couples was less: about £18 a week, shared between two adults. However, to this extent family credit springs the 'unemployment trap' that might otherwise have left many families with higher incomes out of work.

In this way, the optimistic aspect of family credit is that it might act as an up-escalator, drawing families off income support, into work on low wages that employers might find attractive, and supporting them as they become established in work and as they look for improvements in their position as their children grow older.

But while family credit clearly offers help with the first step - getting a job at all - it may act as a hindrance to further steps - improving earnings by overtime, promotion, or a second earner. For example, under certain circumstances a family earning, say, £130 a week net would have been only about £10 a week better off than a family earning £85 a week.

What actually happens? The initial sift provided a glimpse of the total picture. Very few former claimants were found in the upper reaches of the income distribution. In contrast, a quarter of the couples and nearly two-thirds of the lone parents who had once been on family credit were back on income support. In the interview sample, 45 per cent of those who received family credit in its first few months in 1988 were still receiving it in mid-1991, 36 per cent were out of work, 7 per cent were eligible non-claimants, and 12 per cent had got into the moderate income band just above the family credit threshold. The great majority of those making any real progress were couples who had become two-earner families.

Family credit has attracted a loyal core of claimants: 12 per cent had been continuously on FIS and family credit for years. 17 per cent remained solidly on family credit since it arrived; half of those receiving it in 1989 and 60 per cent of those claiming in 1990 were still on benefit in 1991. Thus, if family credit was an up-escalator, it was short, slow moving and led to Bethnal Green rather than Knightsbridge. It was also different for lone parents and for couples: family credit offered lone parents a bigger incentive, but it was among couples that most of the longer-term employment was identified.

The problem is caused by the disincentive effects of the loose relationship between earnings and income created by in-work benefits. The most obvious one is for the *main earner* whose income is being assessed. He or she would have to make a big improvement in earnings in order to enjoy a better standard of living - hence the term, poverty trap. This may discourage people from changing jobs, working for promotion and so on. (Among couples, a male worker would be discouraged only if he took a family view of income: he would retain 66 per cent of any increase in his own earnings; the loss of benefit would be experienced by his wife.)

Second, the offer facing an *unemployed worker* typically increases net income by about £18 for a couple and £30 for a lone parent. The effectiveness of family credit is therefore highly sensitive to the judgement of the amount of extra income which would persuade a breadwinner to accept a job. If that extra income is eroded by higher than average travel costs, for example, the incentive effect provided by the benefit will soon evaporate.

Third, there would be little point in a *partner* of a family credit claimant taking employment, especially if it was part-time. Among couples on family credit, only 12 per cent had a second earner. While family credit may encourage lone parents to go out to work, it encourages married mothers to stay at home and look after their children. 55 per cent of family credit couples had a child under the age of five, the period when the majority of mothers remained out of the labour force.

It remains an open question whether the disincentive for a family receiving family credit, especially a couple, to increase their labour supply is created by the withdrawal rate of benefit as hours of work or pay increase, or by the simple fact of receiving benefit at all. We can ask, solely for the purpose of illustration, would it matter if the rate of withdrawal were 100 per cent? In this case, family credit would, in effect, be converted into a extension of income support: a 'working families premium' awarded to families who work more than 16 hours a week.

Such a change would allow, if this were an aim, a redistribution of benefit from the better off FC recipients with the smaller awards to the worst off recipients with the larger awards. The effect of this would be to increase the step up in income as the 16 hours threshold was passed. (The reduction from 24 hours has, of course, compressed this step because earnings component of income will, on average, be smaller.) As we saw earlier, it is couples with largest awards who have the greatest difficulties on FC and who had most trouble in seeing the advantages of being on FC compared to IS. To strengthen the power of FC to spring the unemployment trap at the expense of steepening once more the poverty trap might be seen by some as an acceptable, if unusual aim. After all, while FC, HB and CCB all remain based on net income, total withdrawal rates cannot exceed 100 per cent as they could under FIS.

The objection is that everyone on family credit (or IS working families premium) would have the same final income, which is said to be unfair and discouraging. Though it might then become difficult to explain why the same 100 per cent rate of withdrawal is now acceptable at working hours between about 3 or 4 and 15 hours. And it would be equally difficult to explain what was so significant about 16 hours to attract such a bonus that was not true of 15 hours, especially if they were 15 better-paid hours.

On the other hand, we saw that the present system withdraws between 70 per cent and 96 per cent of benefit (including HB and CCB) from each new pound earned by FC recipients. Calculations can then be made that, typically, this leaves a family earning £x a week only £z a week better off than a family earning £y. Would anyone notice if that figure was not £z, but zero? And would anyone behave differently if it was?

Some of the evidence from the survey suggests that they might not behave differently. Few families, even the present recipients, have any idea what the rate of withdrawal of FC really is. Many believe it *is* 100 per cent. As the DSS is always keen to point out for other very good reasons, the likely disincentive effects of withdrawal are anyway heavily cushioned by the six months rule. 'Increasing your labour supply' usually means doing overtime. Does anyone really turn down overtime because they are on family credit? Unless they are within 5 weeks of a claim or a renewal, it would not matter in any particular week. Overtime is usually done to oblige (or simply to obey) an employer. Other forms of advancement such as accepting promotion, or looking for a better job seem equally poorly attached to people's perception of family credit withdrawal rates.

For couples, the main disincentive upon wives' chances of part-time work are equally detached from the withdrawal rate *at the margins.* At 70 per cent, 80, 90, or 100 per cent, her options are not very different. Get a full-time job and so spring the whole family clear of the FC threshold altogether, or stay at home. The evidence is that this is how it works. For it to work differently, to work in the way it works for families higher up the income distribution, the withdrawal rate would probably have to be no more than about 30 or 40 per cent. Then part-time work would seem more worthwhile. The problem is that at least a quarter of all families would become entitled to family credit and expenditure would increase five-fold.

The point of this illustration is solely to point out more clearly that, especially for couples, the differences between the problems raised by the poverty trap are really not all that different in work and receiving family credit compared with being out of work and receiving income support, except for the six months security attached to FC. For all its obvious advantage for many, especially lone parents, the change in the hours rule down to 16 hours a week will blur this distinction more. This is why some families seem puzzled that they are not better off on what *appear* to be much larger incomes in work.

For a minority of family credit claimants, the 'up-escalator' self-improvement analogy was entirely wrong. They were going in the other direction, and family credit may have prevented them from falling too far. These were couples who formerly both worked full-time. He lost his job and she then claimed family credit. Lower pay for women increases the likelihood of her eligibility for family credit under these circumstances. The alternative might have been for the wife to give up work too, so that they could claim income support. Family credit was like opening a parachute, preventing or delaying a fall into family unemployment. It kept her job going and the family provided before he could get back into work. If he got back quickly, they would be glad that she retained her job.

Discussion of the incentive effects of family credit should be understood within some severe limits. The majority of lone parents did not work and most of them were resigned to that position for the while, family credit or not. *At the margins of work*, as their children started school, the availability of affordable but preferably free childcare was crucial to whether or not they could move into range of family credit.

There was a fine balance to be struck: to work enough hours to be able to claim, but few enough hours to fit the available childcare. The reduction of qualifying hours to 16 may make this balancing act easier in the sense that less childcare would be needed, though the 16 hours would have to be paid at quite a high rate to bring total incomes up over the levels of out-of-work benefits. More likely, lone parents would be freed to work something like 20 to 24 hours if they had children at primary school. Among all lone parents out of work, 8 per cent said they were seriously thinking about a job *and* were looking to work between 16 and 24 hours a week.

Whereas some lone parents were kept out of range of family credit by the lack of affordable childcare, such lack kept some couples within range. It redoubled the disincentive to work that is common to all wives in benefit families. It was disincentive enough for many to lose 70 or 80 pence in income for each extra pound earned. To pay fares to work and cope with difficult childcare arrangements was a greater disincentive. To pay for childcare as well would have been an indication that the motive to work had little to do with money.

For those lone parents dubious of ever returning to work, it was less a problem of childcare, far more a problem of disability. Again in contrast, disability in couples could create opportunities to claim family credit. If the husband was disabled the wife might be able to work, especially if he did not need regular care

Families, work and benefits

or could even look after the children. Being a woman, she would be more likely than a man to have a wage within the family credit threshold. If he was receiving disability benefits of the kind not counted against family credit entitlement, a considerable incentive could be created. 28 per cent of female full-time workers claiming family credit had disabled husbands.

For many kinds of low income family, on the other hand, the continuing barrier to a smooth transition into work, across the stepping stones provided by family credit and up into average wage levels or better, was a lack of skills that employers value. This weakness in their labour market position left many low income families drifting back and forth from income support to family credit and back again. It was to some extent a characteristic of the moderate income families and the eligible non-claimants that they had sufficient skills to keep them more distant from benefit. Perhaps they also reduced the expectation of being a claimant, even in those times when their income dipped below the eligibility threshold.

How do the families themselves see family credit?

People did not have a clear understanding of family credit. For example, there was a tendency to see their family credit earnings limit as lower than it really was - that they believed the benefit was only for the very poorest families. Few guessed their own limit accurately. On the other hand the reservation wages cited by those out of work were so low as to pitch the prospect of work into their supposed, and certainly into their actual entitlement band for family credit. That is to say, people were generally prepared to work for wages that they thought would qualify them, and actually would qualify them for family credit.

But if they had low reservation wages, many potential workers had high 'reservation security'. A job taken at wages qualifying the family for family credit would have had to be secure for at least a year or two before it was thought worthwhile to abandon a poor but predictable life on income support.

Claimants of family credit showed considerable attachment both to work and to the benefit. Two-thirds expect to continue to claim. Deprived of it, half said they would try to continue in work, a third would seek a better job, and only one in ten said they would stop working. This, despite a majority saying earlier that they could manage without family credit only with the greatest difficulty or not at all.

Among families in work asked to guess about what wages they would consider taking in a new job, family credit families tended more than others to pitch their reservation wages into their range of family credit entitlement. The eligible non-claimants did this less readily and this may account for part of their misapprehensions about their qualification. On the other hand, about one in six of the non-claimants said they intended to claim in the future.

Among those with experience of both benefits, there was a strong tendency for current family credit claimants to say they preferred it to income support. This was specially true of lone parents. It might strike a slightly worrying note, though, that a quarter of the couples currently claiming family credit, but with experience of both, said they preferred income support after all. More seriously perhaps, among those out of work who once claimed family credit in the past, half said they preferred being on income support and only a third said definitely that they had preferred being on family credit.

Overall there appeared to be systematic links between having an incentive to work and claim, and seeing that incentive more accurately. After all, the larger the incentive, the easier it ought to be to see. But it was seen against a background of misapprehension and guesswork. But it was often a positive kind of guesswork. For example, when they thought about their plans for the future, there was a clear connection in people's minds between the ways they positioned themselves toward the labour market, the extent to which this position suggested entitlement to family credit, and the extent to which the families themselves included family credit consciously in their plans, even if they were out of work at the time.

Does family credit improve family welfare?
Yes, it does, but less for couples; lone parents again did better.

Families with children have been at the forefront of the discussion of poverty ever since it was 'rediscovered' in the 1960s. They account for 46 per cent of all individuals living in households with less than half the national average income (HBAI 1991). While earnings are usually sufficient to lift an individual, or even a couple, out of poverty, the 'working poor' consist almost entirely of families with children. FIS, rather than some more universal benefit, was introduced to deal with this problem.

Research in the early 1980s showed that families with children showed far more signs of financial hardship than other out of work claimants of supplementary benefit (Berthoud 1984), and this may have been one of the considerations which directed policy towards treating low income families with children as a priority group. It has been open to debate whether this priority succeeded in delivering more money to families on income support, or merely protected them from the losses experienced by unemployed people without children. Another issue concerns the benchmark: benefits have tended to keep pace with the cost of living during the 1980s, but have fallen behind the increased earnings enjoyed by the better-off half of the population. But there is no doubt that family credit offered more money, to a rather larger group of families, than FIS did. This should have made them better off, at least by comparison with non-working families and with working families entitled to family credit but who fail to claim it.

The survey made no attempt to define 'poverty' in terms of a specific level of income below which people were excluded from an acceptable level of participation. But we asked a series of questions about financial stress and material welfare which between them can be used to show how well- or badly-off people were.

A family was said to be in 'severe hardship' if they scored three or more out of a list of six measures, which were themselves composites of answers given to questions about debt, expenditure, unmet need and anxiety about money. We do not suggest where people 'should' fall on this scale, other than to point out that it has been deliberately chosen as a severe definition. The main purpose of the analysis was to make comparisons between families in different circumstances.

Our sample consisted entirely of families with children, whose income fell below 125 per cent of their family credit threshold. For those out of work, mostly on income support, 28 per cent overall (24 per cent of the couples and 30 per cent of the lone parents) were found to be in 'severe hardship'. At the opposite end of the scale, only 5 per cent of families above the family credit threshold (but between 1 per cent and 25 per cent above it) were as badly off as that. This was entirely as might have been expected.

Were people on family credit much better off, in these terms, than out-of-work families? 20 per cent of claimants were in severe hardship, according to our definition; only 8 per cent fewer than among the non-working families. Most of this small improvement was accounted for by lone parents. Claimant couples were no better off than those out of work. When this comparison was restricted to families either working and getting family credit, or being entirely without work, the narrow advantage of the family credit families becomes a little more pronounced. But this advantage still lay most strongly with the lone parent claimants by a margin of 15 per cent in severe hardship compared with 31 per cent of the lone parents who had no work at all. The in-work claimant couples were hardly any better off than the couples with no work at all (24 versus 28 per cent).

The reason is that although the apparent incomes of family credit claimants - earnings plus family credit -were higher than the income support they would have received by an average of £61 per week, it came to only an extra £23 once the loss of rent rebate and community charge benefit was taken into account, and to only £15 when travel fares and childcare costs were added in. Moreover, this net gain from work was much smaller for couples than for lone parents, and it showed.

All this was much as might have been expected. The real surprise came when we turned to families who appeared to be eligible for family credit, but were not receiving it. Their total income should have been lower than that of the claimants, and so it proved. Every logic suggests that they should therefore have experienced more hardship than the claimants, but this was not true. Only 11 per cent of them were within our definition of 'severe hardship', not many more than among the families whose incomes took them just above the threshold. The best off among these were ENCs who had *never* claimed family credit. The eligible non-claimants seemed to be far better off than their relative incomes would predict.

This finding was observed for every indicator of financial and material stress included in the questionnaire, so it cannot be explained in terms of the detailed definition of hardship. There are a number of possible reasons for this finding. For example:

- Some of the non-claimants may have under-reported their true income. This, if true, would have important implications for the take-up rate, which would be higher than the underlying rates suggested earlier.
- The non-claimants may have had higher incomes in the past, and this may have put them in a position to ride out a period of low income with relatively little hardship.
- The non-claimants may have been drawing on resources which were not counted for benefit purposes, nor in the questionnaire.
- The non-claimants may have been more skilful than other people at managing on a low income, and avoiding hardship.

Whichever of these hypotheses is true, the explanation has to include the reason why these families did not claim their benefit. The first hypothesis would explain that easily enough; if respondents understated their income, they may not have been eligible after all. The problem is that such an explanation would also have to allow that claimants also underestimated their income. They would be fewer but they do have, after all, a better motive for keeping quiet about extra cash.

The other three hypotheses would have to explain non-take-up on the basis that people who did not experience hardship did not feel the need to claim. But there was no direct evidence for such an explanation. And if they were such good managers, why did they turn away good money?

The material well-being data also shed an interesting light on incentives. If people did not experience better times on family credit than they did out of work, then marginal differences in incomes in and out of work created by family credit would not work as incentives at all effectively. They might once, but not twice. Might not the apparent lack of a clear gain in living standards on family credit, compared with life on income support, tend to discourage such families from working and claiming family credit?

There was some evidence for this. There was a group of families, usually the lowest paid, usually couples, for whom family credit did not work. Those who had returned to income support from a spell on family credit tended to have very unfavourable scores on the index of hardship. Those who did so *and* said they now preferred being on income support, had dreadful hardship scores. Among couples in this position, half were in severe hardship. They went to work on family credit, took a beating, slumped back onto income support and resigned themselves to it. (As many of them said, at least you know where you are on IS.) Why does this happen?

It has something to do with debt, among other things. Debt forms a large part of the index of relative material well-being that supports the above conclusion. There was a substantial minority of people, again usually couples, who got floated into work by family credit with a heavy burden of debt. Often, they sank. It seems likely that they preferred income support because debt was easier to manage, sometimes through direct payments or deductions. They could hope to earn a moratorium on some personal debts and on their rent arrears too. These debts would be reactivated if they went to work. For a few low-income families, debt could be a disincentive to work that the marginal benefits of family credit, especially for couples, could not compete with for long.

What are the most important conclusions from the survey?
Family credit appeared to be making an important contribution to the labour market participation of *lone parents*. If it was not there, the already large numbers of lone parents living on income support would probably increase.

The majority of lone parents were unable to contemplate the idea of full-time work yet, but among those with any motive and opportunity to work, family credit offered a strong incentive just as soon as they could sort out their childcare. Those whose attention it attracted, saw the incentive clearly. Significantly, the great majority of those contemplating work from a position on income support, included family credit in their plans. When they worked and claimed, it improved their material circumstances compared with those out of work. As a result, their take-up was high. A third of working lone parents claimed family credit and they made up four out of ten claimants. The reduction in qualifying hours and the new £15 a week disregard for maintenance payment can only increase these figures.

The position of couples was more problematic. They did not have the lone parents' problems with childcare but family credit provided them with weaker incentives. They got half the amount of additional income in work compared with the gains offered to lone parents. As a result, those couples who did claim got, on average, relatively little improvement in their material well-being compared with out of work families. There was a degree of awareness of this and those who had had a bad time on family credit tended to prefer being on income support. Couples' take-up rate remained relatively low. Their 'underlying' take-up rate was still only 60 per cent, compared with lone parents' 78 per cent.

Low take-up had less to do with the complexities of claiming, or with ignorance or stigma, than with misunderstandings about eligibility, though the passage of time helped.

These misunderstandings tended to arise more often among people who were socially located at a distance from the world inhabited by social security claimants. They arose among low-income home owners and among more skilled workers, earning more (though still actually within range of family credit), yet who tended to feel that people like themselves, income tax and MIRAS-mortgage payers and all, would not be eligible for a means-tested social security benefit. For some (40 per cent) this was a view reinforced by recent rejection in a claim for family credit. Rejection may be a disincentive. It may also be evidence of ineligibility.

More than anything, misunderstandings arose among families who were not apparently experiencing much severe hardship, less in fact than the problems experienced by claimants, despite their having lower incomes than the claimants. False belief in ineligibility for reasons such as these is the kind of conclusion that couples might convince each other of. Lone parents are much more in the habit of going and finding out what they might be due.

The strengths of family credit, therefore, have been to create a single system of in-work benefits for families that is rational on paper and fairly rational in the field. The arithmetic works. For lone parents, the sums come out well and it has helped significant numbers of them into work. But the majority of lone parents have problems with work that are far greater than the incentive effects of marginal variations in family credit. It also helps significant numbers of two parent families to get and keep paid work. There was much evidence for this in the survey and, besides, they told us so.

The administration of the benefit also seemed to be working better than was supposed. The procedures are complicated and people with experience of them said they could cause problems. But they also said they found ways to solve them. The benefit was also reaching more of the eligible population than was feared: not half, perhaps as many as two-thirds. Broadly, as Anne Corden foretold, the more that was learned about non-claimants, the less eligible they turned out to be. A problem remains, especially among owner occupier couples, but the trend appears to be in the right direction.

The weaknesses of family credit are twofold. The first is connected to an inevitable consequence of its strengths. The greater an incentive is created, in the form of an improvement in final income in work, the steeper tends to be the rate of withdrawal of benefit against extra earnings. The switch to family credit all but eliminated the absurdities of FIS and that could withdraw more than a pound for each new pound of earnings for some people. But it actually increased the proportions having marginal rates of withdrawal over 80 per cent. This provides too little incentive for many families to seek marginal improvements in work, though it is also true that this disincentive effect is blunted rather by the one to six month time lag between an increase in income and its likely effects on benefit levels. But as the data seem to show, it keeps many wives of claimants out of part-time work - their traditional path towards full-time work and becoming dual earner families. Possibly as a consequence of this, too few ex-claimants of family credit seem to penetrate into the higher income strata. Almost none seem to get beyond average family earnings, though this may improve as time goes on.

The second weakness is connected both to the levels of final income and the social and economic isolation typical of many families who claim social security benefits. Many families, often living on council estates, often those relying most heavily on family credit, have a lot of trouble seeing much reward for their enterprise. The worst paid couples, in particular, see least improvement in their standards of living compared to life out of work. They are the same unskilled families who face the greatest difficulties in getting into work, staying in work, and in getting on better in work. They are the same families who face the highest losses from additional income. And they are the same families who tend to have brought into work a degree of material disadvantage and debt accumulated over spells on income support. These families, still a minority of low income families, experience hardship both in and out of work. It is significant that those who struggle most do so more often against a background of a history of receipt of income support than as a direct result of difficulties with family credit. Where severe hardship persists, it appears to be an outcome of difficulties over a long period of time, rather than an immediate result of current income.

Those who would use this report to judge the usefulness of in-work benefits for families must distinguish carefully between a judgement about the effectiveness of family credit (plus other benefits) *in the field*, and a judgement about the wider effectiveness of a policy that relies on income-related benefits like family credit, rather than on some other policy. It is easy, but unhelpful, to confuse the two.

In the field, the system seems to be working better than earlier information had suggested. If targeting is the aim, family credit hits its targets more often and more effectively than earlier research has suggested, and probably a lot more effectively than its predecessor - family income supplement - ever did. But they are moving targets: family credit is a transitional benefit that families move through on their way to and from work, up and down the income range, and in and out of parenthood, of course. This means that the effectiveness of the delivery of family credit must be continually renewed.

Overall though, the main advantage of family credit is that its strengths assist many while its weaknesses affect relatively few. Most benefit, to a greater or lesser extent, though some struggle.

In the longer view, one of the more significant outcomes of this study has been to show the extent to which severe hardship among low income families is socially structured. Low income families are not all the same even if they do have similar equivalent incomes. There is a difference between low income and social disadvantage. Most low income families face material difficulties of one kind or another. When the lowest incomes have to be supported by income-related benefits and when these coincide with social tenancy, poor education and unskilled work, hardship increases sharply. When they do not coincide, it does not. The strength of this social structuring will place limits on the effects of *levels* of social security benefits in their income. This makes it hardest to help the poorest, though family credit is getting through effectively because families with the greater entitlements and the greater need, have the higher take-up rates.

As part of this process, the paradox of family credit is that receiving it is one of the indicators that tends to place a family on the disadvantaged side of what we have called the benefit fault line. But receiving it is undoubtably an advantage for most who do. Even if material circumstances in many cases are slow to improve in response to family credit, the family *is* in work and has better reason to expect improvement than will a family out of work. Paid work is still at the centre of life. Access to it, for most people, is the only route away from hardship. To the extent that family credit improves that access for people with dependent children, it succeeds in its longer term aims.

The wider judgement - the wisdom of a policy to use family credit to supplement the incomes of working families - depends on a political choice between targeted and universal benefits. No wider view of this kind is taken here because, if for no other reason, this study has focused on the practical outcomes of the policy and not on its strategic value.

But it is a judgement that is influenced to some extent by an assessment of the benefit's practical strengths and weaknesses. If we had found that family credit did not work, it would be harder to defend the wider policy of having it at all. Imagine, for example, that we had found eligible non-claimants more numerous than feared, that they had larger entitlements than recipients and they suffered the greater hardship, and so on. But we found the opposite.

We can also comment on one other important aspect. An objection to targeting that is often made is that it is unfair to those who are just out of range. In our sample design, these people are the 'moderate income' families, below average income but above family credit entitlement. We found that they were not strangers to material difficulties, but their advantage over the family credit families was pronounced.

It is unlikely that the population of low income families will shrink dramatically over the next few years. Continuing low demand for less skilled labour and, hence, low pay, will increase the strain. It is equally unlikely that universal forms of family income support will suddenly be preferred to targeted forms. For these reasons, large numbers of low income families will continue to count income-related social security benefits an important source of income, in and out of work, for the foreseeable future.

The findings of this study certainly support the view that family credit, and other in-work benefits, will continue to have an important place in a policy of targeting resources to families with children. As average family living standards grow in the future, the real cost that low income families must meet to provide an acceptable minimum standard of living will also grow. In this way, the need for the most effective possible delivery of family credit and other in-work benefits must also increase.

References

Ashworth, K. and Walker, R. (1992) *The Dynamics of Family Credit* CRSP Paper 172

Berthoud, R. (1984) *The Reform of Supplementary Benefit* London: PSI

Berthoud, R. and Kempson, E. (1992) *Credit and Debt: The PSI Report* London: PSI

Blundell R., Fry, V. and Walker, I. (1988) "Modelling the Take-up of Means-Tested Benefits: the Case of Housing Benefits in the United Kingdom" *Economic Journal* 98 pp 58-74

Bradshaw, J. and Millar, J. (1991) *Lone Parent Families in the UK* London: HMSO

Brown, J. (1983) *Family Income Supplement* London: PSI

Brown, J. (1987) *The Future of Family Income Support* London: PSI

Corden, A. (1983) *Taking up a means-tested benefit: the process of claiming FIS* London: HMSO

Corden, A, (1987) *Disappointed Applicants: A study of unsuccessful claims for Family Income Supplement* Avebury

Corden, A. and Craig, P. (1991) *Perceptions of Family Credit* London: HMSO

Craig, P. (1991) "Costs and Benefits: A Review of Research on Take-up of Income-Related Benefits" *Journal of Social Policy* 20 (4) pp 537-565

Daniel, W. (1990) *The Unemployed Flow* London: PSI

Deacon, A. and Bradshaw, J. (1983) *Reserved for the Poor: The Means Test in British Social Policy* Oxford: Basil Blackwell & Martin Robertson

Department of Health and Social Security (1985) *Reform of Social Security* (Green Paper) London: HMSO

Department of Social Security (1991) *Family Income Supplement: Estimates of Take-Up 1986-87 Technical Note* London: Analytical Services Division

Department of Social Security (1991) *Income Support Statistics 1990* London: DSS

Department of Social Security (1992) *Social Security Statistics 1991* London: HMSO

Department of Social Security (1993) *Income Related Benefits Estimates of Take-up in 1989* London: Government Statistical Service

Dilnot, A. and Morris, C. N. (1983) "Private costs and benefits: measuring replacement rates" in Greenhalgh, C., Layard, R. and Oswald, A. (eds) *The Causes of unemployment* Oxford: Clarendon Press

Hansard (1987) 21 October col 809; 19 November cols 647-648

Heady, P. and Smyth, M. (1989) *Living Standards During Unemployment* London: HMSO

Jenkins, S. and Millar, J. (1989) "Income risk and income maintenance: implications for incentives to work" in Dilnot, A. and Walker, I. (eds) *The Economics of Social Security* Oxford: Oxford University Press

Kemp, P. 1992) *Housing Benefit: An Appraisal* Social Security Advisory Committee Research Paper 4, London: HMSO

Kerr, S. (1983) *Making Ends Meet* London: Bedford Square Press

Knight, I. (1981) *Family Finances* OPCS Occasional Papers No. 26 London: HMSO

McLaughlin E., Millar, J. and Cooke, K. (1988) *Work and Welfare Benefits* Avebury

Mack, J. and Lansley, S. (1985) *Poor Britain* London: Allen and Unwin

Mack, J. and Lansley, S. (1992) *Breadline Britain in the 1990s* London: Harper Collins

Marsh, A. and McKay, S. (1993) "Families, work and the use of childcare" *Employment Gazette*, August, forthcoming

National Audit Office (1991) *Support for Low Income Families* London: HMSO

Noble, M., Smith, G. and Munby, T. (1992) *The Take-up of Family Credit* Oxford: Department of Applied Social Studies and Social Research

Parker, H. (1989) *Instead of the Dole: An enquiry into integration of the tax and benefit systems* London: Routledge

Perkins, E., Roberts, S. and Moore, N. (1992) *Helping Clients Claim Their Benefits: The information needs of informal benefits advisers* London: PSI

Piachaud, D. (1971) "Poverty and Taxation" *Political Quarterly* 42 (1) pp 31-44

Social Security Committee (1991) *Households Below Average Income 1979-1988*

Walker, R. (1980) "Temporal Aspects of Claiming Behaviour: Renewal of Rent Allowances" *Journal of Social Policy* 9 (2) pp 207-222